Full Color on Every Page!

PC Upgrade & Repair Simplified®

2nd Edition

From

maranGraphics®

&

HUNGRY MINDS, INC.

New York, NY • Cleveland, OH • Indianapolis, IN

Chicago, IL • Foster City, CA • San Francisco, CA

PC Upgrade & Repair Simplified® 2nd Edition

Published by
Hungry Minds, Inc.
909 Third Avenue
New York, NY 10022
www.hungryminds.com

Library of Congress Control Number: 00-193098

ISBN: 0-7645-3560-9

Printed in the United States of America

10 9 8 7 6 5 4 3 2 1

2K/ST/QS/QR/MG

Distributed in the United States by Hungry Minds, Inc.
Distributed by CDG Books Canada Inc. for Canada; by Transworld Publishers Limited in the United Kingdom; by IDG Norge Books for Norway; by IDG Sweden Books for Sweden; by IDG Books Australia Publishing Corporation Pty. Ltd. for Australia and New Zealand; by TransQuest Publishers Pte Ltd. for Singapore, Malaysia, Thailand, Indonesia, and Hong Kong; by Gotop Information Inc. for Taiwan; by ICG Muse, Inc. for Japan; by Intersoft for South Africa; by Eyrolles for France; by International Thomson Publishing for Germany, Austria and Switzerland; by Distribuidora Cuspide for Argentina; by LR International for Brazil; by Galileo Libros for Chile; by Ediciones ZETA S.C.R. Ltda. for Peru; by WS Computer Publishing Corporation, Inc. for the Philippines; by Contemporanea de Ediciones for Venezuela; by Express Computer Distributors for the Caribbean and West Indies; by Micronesia Media Distributor, Inc. for Micronesia; by Chips Computadoras S.A. de C.V. for Mexico; by Editorial Norma de Panama S.A. for Panama; by American Bookshops for Finland.
For U.S. corporate orders, please call maranGraphics at 800-469-6616 or fax 905-890-9434.
For general information on Hungry Minds' products and services, please contact our Customer Care Department within the U.S. at 800-762-2974, outside the U.S. at 317-572-3993 or fax 317-572-4002.
For sales inquiries and reseller information, including discounts, premium and bulk quantity sales, and foreign-language translations, please contact our Customer Care Department at 800-434-3422, fax 317-572-4002, or write to Hungry Minds, Inc., Attn: Customer Care Department, 10475 Crosspoint Boulevard, Indianapolis, IN 46256.
For information on licensing foreign or domestic rights, please contact our Sub-Rights Customer Care Department at 650-653-7098.
For information on using Hungry Minds' products and services in the classroom or for ordering examination copies, please contact our Educational Sales Department at 800-434-2086 or fax 317-572-4005.
Please contact our Public Relations Department at 212-884-5163 for press review copies or 212-884-5000 for author interviews and other publicity information or fax 212-884-5400.
For authorization to photocopy items for corporate, personal, or educational use, please contact Copyright Clearance Center, 222 Rosewood Drive, Danvers, MA 01923, or fax 978-750-4470.

Trademark Acknowledgments

The 3-D illustrations are the copyright of maranGraphics, Inc.

U.S. Corporate Sales
Contact maranGraphics at (800) 469-6616 or fax (905) 890-9434.

U.S. Trade Sales
Contact Hungry Minds at (800) 434-3422 or fax (317) 572-4002.

Some comments from our readers...

"Compliments To The Chef!! Your books are extraordinary! Or, simply put, Extra-Ordinary, meaning way above the rest! THANKYOUTHANKYOU THANKYOU! for creating these. They have saved me from serious mistakes, and showed me a right and simple way to do things. I buy them for friends, family, and colleagues."

–Christine J. Manfrin (Castle Rock, CO)

"Thank you, thank you, thank you....for making it so easy for me to break into this high-tech world. I just got started on the net and e-mail a year ago. I was overwhelmed by the instructional booklets that came with my computer and printer. I struggled for months. Then, one day I came across your manual and as I leafed through it, a huge sigh of relief swept over me. At last I had found an instruction manual that WAS simple to use! I now own 4 of your books. I recommend them to anyone who is a beginner like myself. Now....if you could just do one for programming VCR's, it would make my day!"

–Gay O'Donnell (Calgary, Alberta, Canada)

"What fantastic teaching books you have produced! Congratulations to you and your staff. You deserve the Nobel prize in Education in the Software category. Thanks for helping me to understand computers."

–Bruno Tonon (Melbourne, Australia)

"I was introduced to maranGraphics about 4 years ago and YOU ARE THE GREATEST THING THAT EVER HAPPENED TO INTRODUCTORY COMPUTER BOOKS!"

–Glenn Nettleton (Huntsville, Alabama)

"I'm a grandma who was pushed by an 11-year-old grandson to join the computer age. I found myself hopelessly confused and frustrated until I discovered the Visual series. I'm no expert by any means now, but I'm a lot further along than I would have been otherwise. Thank you! To date, I have purchased 3 of your publications and am looking forward to more."

–Carol Louthain (Logansport, IN)

"I write to extend my thanks and appreciation for your books. They are clear, easy to follow, and straight to the point. Keep up the good work! I bought several of your books and they are just right! No regrets! I will always buy your books because they are the best."

–Seward Kollie (Dakar, Senegal)

"Just finished my third maranGraphics book and wanted you to know that your books are superior! An avid reader since childhood, I've consumed literally tens of thousands of books, a significant quantity in the learning/teaching category. Your series is the most precise, visually appealing and compelling to peruse. Kudos!"

–Margaret Rose Chmilar (Edmonton, Alberta, Canada)

"I just want tell you how much I, a true beginner, really enjoy your books and now understand a lot more about my computer and working with Windows. I'm 51 and a long time out of the classroom, but these books make it easier for me to learn. Hats off to you for a great product."

–William K. Rodgers (Spencer, NC)

"I commend your efforts and your success. I teach in an outreach program for the Dr. Eugene Clark Library in Lockhart, TX. Your Teach Yourself VISUALLY books are incredible and I use them in my computer classes. All my students love them!"

–Michele Schalin (Lockhart, TX)

"I would like to take this time to thank you and your company for producing great and easy to learn products. I bought my first computer in Dec. of '99 and I was pretty lost. I bought two of your books from a local bookstore, and it was the best investment I've ever made! Thank you for thinking of us ordinary people and helping us understand the world in which we live."

–Jeff Eastman (West Des Moines, IA)

"I would like to take this time to compliment maranGraphics on creating such great books. Thank you for making it clear. Keep up the good work."

–Kirk Santoro (Burbank, CA)

maranGraphics is a family-run business located near Toronto, Canada.

At **maranGraphics**, we believe in producing great computer books–one book at a time.

Each maranGraphics book uses the award-winning communication process that we have been developing over the last 25 years. Using this process, we organize screen shots, text and illustrations in a way that makes it easy for you to learn new concepts and tasks.

We spend hours deciding the best way to perform each task, so you don't have to! Our clear, easy-to-follow screen shots and instructions walk you through each task from beginning to end.

Our detailed illustrations go hand-in-hand with the text to help reinforce the information. Each illustration is a labor of love–some take up to a week to draw!

We want to thank you for purchasing what we feel are the best computer books money can buy. We hope you enjoy using this book as much as we enjoyed creating it!

Sincerely,

The Maran Family

Please visit us on the Web at:

www.maran.com

Credits

Author:
Paul Whitehead

Copy Development Director:
Kelleigh Johnson

Copy Developer:
Luis Lee

Project Manager:
Judy Maran

Editors:
Teri Lynn Pinsent
Stacey Morrison
Norm Schumacher
Faiza Jagot

Layout Designer & Illustrator:
Treena Lees

Illustrators:
Russ Marini
Sean Johannesen
Dave Thornhill
Natalie Tweedie

Indexer:
Teri Lynn Pinsent

Permissions Coordinator:
Jennifer Amaral

Senior Vice President and Publisher, Hungry Minds Technology Publishing Group:
Richard Swadley

Publishing Director, Hungry Minds Technology Publishing Group:
Barry Pruett

Editorial Support, Hungry Minds Technology Publishing Group:
Martine Edwards
Lindsay Sandman
Sandy Rodrigues

Post Production:
Robert Maran

Acknowledgments

Thanks to the dedicated staff of maranGraphics, including Jennifer Amaral, Roderick Anatalio, Cathy Benn, Faiza Jagot, Sean Johannesen, Kelleigh Johnson, Wanda Lawrie, Luis Lee, Treena Lees, Jill Maran, Judy Maran, Robert Maran, Ruth Maran, Russ Marini, Suzana G. Miokovic, Stacey Morrison, Teri Lynn Pinsent, Steven Schaerer, Norm Schumacher, Raquel Scott, Dave Thornhill, Natalie Tweedie, Roxanne Van Damme and Paul Whitehead.

Finally, to Richard Maran who originated the easy-to-use graphic format of this guide. Thank you for your inspiration and guidance.

Permissions

Alta Vista

Digital, AltaVista and the AltaVista logo are trademarks or service marks of Digital Equipment Corporation. Used with Permission.

AMD

AMD, the AMD logo, and combinations thereof as well as certain other marks listed at http://www.amd.com/legal/trademarks.html are trademarks of Advanced Micro Devices, Inc.

Cyrix

Cyrix is a registered trademark of VIA Technologies, Inc.

Imation Corp.

SuperDisk
SuperDisk is a trademark of Imation Corporation.

Travan Tape Drive
Travan is a trademark of Imation Corporation.

Intel

Courtesy of Intel Corporation.

Microsoft

© 2001 Microsoft Corporation. All rights reserved.

Rambus

Rambus®, RDRAM and the Rambus logo are registered trademarks and RIMM is a trademark of Rambus Inc.

Yahoo

Reproduced with permission of Yahoo! Inc. 2001 by Yahoo! Inc. YAHOO! and the YAHOO! logo are trademarks of Yahoo! Inc.

Permissions Granted:

Dell

ENERGY STAR

iomega

Sony

Sunkist

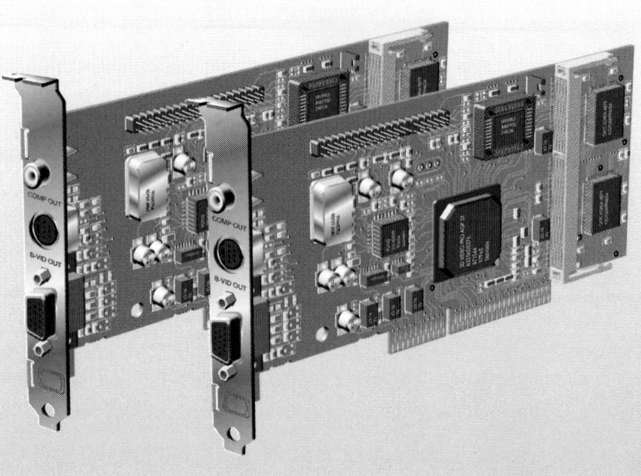

Table of Contents

Table of Contents

CHAPTER 1

UPGRADE AND REPAIR BASICS

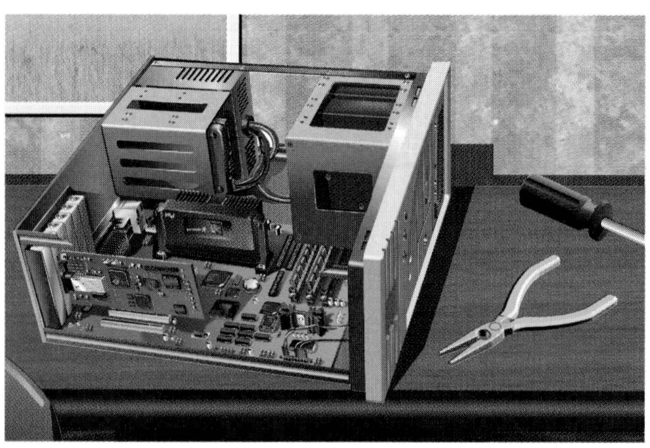

CHAPTER 2

COMPUTER ESSENTIALS

CHAPTER 3

INPUT AND OUTPUT DEVICES

CHAPTER 4

COMMUNICATION DEVICES

CHAPTER 5

STORAGE DEVICES

Table of Contents

CHAPTER 6

UPGRADE A COMPUTER

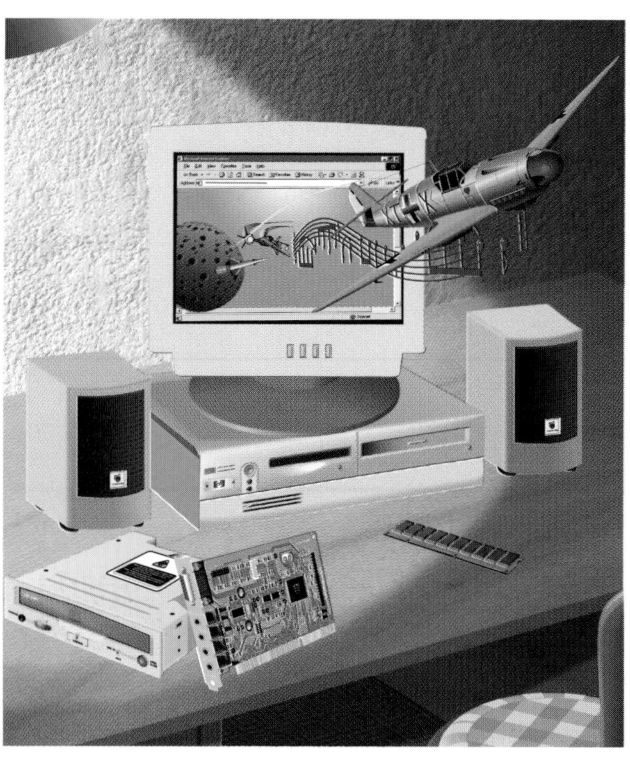

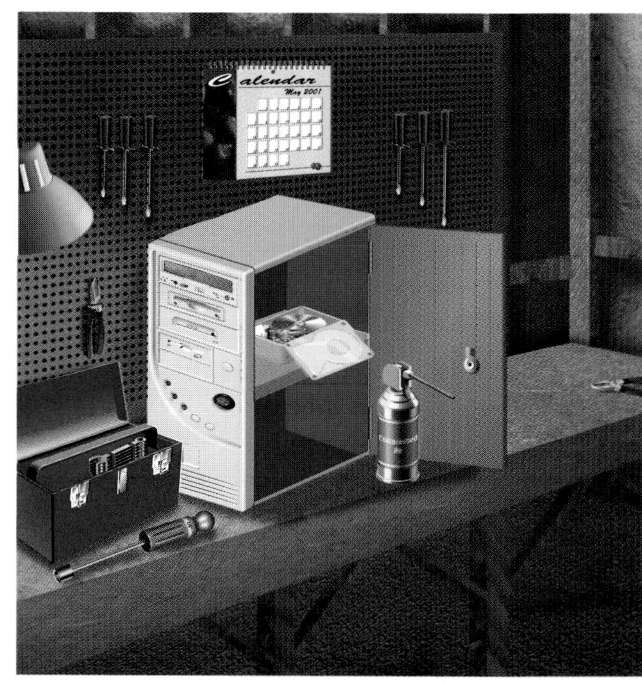

CHAPTER 7

REPAIR A COMPUTER

CHAPTER 8

PURCHASE A NEW COMPUTER

CHAPTER 9

CREATE A HOME NETWORK

APPENDIX

INTRODUCTION TO PC UPGRADE AND REPAIR SIMPLIFIED

PC Upgrade and Repair Simplified, 2nd Edition is for anyone who wants to learn computer upgrade and repair techniques. Performing your own upgrades and repairs can save you money and increase your knowledge about computers and computer components.

Learn to Upgrade and Repair

This book will teach you how to keep your computer up-to-date by upgrading components and devices. You will also learn how to determine the cause of common computer problems and how to repair those problems.

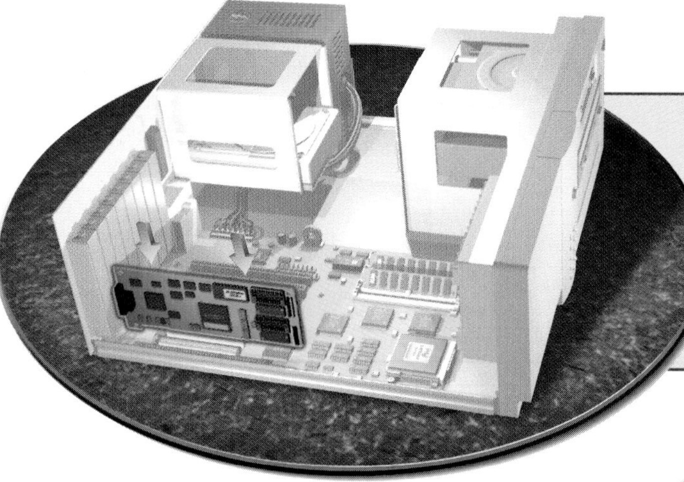

Install Components and Devices

PC Upgrade and Repair Simplified, 2nd Edition uses pictures to guide you step by step through installing internal components, such as an expansion card or a CPU. You will also learn how to connect external devices, such as a keyboard or scanner.

Set Up a Home Network

If you have more than one computer at home, you can use this book to learn the basics you need to set up a home network. A home network enables you to access information and resources from another computer, share an Internet connection and play multi-player games.

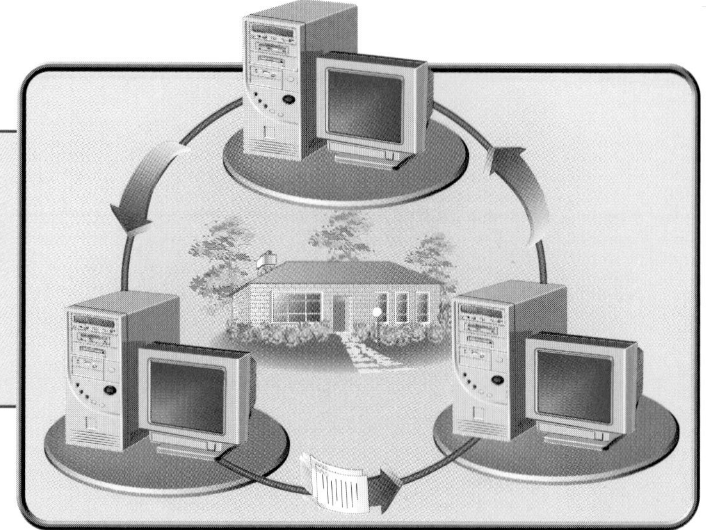

CONSIDERATIONS

Type of Computer

You do not need a particular type of personal computer to complete the tasks shown in this book. *PC Upgrade and Repair Simplified, 2nd Edition* can help you upgrade and repair a wide variety of computer components and devices.

Computer Experience

You do not need any previous computer upgrade or repair experience to use this book, but you should be familiar with the major components of the computer. You should also be familiar with the features and capabilities of your computer's operating system.

Computer Tools

You can use common tools, such as a screwdriver, to perform most computer upgrades and repairs. Some tasks, however, may require you to use special tools, such as grounding devices. Grounding devices protect computer components from being damaged by static electricity. For information about computer tools, see page 4.

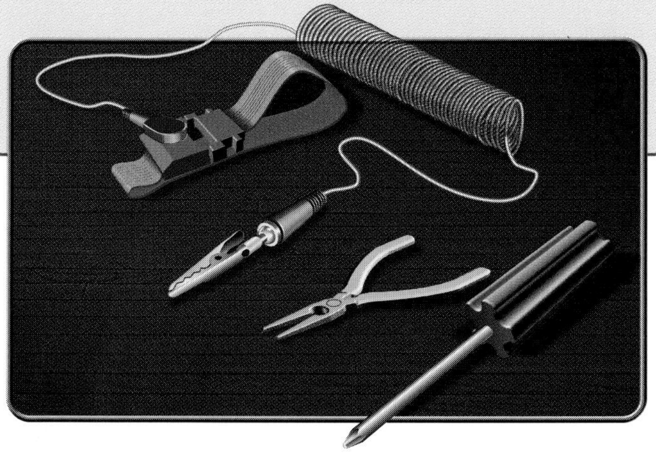

Warranty

You should check your computer warranty before attempting to upgrade or repair the computer. Some warranties can last up to three years and may be voided if you open the computer case.

There are several tools you can use to upgrade or repair your computer safely and efficiently. You can purchase a kit of commonly used computer tools at most computer stores.

Screwdriver

You can use a slotted or Phillips screwdriver to insert and remove the screws on most computers. If you use a power screwdriver, choose one with torque control to avoid over-tightening screws. Some computers have screws that require a star-shaped screwdriver, called a Torx driver. The most common Torx driver sizes you need are T10 and T15.

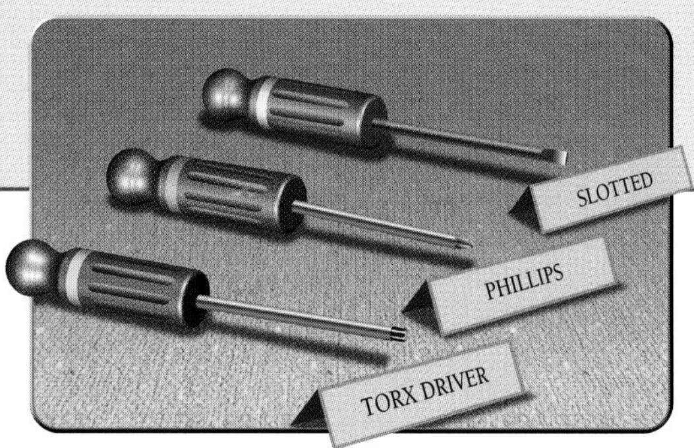

Nut Drivers

Small nut drivers can be used instead of a screwdriver for many screws. The most common nut driver sizes you need are 3/16-inch and 1/4-inch.

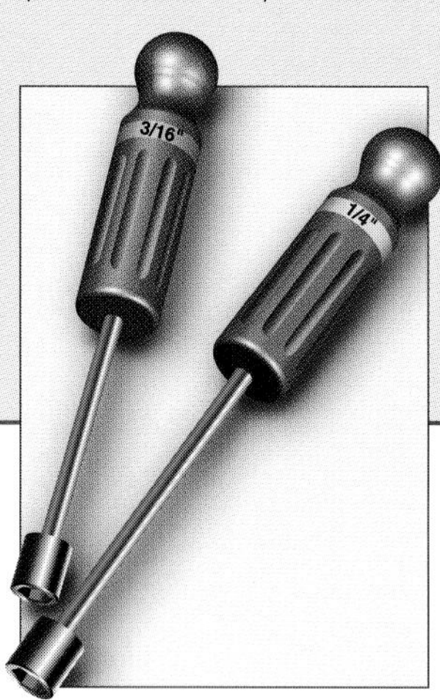

Pliers or Tweezers

You can use a small set of needle nose pliers or a sturdy pair of tweezers to adjust the jumpers on a system board or on a device such as a hard drive.

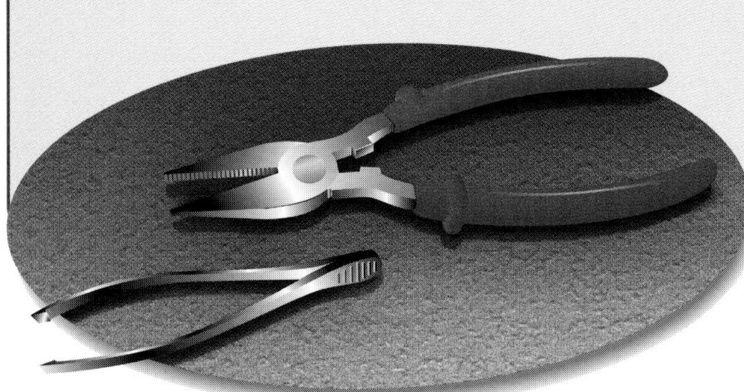

Chip Remover

A chip remover is a device you can use to remove a damaged chip from its socket on a circuit board. A chip remover is often referred to as a chip extractor or chip puller.

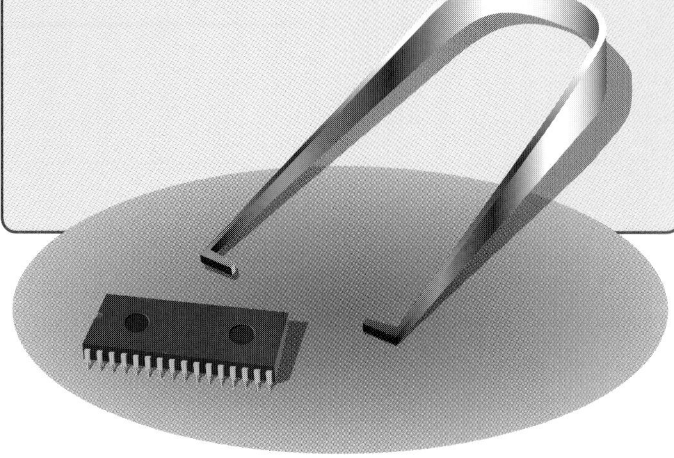

Magnet and Grabber

Computer screws and other small parts can often fall into hard-to-reach places inside the computer case. You can use a small magnet on the end of an extending rod to retrieve screws you have dropped. A grabber can be used to retrieve non-metallic parts.

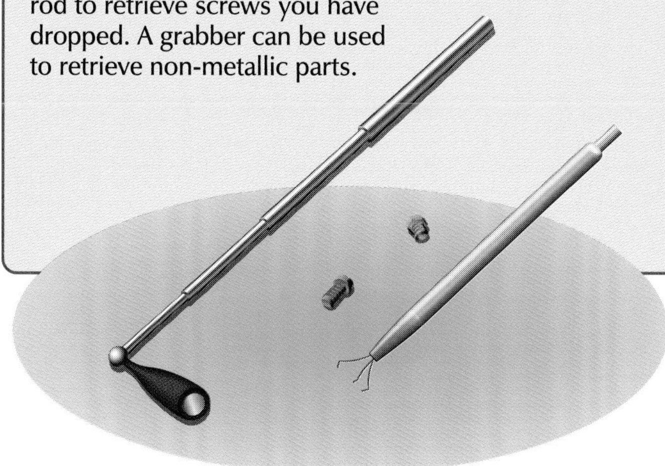

Grounding Strap

Computer components can be damaged by static electricity. While repairing a computer, you should wear a grounding strap to prevent the transfer of static electricity from your body to the computer. For information about protecting components from static electricity, see page 6.

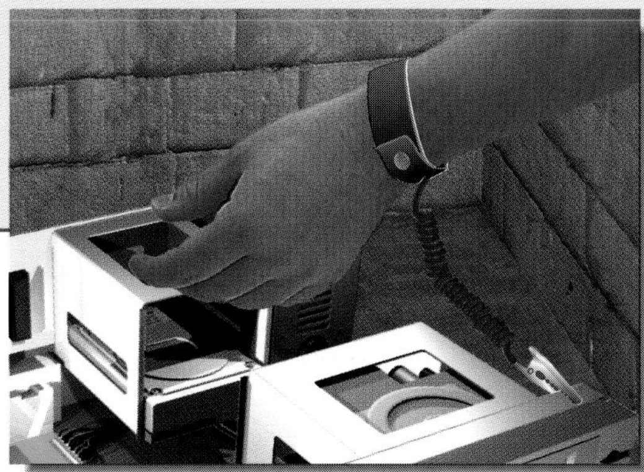

Compressed Air

You can use a can of compressed air to blow dust and dirt from inside a computer case. This can make components easier to see and work with.

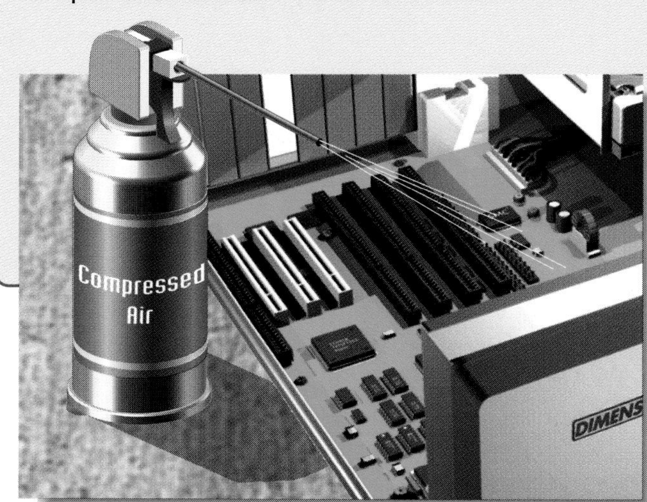

Flashlight

You can use a flashlight to illuminate the inside of a computer case. This helps you easily see components while repairing a computer. Using a small mirror with the flashlight helps you get a better view of obstructed components.

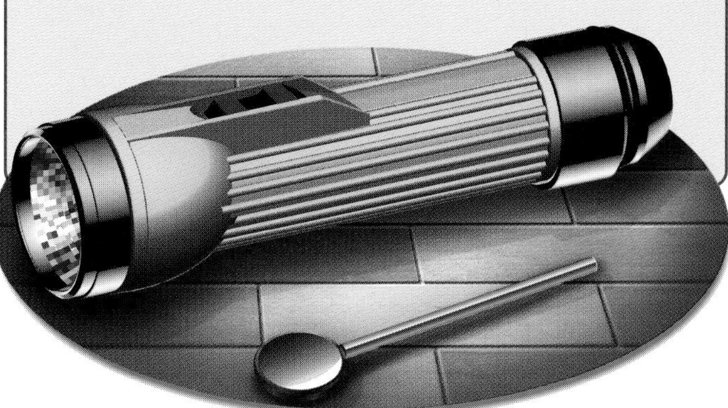

PROTECT COMPONENTS FROM STATIC ELECTRICITY

Static electricity can damage computer components, especially those with complex circuits, such as a system board or CPU chip. When upgrading or repairing your computer, you must take precautions to protect the components.

Static Electricity

Your body generates static electricity. Although you may not be able to detect the static electricity you generate, it is always present. You can transfer static electricity from your body to computer components just by touching them. ElectroStatic Discharge (ESD) is the term used to describe the transfer of static electricity from one object to another.

Grounding

When upgrading or repairing a computer, you should not touch the computer unless you and the computer are grounded. To ground yourself and the computer, you can use devices such as grounding wires, ground straps and grounding mats.

You should not attempt to ground a computer by leaving the power cord plugged into an outlet. Even when the power is turned off, newer computers supply a constant current to the system board when plugged in. This current could damage your computer or components when you try to upgrade or repair the computer.

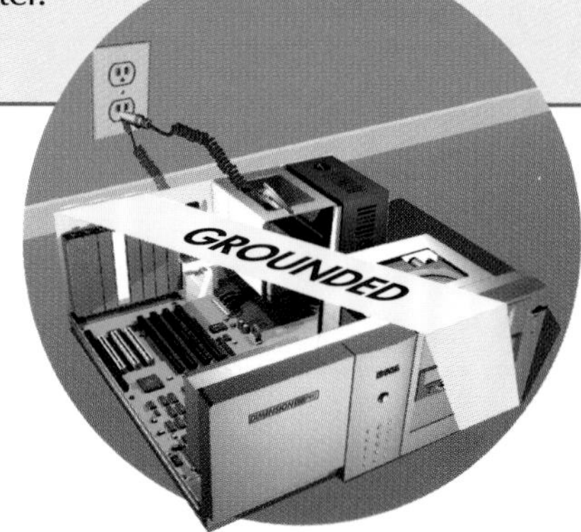

GROUNDING DEVICES

Many grounding devices plug into the third hole on an electrical outlet. Grounding devices are available at most computer stores.

Grounding Wire

You should always connect a metal part of the computer case to a grounding wire. When the computer case is grounded, you can touch a metal part of the computer case to ground yourself.

Grounding Strap

You can wear a grounding strap on your wrist to prevent the transfer of static electricity from your body to computer components. Disposable grounding straps are available at most computer stores.

Grounding Mat

You can use a grounding mat to protect individual components from static electricity. You can position a grounding mat beside a computer and then place individual components on the mat.

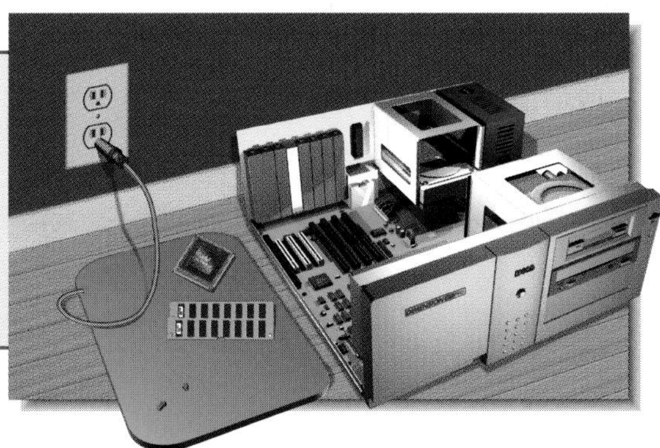

ANTI-STATIC BAGS

If you are removing a component from a computer for an extended period of time, you should store the component in an anti-static bag. Anti-static bags come in different sizes and are available at most computer stores.

You can use cables and connectors to connect devices to your computer. Connectors with holes are called female connectors. Connectors with pins are called male connectors.

Most cables and connectors are unique and can connect only specific devices to a computer.

EXTERNAL CONNECTORS

Most external connectors are located at the back of the computer case. Some external connectors use screws or small clips to secure a connection.

Keyboard Port

A keyboard port is a female connector with 6 holes, which allows you to connect a keyboard to the computer. This is known as a mini-DIN or PS/2 connector. Older computers have a larger keyboard port with five holes, known as a DIN connector.

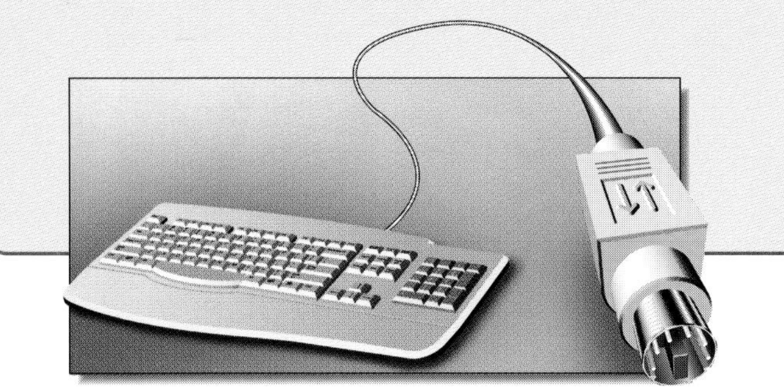

Mouse Port

A mouse port is a female connector with 6 holes and is found on newer computers. Also known as a mini-DIN or PS/2 connector, a mouse port allows you to connect a mouse to the computer. The mouse port looks identical to the keyboard port. Manufacturers often use labels or color-coding to help you distinguish the mouse port from the keyboard port.

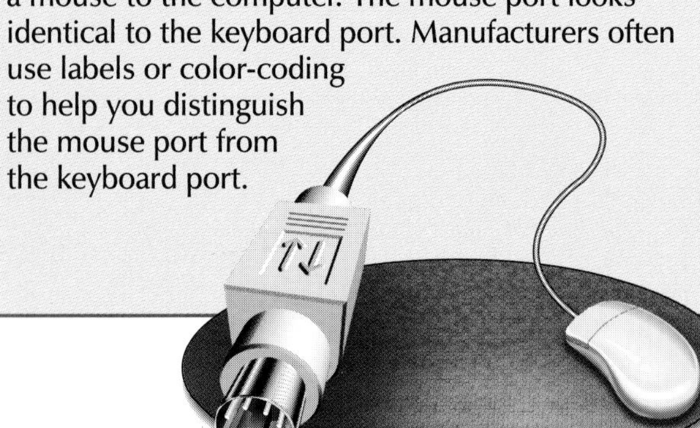

Serial Port

A serial port can be a 9 or 25-pin male connector. A serial port allows you to use a serial cable with a 9 or 25-hole female connector to connect a device such as a mouse or external modem to the computer. Most computers have two serial ports.

Parallel Port

A parallel port is a female connector with 25 holes. A parallel port allows you to use a parallel cable with a 25-pin male connector to connect a device such as a printer to the computer. Most computers have only one parallel port.

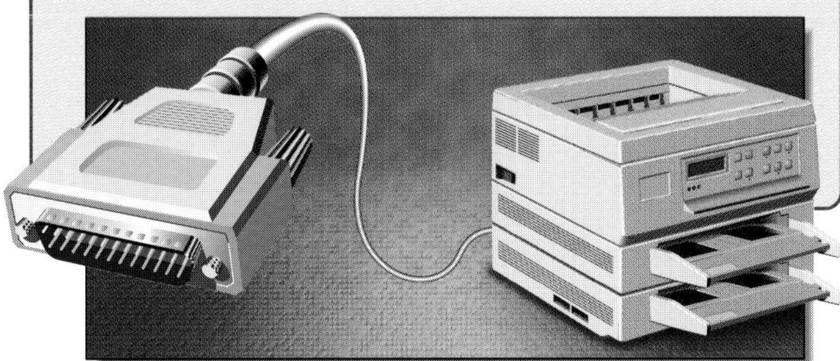

Monitor Port

A monitor port is a female connector with 15 holes. A monitor port allows you to use a monitor cable with a 15-pin male connector to connect a monitor to the computer. Some computers have multiple monitor ports.

Power Connector

A power connector is a 3-prong male connector. A power connector allows you to use a power cable with a 3-hole female connector to connect the computer to an electrical outlet on the wall.

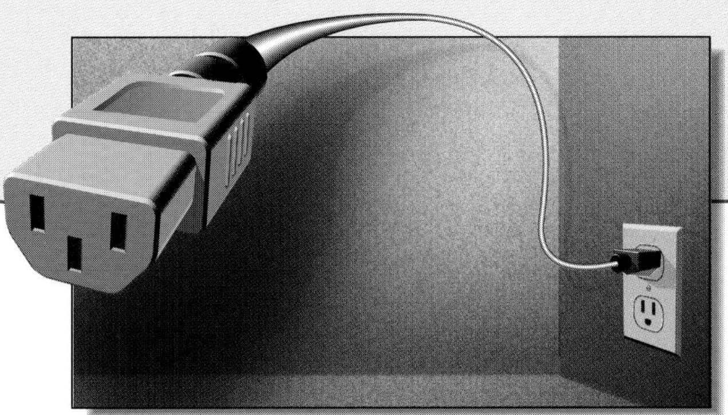

EXTERNAL CONNECTORS (CONTINUED)

Audio Jack

Most computers have a sound card that contains several small, round audio jacks. Audio jacks allow you to connect devices such as speakers, headphones or a microphone to the computer.

Joystick Port

A joystick port is a female connector with 15 holes and is usually found on a sound card. A joystick port allows you to connect a joystick to the computer to play games. You can also use a joystick port to connect a musical instrument, such as an electronic synthesizer, to the computer.

Modem Jack

A modem jack is the same type of connector as a telephone jack. A computer with an internal modem has two modem jacks. One jack allows you to plug a telephone line into the computer, while the other jack allows you to connect a telephone to the computer.

USB Port

A Universal Serial Bus (USB) port is a small, rectangular connector that can support up to 127 devices, such as a printer, digital camera and scanner. Most new computers have two USB ports.

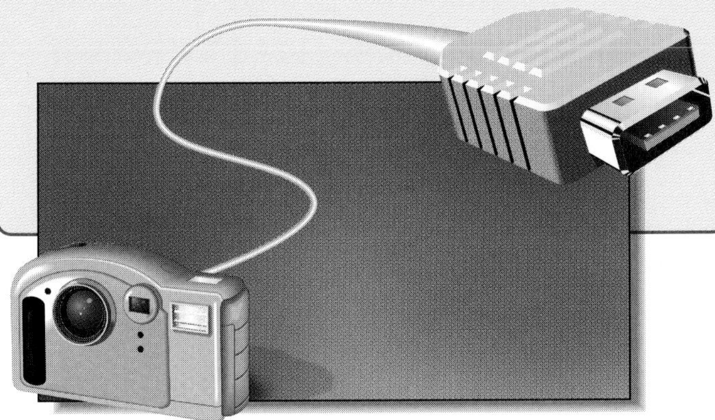

Coaxial Connector

A coaxial connector is a small, round, metal connector found on a network interface card. A coaxial connector allows you to use coaxial cable to connect the computer to a network.

RJ-45 Jack

An RJ-45 jack looks like a large telephone jack and is found on a network interface card. An RJ-45 connector allows you to use twisted pair cable to connect the computer to a network.

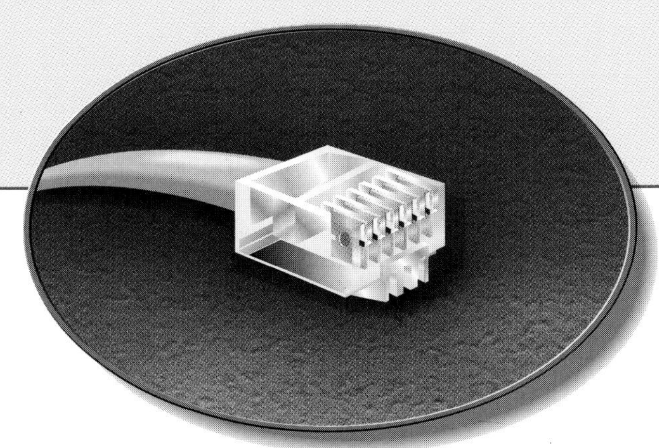

SCSI Port

A Small Computer System Interface (SCSI, pronounced "scuzzy") port is a female connector with 50 or 68 holes. A SCSI port allows you to use a SCSI cable with a 50 or 68-pin male connector to connect devices such as an external hard drive, tape drive or scanner to the computer.

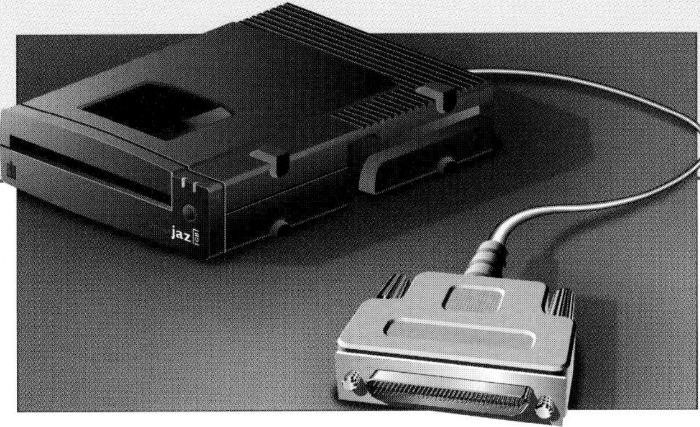

INTERNAL CONNECTORS

Most internal connectors in new computers are located on the system board, but some are found on expansion cards.

Most internal devices connect to the computer using a ribbon cable. The connector on the ribbon cable must be properly aligned with the connector on the system board or expansion card. To properly attach the connectors, align the red colored edge of the ribbon cable with pin 1 on the system board or expansion card. A number 1 or a dot is printed near the connector to indicate the location of pin 1.

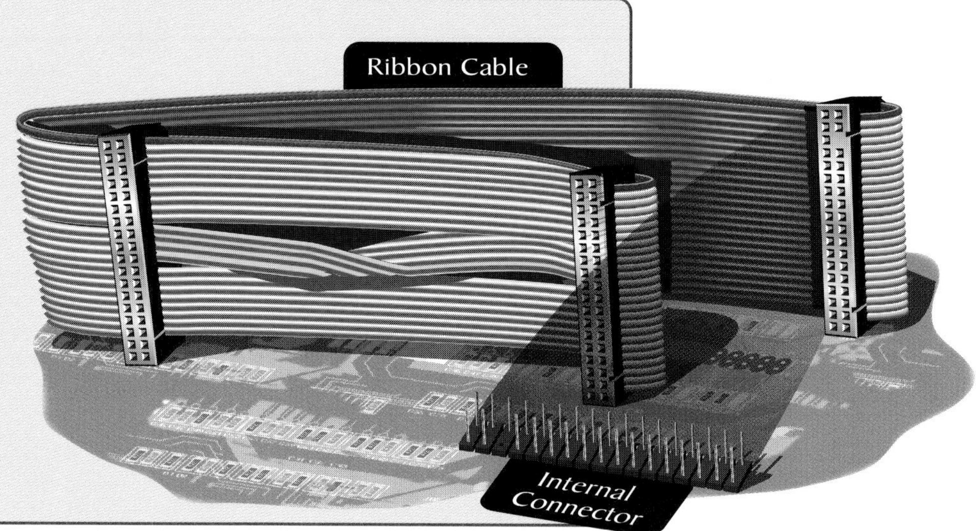

EIDE

An Enhanced Integrated Drive Electronics (EIDE) connector is a 40-pin male connector. Many new computers have two EIDE connectors. An EIDE connector allows you to use an EIDE ribbon cable to connect two devices, such as a hard drive and CD-ROM drive, to the computer.

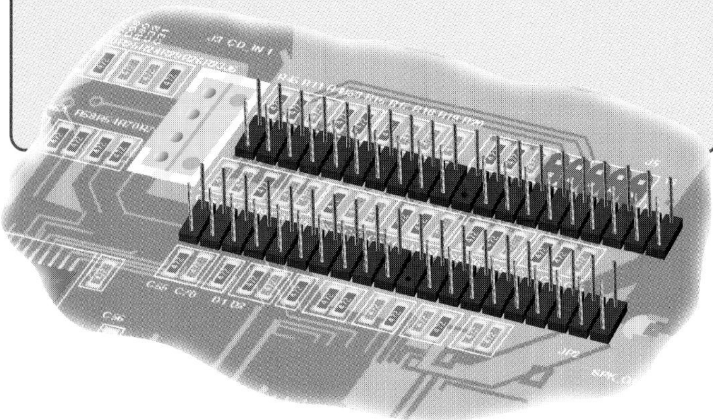

SCSI

An internal Small Computer System Interface (SCSI) connector is a 50-pin male connector and is usually found on a SCSI expansion card. An internal SCSI connector allows you to use a SCSI ribbon cable to connect multiple storage devices, such as a hard drive and tape drive, to the computer.

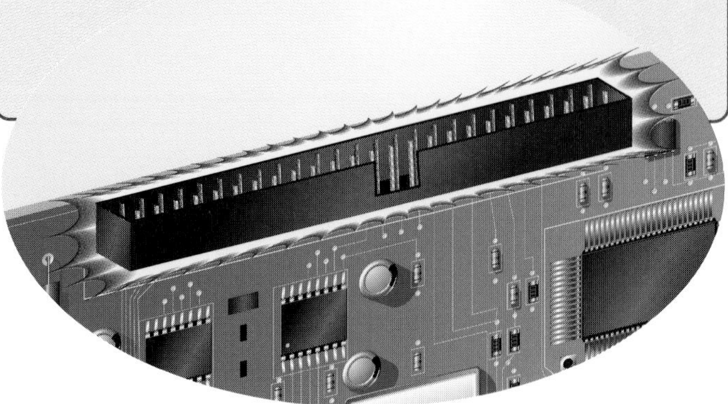

Floppy Drive

A floppy drive connector is a 34-pin male connector. All computers have a floppy drive connector. A floppy drive connector allows you to use a floppy drive ribbon cable to connect two devices, such as a floppy drive and a tape drive, to the computer.

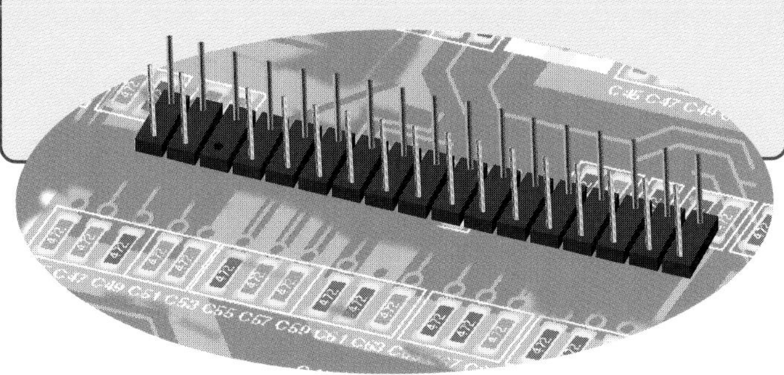

Parallel

An internal parallel connector is a 26-pin male connector. You can use an internal parallel connector to connect a parallel port to the computer. Many new computers do not have an internal parallel connector because the parallel port is built into the system board.

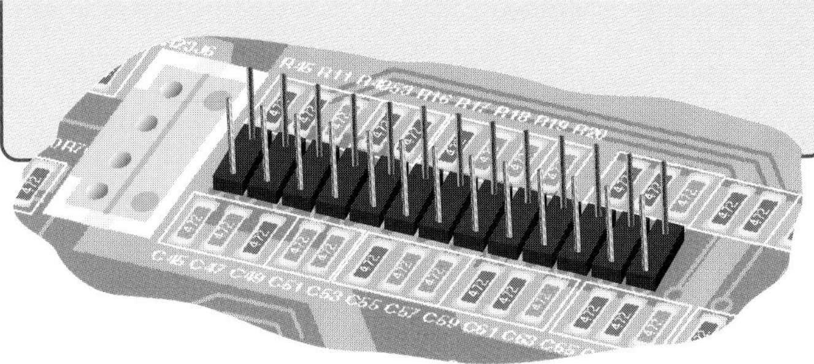

Serial

An internal serial connector is a 10-pin male connector. You can use an internal serial connector to connect a serial port to the computer. Many new computers do not have an internal serial connector because the serial port is built into the system board.

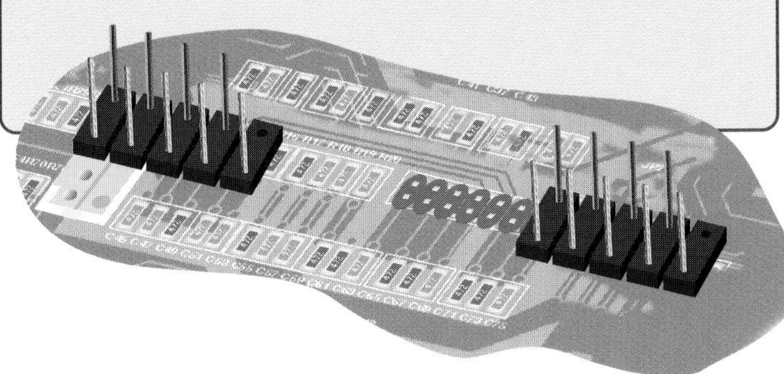

Pin Connectors

Most pin connectors are 2 or 4-pin male connectors. A pin connector allows you to use a wire to connect an item on the front of the case, such as the power switch or hard drive activity light, to the computer.

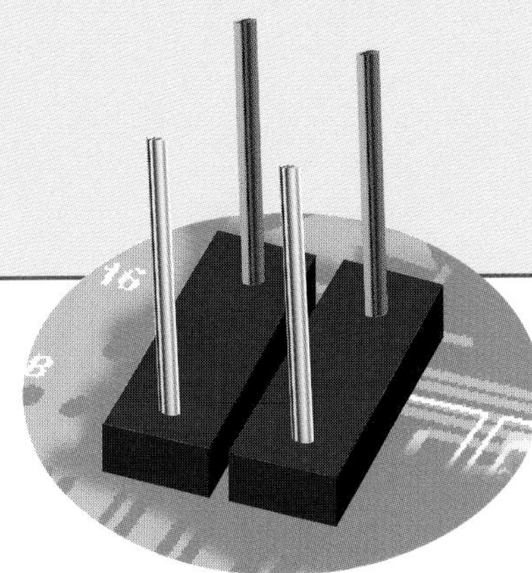

REFERENCE MATERIAL

There are many sources of reference material about upgrading and repairing computers. You can find information about your computer or the particular upgrade or repair you want to perform.

SOURCES OF REFERENCE MATERIAL

Documentation

When gathering reference material, you should start by reviewing the documentation that came with the computer. Computer documentation usually contains information about the system specifications and common error messages. The documentation also often has a troubleshooting section that can help you solve common problems. This type of reference material is often provided in a printed manual, but may also be found on floppy disks or a CD-ROM disc.

Internet

The Internet is an excellent source of up-to-date reference material about computers. Almost all computer manufacturers have Web sites where you can review product information and contact technical support representatives. Many computer-related Web sites also provide a wide variety of information about upgrading and repairing computers.

Computer-related newsgroups are another good source of reference material on the Internet.

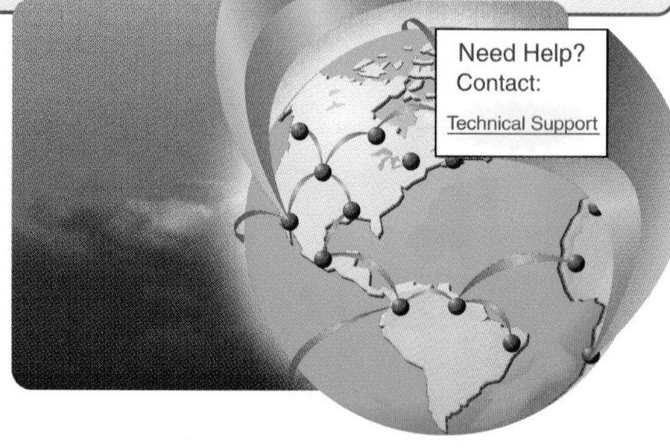

Computer Clubs

Joining a computer club in your area allows you to exchange ideas with other people who are interested in computer upgrade and repair. Some computer clubs offer classes on computer maintenance and repair.

Computer Stores

If you have specific questions, you can try calling the store where you purchased the computer or equipment. Computer stores often provide technical support for their customers.

Computer Shows

Computer shows, where manufacturers display and sell computer hardware and software, are a good source of information. At these shows, you can speak with people who are knowledgeable about upgrading and repairing computers. Many computer shows also provide workshops that teach you how to perform basic computer maintenance and repair.

CD-ROM Discs

There are many CD-ROM discs available that contain computer reference material. For example, you can purchase a CD-ROM disc that contains frequently asked questions about computer repair or a collection of articles related to computer hardware and software. You can also find product specifications, hardware settings and solutions to common computer problems on CD-ROM discs.

PREPARE TO UPGRADE OR REPAIR A COMPUTER

There are several things you can do to prepare for an upgrade or repair. Proper preparation can help make upgrading or repairing your computer easier.

Schedule Time

You should schedule an upgrade or repair for a time when you will not need your computer. You may want to choose a time when sources of help and technical support are available.

When scheduling an upgrade or repair, make sure you set aside enough time to complete the task. Replacing or adding a component may not take very long, but setting up the computer to work with a new component can be time-consuming. You should also allow time for any problems that may arise.

Record the Computer Settings

The computer settings store information about the devices installed on a computer and are essential to the proper functioning of the computer. You should write down the computer settings before you begin to upgrade or repair a computer, as this information may be erased during the upgrade or repair. For information about computer settings, see page 146.

Perform Benchmark Tests

You should run benchmark software on your computer to determine the current performance levels of the system. After the upgrade or repair is complete, you can perform the benchmark tests again. Comparing the tests performed before and after the upgrade or repair can help you determine the success of your work.

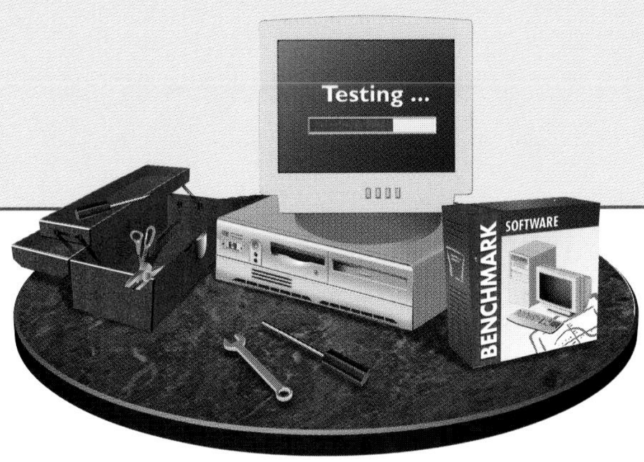

Back Up Information

When upgrading or repairing a computer, you risk losing or damaging information stored on the computer. You should always make a backup copy of the information stored on the computer before you begin. For more information, see page 24.

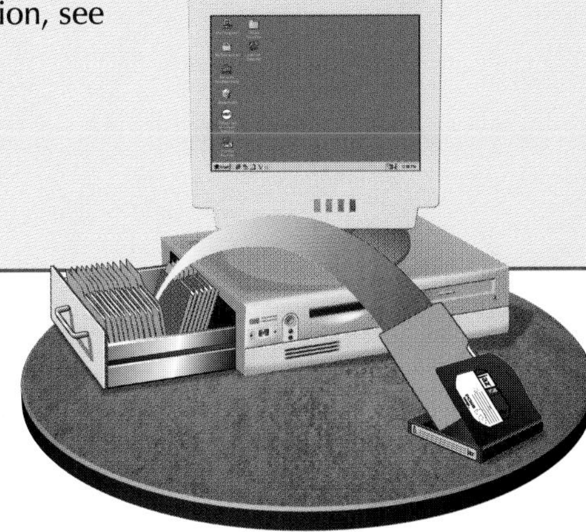

Gather Software

Make sure you have a startup disk, the CD-ROM disc for the operating system and the installation disks for the backup software. In the event of a problem, you may need to re-install the operating system and backup software before you can restore your information.

Gather Reference Material

You should gather any reference material you will need to perform the upgrade or repair, such as the documentation that came with the computer or component. You may need to refer to this information if a problem arises.

PREPARE TO UPGRADE OR REPAIR A COMPUTER (CONTINUED)

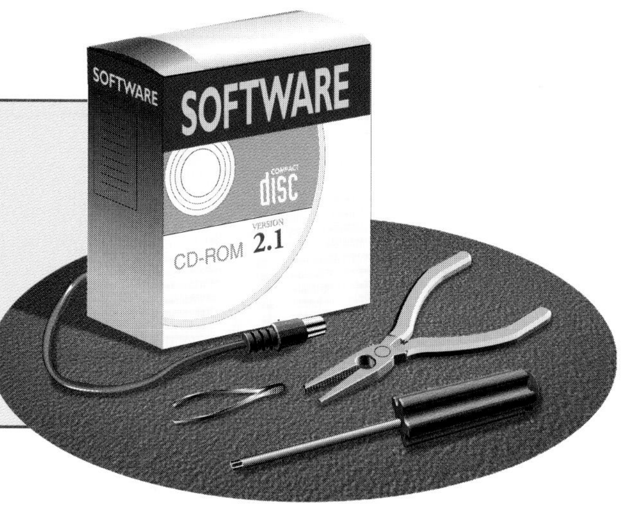

Gather Equipment and Tools

Before you begin upgrading or repairing a computer, you should make sure you have all the necessary equipment to perform the task, such as cables or software. You should also gather any computer tools you may need, such as screwdrivers and pliers. For more information about computer tools, see page 4.

Gather Cleaning Equipment

You may also want to gather your computer cleaning supplies before you begin. Disassembling a computer for upgrade or repair is a great opportunity to clean the internal components of the computer. For information about computer cleaning supplies, see page 20.

Prepare a Work Area

Clear a work area where you can perform the upgrade or repair. Disassembling a computer can be awkward and usually requires a lot of space. If your computer is in a cramped location, you should move it to a more accessible area. You should choose a well-lit area so you can clearly see the inside of the computer.

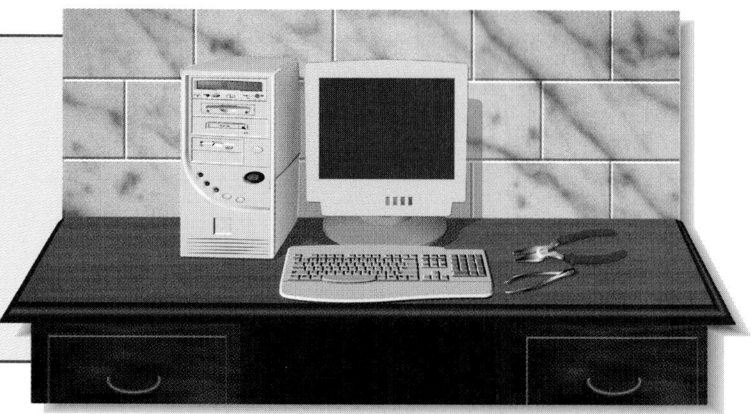

Protect Components From Static Electricity

Static electricity can damage the components in a computer. When upgrading or repairing a computer, you should take precautions to protect the components from damage caused by static electricity, such as using a grounding mat or wearing a grounding strap. For more information, see page 6.

Prepare Components

Many components require some assembly before they can be installed in a computer. For example, you may need to attach a mounting bracket to a storage device before you can install it. Consult the documentation included with the component to determine if assembly is required.

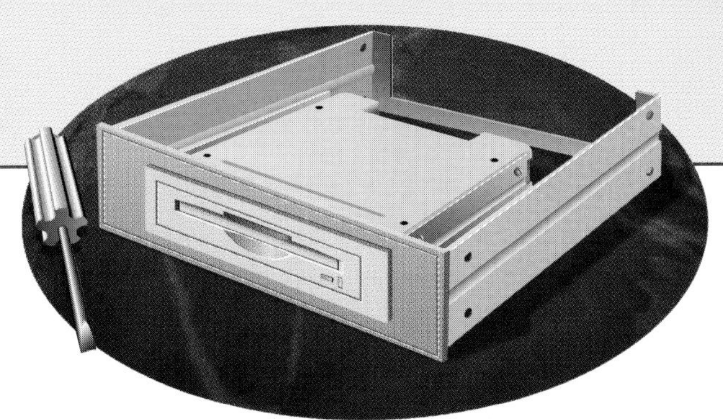

Take Notes and Make Drawings

While disassembling a computer, you should take notes and make drawings to record information such as where cables are connected, the order you remove components and how jumpers and switches are set on components. This information can help you later re-assemble the computer.

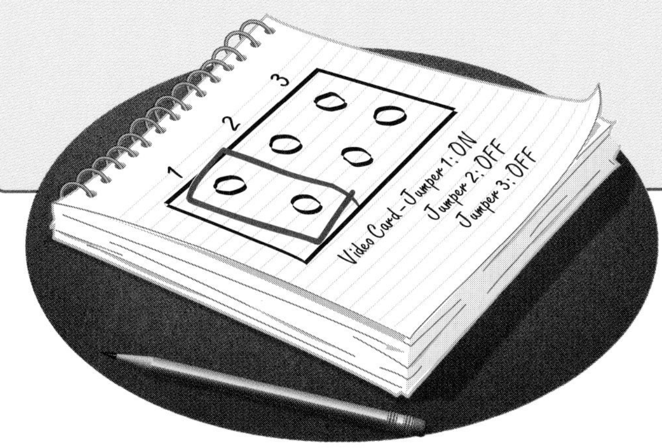

Record Model and Serial Numbers

You should record the model and serial numbers of all the components in your computer. An accurate listing of this information can help make upgrading and repairing the computer an easier task.

There are many items you can use to clean a computer. Cleaning your computer on a regular basis can help keep the computer in good working order.

Most computer and electronics stores carry computer cleaning supplies.

Cleaning Fluid

You can use cleaning fluid to clean the plastic surfaces on the outside of a computer. Computer cleaning fluid usually comes in a spray bottle. You should always spray cleaning fluid on a cloth rather than directly on a computer. This will prevent the fluid from leaking inside the computer and causing electrical problems.

Vacuum Cleaner

You can remove dust and dirt from inside a computer using a specially designed vacuum cleaner. A computer vacuum cleaner is useful when you want to avoid blowing dust on other components. These vacuum cleaners often come with attachments you can use to clean very small areas of a computer, such as between the keys on a keyboard or between expansion slots.

Compressed Air

You can use a can of compressed air to blow dirt, debris and dust from inside a computer. Cans of compressed air are inexpensive.

Brush

You can use a small brush, such as a makeup brush or paintbrush, to remove dirt and debris from inside a computer. You may also want to use a brush to loosen accumulated dust before removing the dust with a computer vacuum cleaner or a can of compressed air. You should not use a brush on the circuit boards inside a computer.

Contact Cleaner

You can use contact cleaner to clean the connectors in a computer, such as expansion slot connectors and the metal contacts on memory modules. Cleaning connectors helps ensure a reliable connection between a component and the computer.

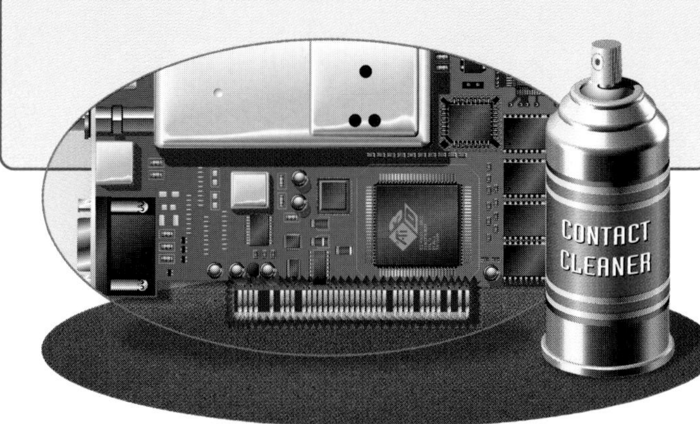

Lubricant

You can use a silicone lubricant to lubricate mechanical components, such as the computer case hinges or floppy drive eject button. Some lubricants also have cleaning capabilities, similar to contact cleaner. You should use a swab to apply lubricant to computer components.

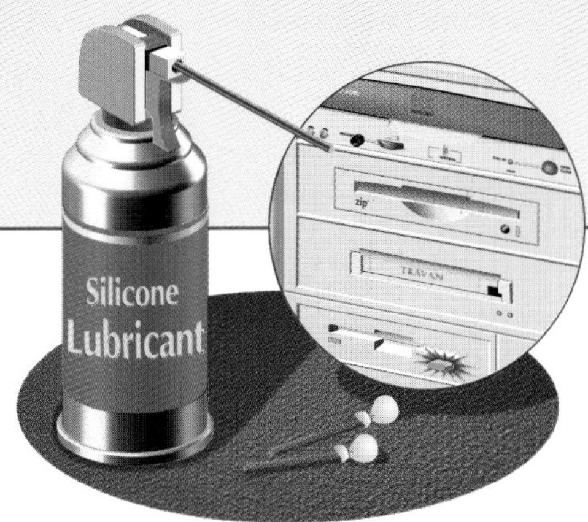

A virus is a program that can disrupt the normal operation of a computer. There are several ways you can protect your computer from viruses.

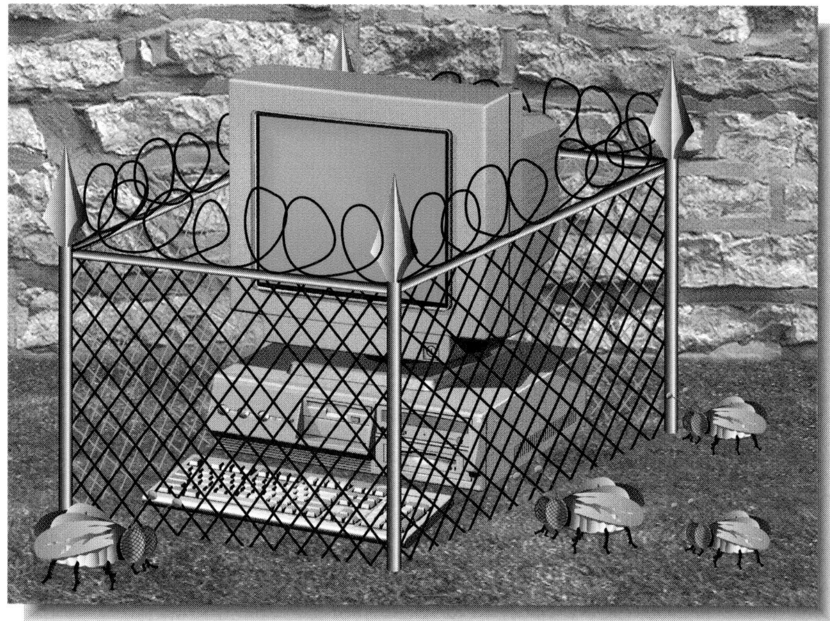

Symptoms of a virus, such as computer lockups, data loss, program crashes, unusual messages and reduced computer performance, are often mistaken for hardware or software problems.

HOW VIRUSES SPREAD

Floppy Disk

Floppy disks are a common way that viruses spread between computers. You should not use a floppy disk you receive from another person unless you are certain the disk does not contain a virus. You should also never start a computer when the floppy drive contains a disk that has been used by another computer.

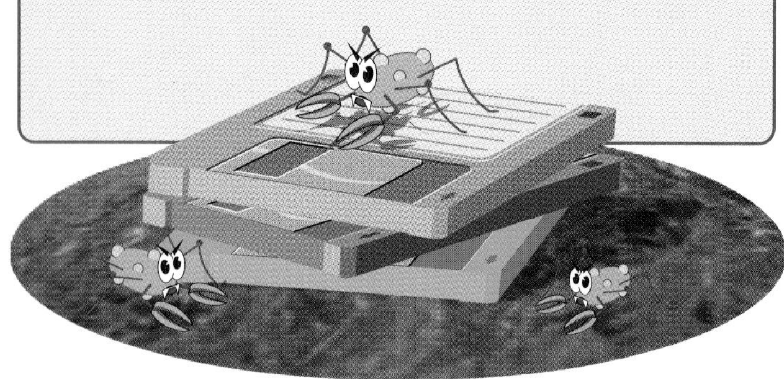

Internet

The Internet has made it possible for viruses to spread quickly to many computers. You should only download programs or other information from reputable sources on the Internet.

You should also be careful of files you receive attached to e-mail messages. You should only open files sent by people you trust.

CHOOSE AN ANTI-VIRUS PROGRAM

Scanner

An anti-virus program with a virus scanner feature allows you to check the files on a hard drive or floppy disk for viruses as a preventative measure or when symptoms of a virus are present.

Constant Scanning

Some anti-virus programs constantly check for viruses on your hard drive and in any new files you download or programs you install. This allows you to detect a virus before the virus can do serious damage.

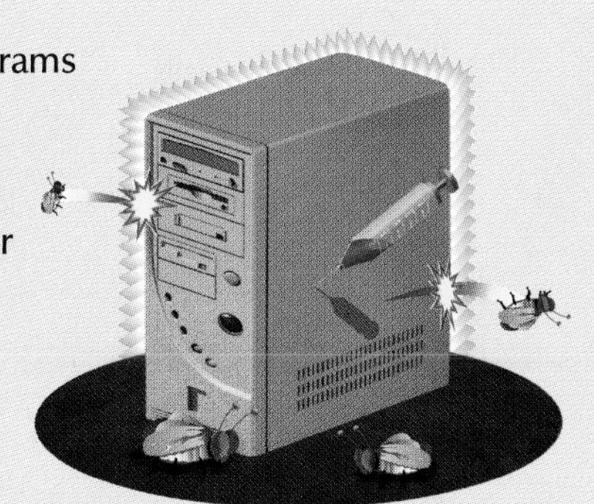

Virus Removal

A virus removal feature removes any viruses found by the anti-virus program. Some viruses can be removed without damaging the infected file, but sometimes the file may become unusable.

Intrusion Detection

Most high-speed Internet connections can make your computer vulnerable to access by unauthorized users who may infect your computer with viruses. An intrusion detection feature protects your computer from unauthorized access.

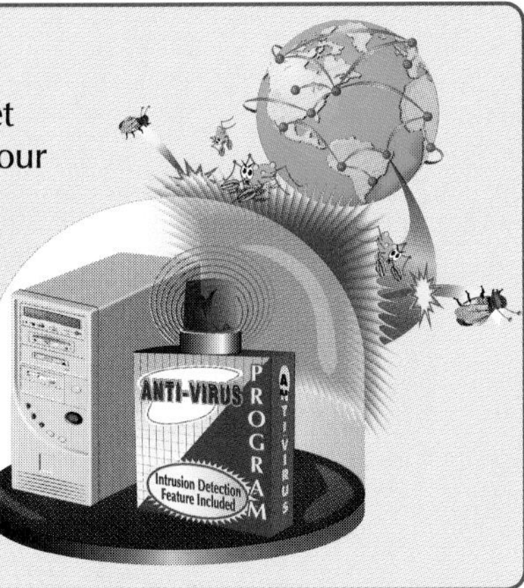

Updates

Anti-virus program updates allow programs to detect the latest known viruses. Anti-virus program manufacturers regularly make updates available on their Web sites. Some anti-virus programs also have an automatic update feature.

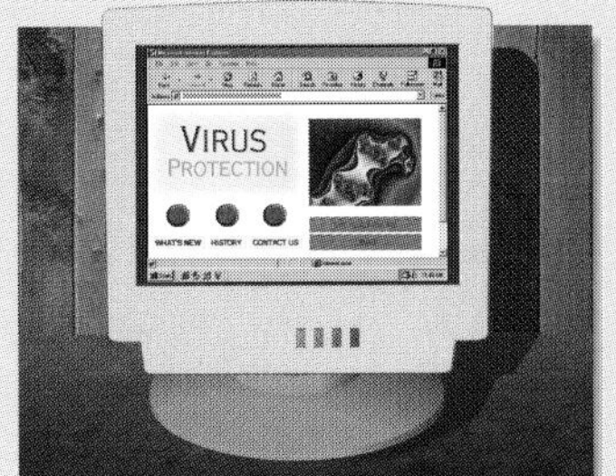

BACK UP INFORMATION

Before you upgrade or repair your computer, you should ensure you have a backup copy of all the information stored on the computer.

You are more likely to lose or damage information on a hard drive while upgrading or repairing a computer than at any other time.

BACKUP PROGRAMS

A backup program copies the files stored on a computer to a storage device, such as a tape drive. Most storage devices come with a backup program specifically designed for use with the storage device. Most backup programs compress the data being backed up to save space on the storage media, such as tape cartridges.

BACKUP MEDIA

You can back up information onto media such as floppy disks, tape cartridges or removable disks. You should store your backup media in a safe, dry location out of direct sunlight. You should also regularly test your backups to ensure that the backup media you use has not become damaged over time.

BACKUP PROCEDURES

Types of Backups

A full backup backs up all the programs and information on a computer. Before upgrading or repairing your computer, you should perform a full backup. A differential backup backs up only the information that has changed since the last full backup. An incremental backup backs up only the information that has changed since the last time you performed any type of backup. The types of backups you can perform depend on the capabilities of your backup program.

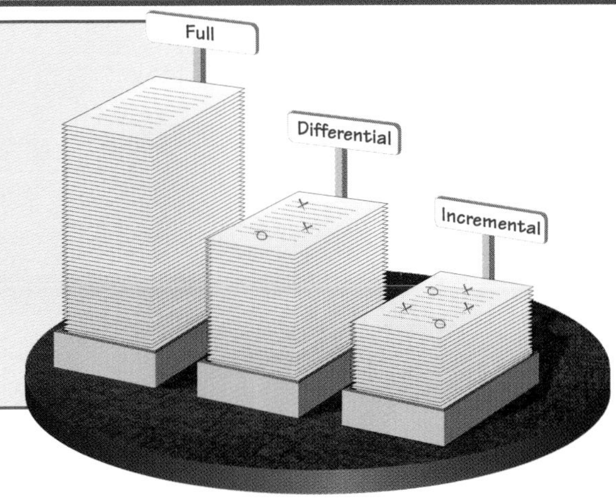

BACKUP CALENDAR

Backup Schedule

You should create and then strictly follow a backup schedule. To determine how often you should back up the information on a computer, consider the importance of the information and the time it would take to recreate your work. In the event of a hard drive failure, you will lose all the work you have accomplished since the last backup you performed.

Duplicate Backups

To minimize the chances of losing information, you should make two backup copies of your information. Keep one copy near your computer and the second copy in a separate location where it will not be affected by fire or theft.

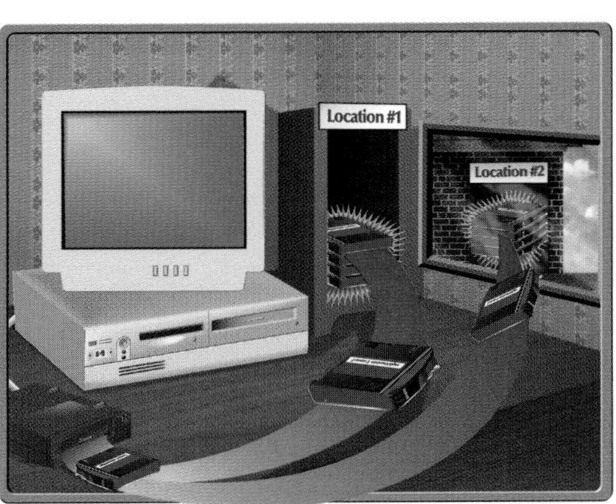

Training will teach you how to upgrade and repair your computer more efficiently.

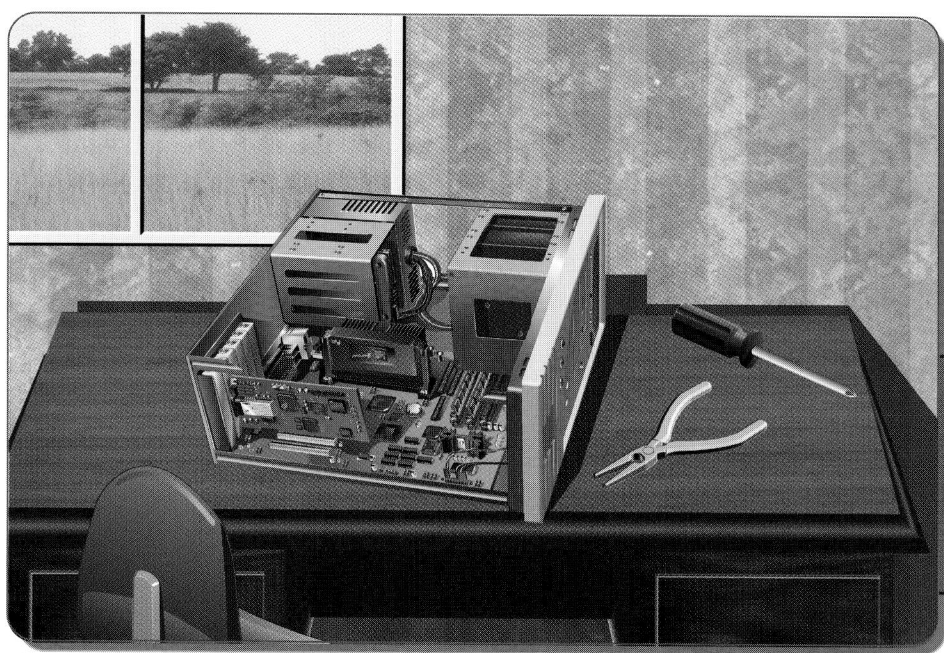

One of the best ways to learn about upgrading and repairing a computer is to work on your own computer to gain hands-on experience.

Benefits of Training

Computer upgrade and repair skills are valuable both at home and in the workplace. Learning how to upgrade and repair a computer allows you to effectively troubleshoot computer problems and enables you to customize a computer to suit the needs of the user. The ability to upgrade and repair your computer also saves you from having to find a reliable repair service and can save you money.

Up-To-Date Information

You should continue to educate yourself on new developments in the computer industry after you finish your training. The information you learn while training can become obsolete if you do not keep up-to-date with current computer products, trends and information. Computer magazines, which are available at most computer stores, and Web sites on the Internet are good sources of current information.

TYPES OF TRAINING

Computer Stores

Many computer stores, especially large chain stores, offer classes in computer upgrade and repair. The classes are usually inexpensive and some stores even offer free classes to regular customers.

Computer and Business Schools

Many specialized schools, such as computer and business schools, offer computer upgrade and repair classes. You may be able to receive certification when you complete a training course at a computer or business school.

Computer-Based Training

Computer-Based Training (CBT) allows you to use your computer to learn at home at your own pace. Computer-based training courses are available in a package containing a book and CD-ROM disc at most computer stores. You can also find courses on the Internet.

Computer-based training courses contain step-by-step instructions with detailed illustrations and diagrams. There are also questions you can answer to receive feedback about your progress. You may be able to receive certification when you complete computer-based training.

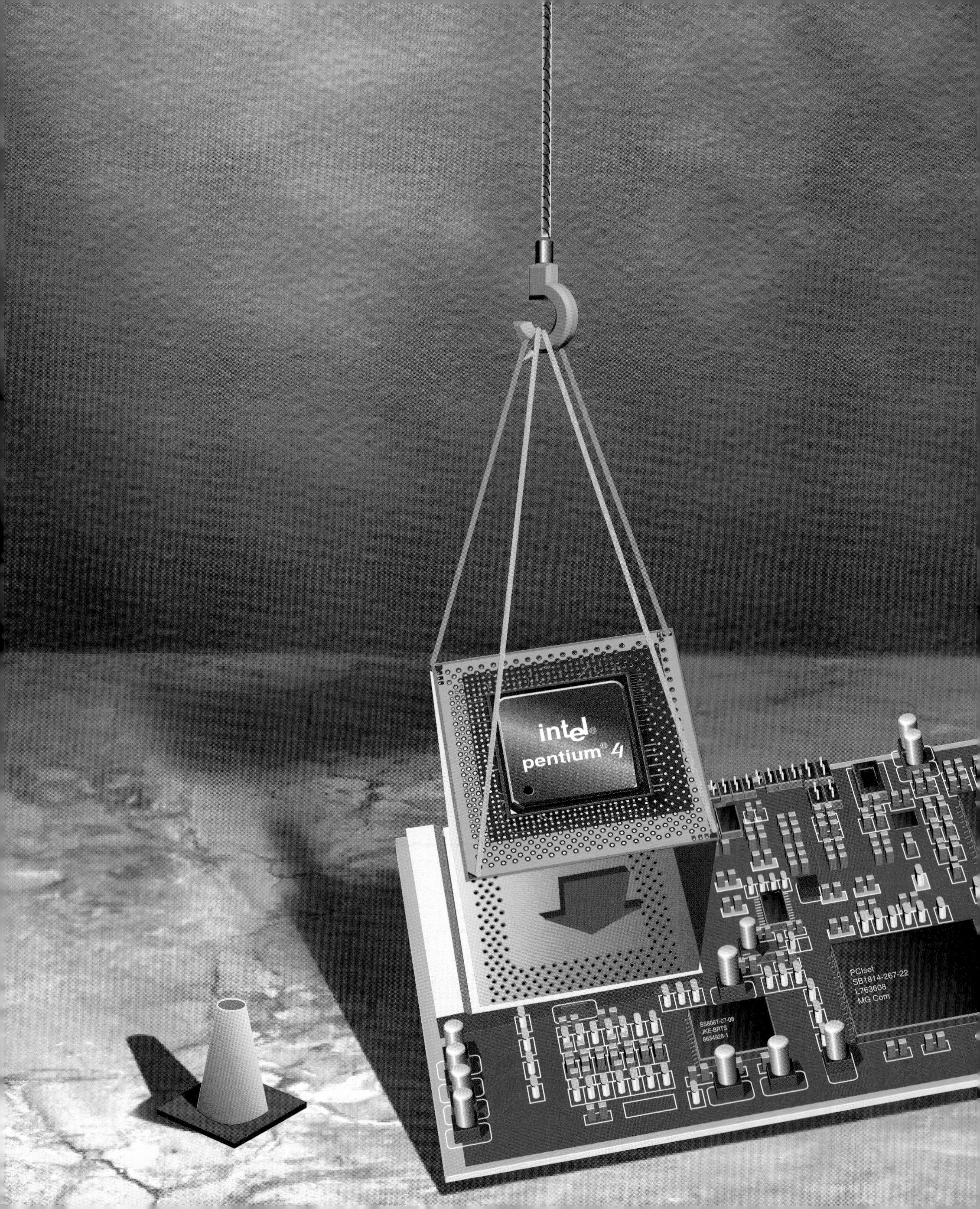
intel
pentium 4
PCIset
SB1814-267-22
L763608
MG Com
SS8087-07-08
JKE-BRTS
8634928-1

CHAPTER 2

COMPUTER ESSENTIALS

Do you want to familiarize yourself with the components a computer requires to operate before you begin an upgrade or repair? This chapter explains the system board, central processing unit and much more.

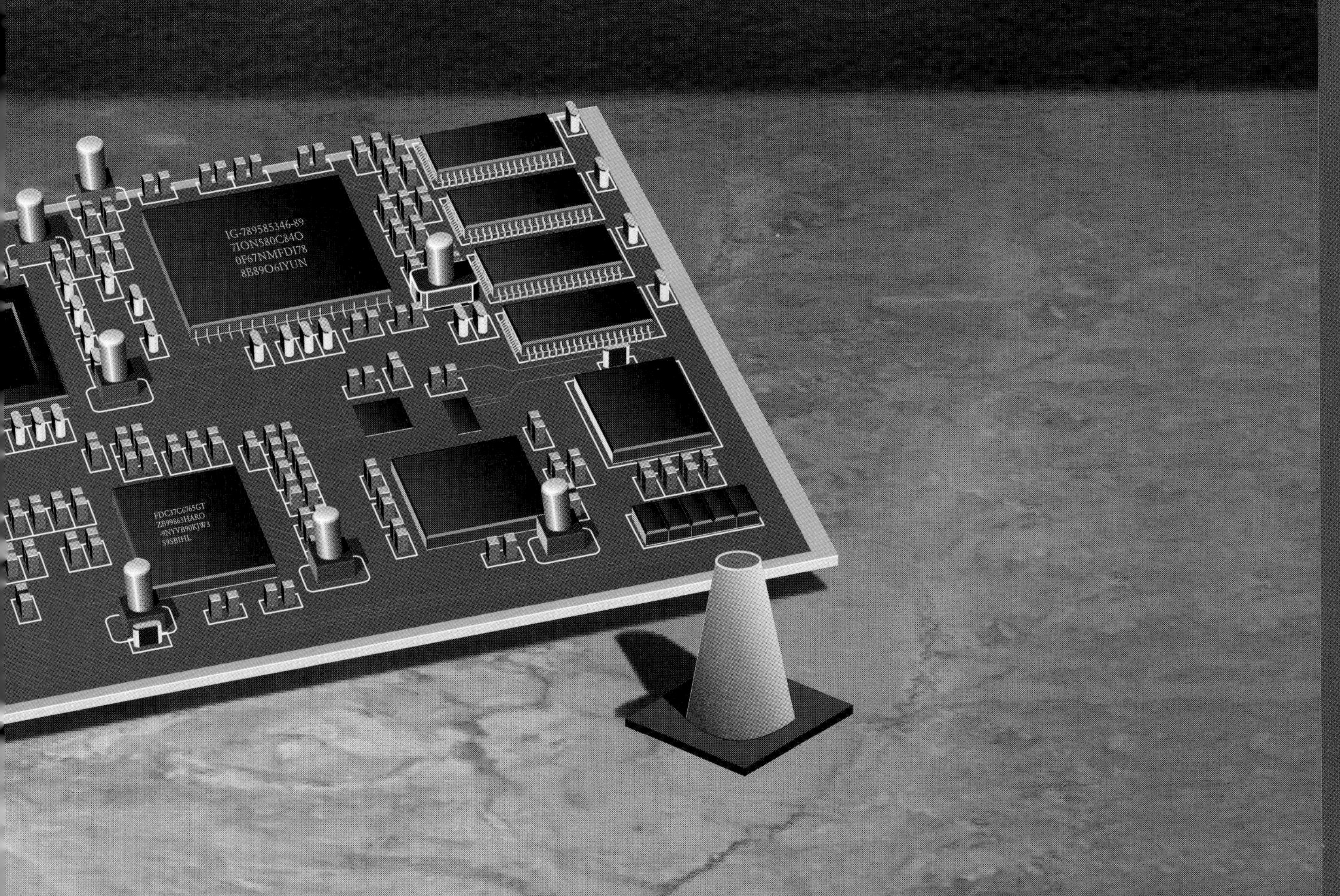

COMPUTER CASE

A computer case is a box that contains most of the major components of a computer system. A computer case provides a solid structure that protects components from dirt and damage.

When upgrading or repairing a computer, you will often need to remove the computer case cover.

REMOVE A COMPUTER CASE COVER

Before removing the computer case cover, turn off the computer and unplug the power cable.

1

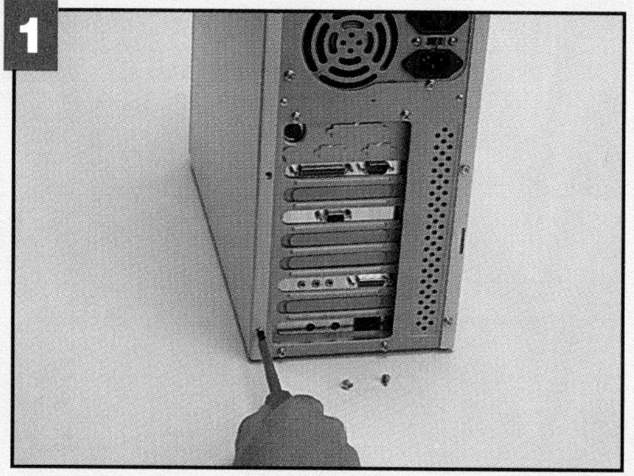

Remove the screws that hold the computer case cover in place. Most covers are held in place by four screws at the back of the computer.

You can check your computer's documentation to determine which screws to remove. Some of the screws at the back of the computer secure internal devices, such as the power supply, to the computer.

2

Slide the cover backward or forward a short distance. Then lift the cover straight up.

SET UP A COMPUTER CASE

Most computer cases have items, such as the power button and indicator lights, which attach to pin connectors on the system board. To avoid problems, make sure you connect all the items properly.

CHOOSE A COMPUTER CASE

Computer Case Style

There are two main styles of computer cases—desktop and tower. A desktop case is wider than it is tall and usually sits on a desk, under a monitor.

A tower case often sits on the floor. This provides more desk space, but can be less convenient for inserting and removing floppy disks and CD-ROM discs.

Form Factor

A form factor is a set of specifications that determines the internal size and shape of a computer case. The two most popular computer case form factors are ATX and Baby AT. The computer case must use the same form factor as the power supply and system board.

Power Supply

Computer cases are often sold with a power supply already installed. When purchasing a new computer case, you should ensure that the power supply meets your power requirements. For more information about power supplies, see page 38.

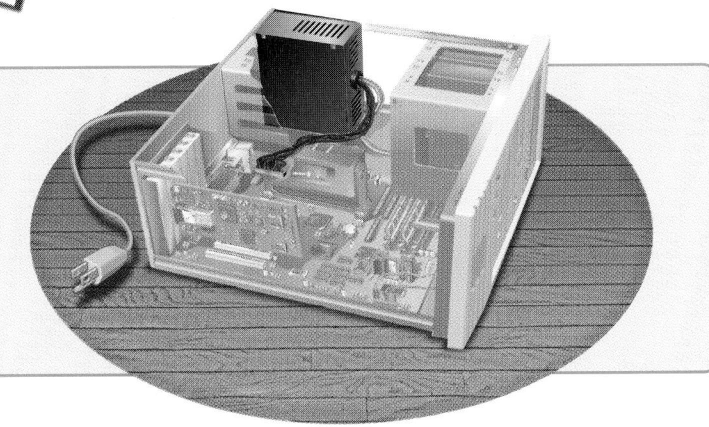

SYSTEM BOARD

A system board is the largest and most complex component in a computer.

REPLACE A SYSTEM BOARD

Before replacing a system board, turn off the computer, unplug the power cable and remove the cover from the computer case. Then ground yourself and the computer case. For information about grounding, see page 6.

Disconnect the cables from the back of the computer. Then remove the expansion cards from the system board.

Disconnect all the cables from the system board.

Remove all the screws that secure the system board in the computer case.

Slide the system board slightly sideways to release the small plastic spacers, called standoffs, that prevent the system board from touching the computer case. Then lift the system board out of the computer case.

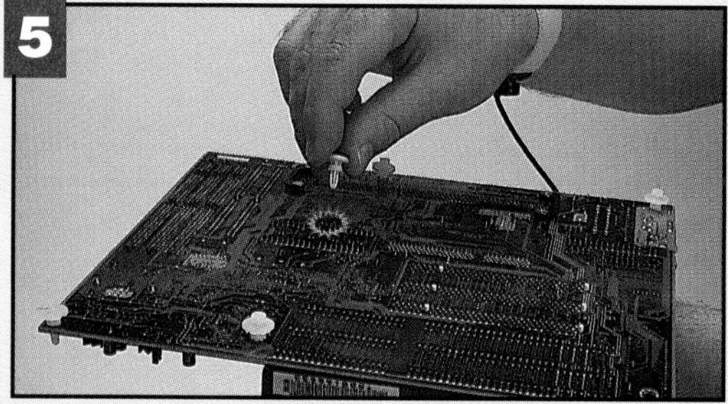

If necessary, add the standoffs from the old system board to the new system board.

Place the new system board in the computer case, slide the system board into position and secure it with screws. Then reconnect all the cables, re-install the expansion cards and replace the cover on the computer case.

MAIN SYSTEM BOARD COMPONENTS

A **port** allows the system board to communicate with an external device, such as a printer.

A **memory slot** is a socket on the system board. A memory module, which holds memory chips for storing data, sits in a memory slot.

A **chipset** is a series of chips that contains instructions for controlling the movement of data through the system board.

The **power connector** is a socket on the system board. The system board power cable attaches to the power connector.

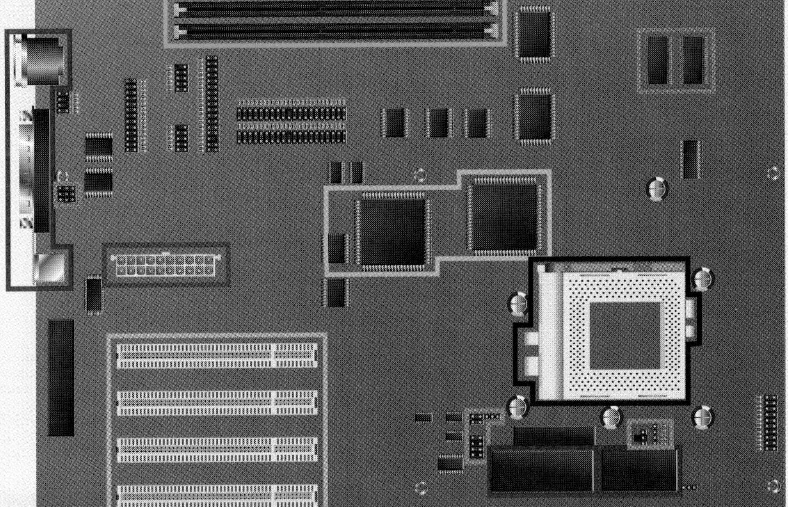

Cache memory stores recently used data.

An **expansion slot** is a socket on the system board. An expansion card, which lets you add features to a computer, plugs into anexpansion slot.

Jumpers allow you to adjust the settings for the system board.

The **Basic Input/Output System (BIOS) chip** controls the transfer of data between devices attached to the system board.

The **Complementary Metal Oxide Semiconductor (CMOS) chip** saves the time and the computer's BIOS settings. A battery provides power to the CMOS chip when the computer is turned off.

The **processor socket** holds the CPU, which is the main chip in a computer.

CHOOSE A SYSTEM BOARD

Form Factor

A form factor is a set of specifications that determines the general size and shape of a system board. The Baby AT form factor is found in many older computers, but most newer computers use the ATX form factor. The system board you choose must use the same form factor as the computer case and power supply.

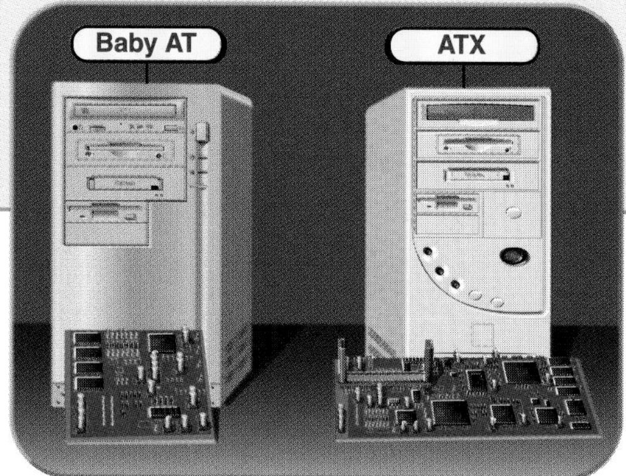

Power Management

Most system boards offer Advanced Power Management (APM) features, which allow you to conserve energy by controlling how a computer uses power after a period of inactivity. For example, you can have your hard drive, monitor and other devices shut down when they are not in use.

Processor Socket

The type of processor socket determines the type of CPU you can use in the computer. A square, two-inch socket, called Socket 7, holds a Pentium CPU. Pentium II, Celeron and Pentium III CPUs fit into a socket similar to an expansion slot, called Slot 1.

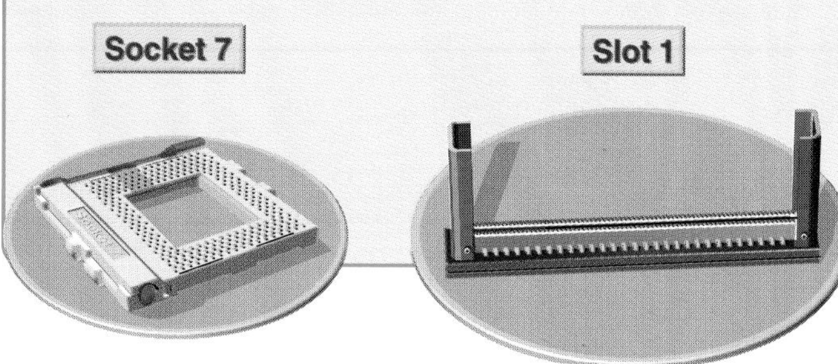

Chipset

Each system board has a series of chips that contains instructions to control the movement of data through the system board. When you purchase a system board, make sure the chipset is compatible with your CPU.

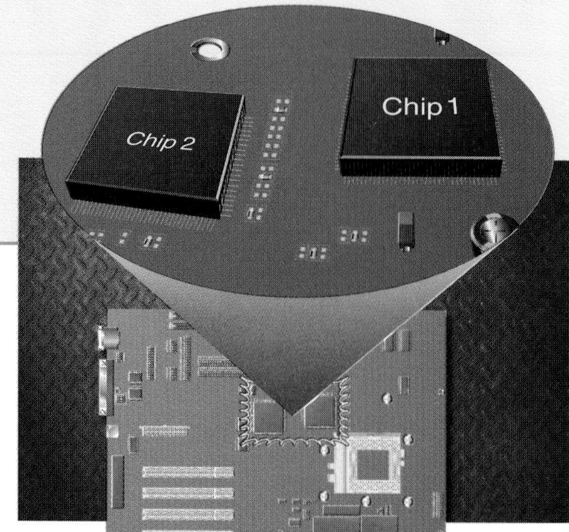

Cache Memory

Cache memory is used to speed up the transfer of data by storing data the computer has recently used. Cache memory is faster and more expensive than main memory. Many new system boards come with 512 K of cache memory.

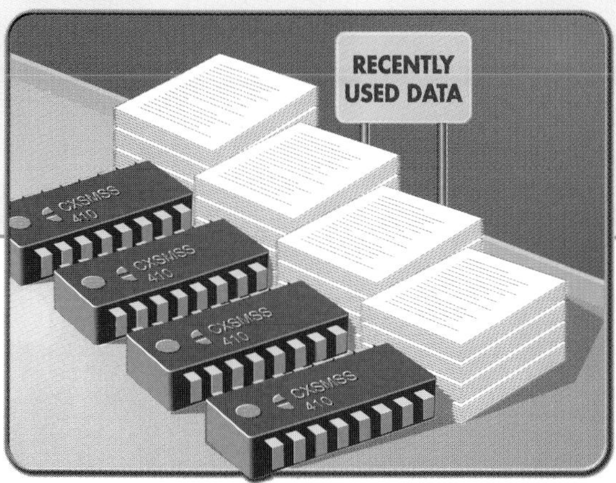

Memory Speed

Depending on the type of memory in the computer, memory speed may be measured in nanoseconds (ns) or megahertz (MHz). When upgrading your system board, make sure the system board supports the speed of your existing memory. For information about memory, see page 46.

Buses

The system bus carries data between components on the system board. Most new system boards support bus speeds of 100 and 133 megahertz (MHz). System boards that use Pentium 4 CPU chips can support bus speeds starting at 400 MHz.

Expansion buses carry data between devices in a computer. There are three common types of expansion bus—Industry Standard Architecture (ISA), Peripheral Component Interconnect (PCI) and Accelerated Graphics Port (AGP).

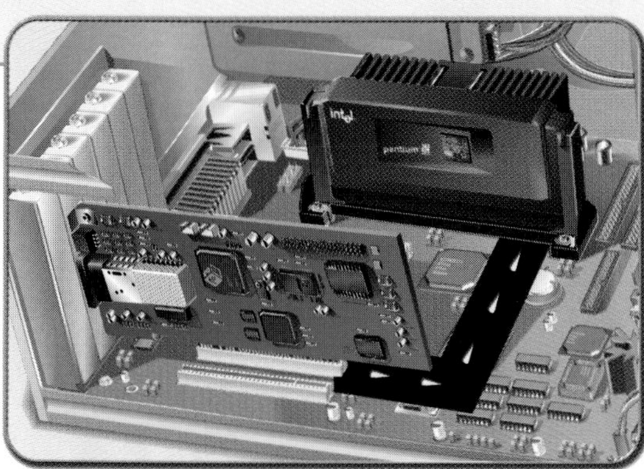

BIOS

The Basic Input/Output System (BIOS) chip controls the transfer of data between devices. When you turn on the computer, the BIOS chip automatically examines each device and adjusts the system board settings to ensure the devices work properly. For information about BIOS settings, see page 146.

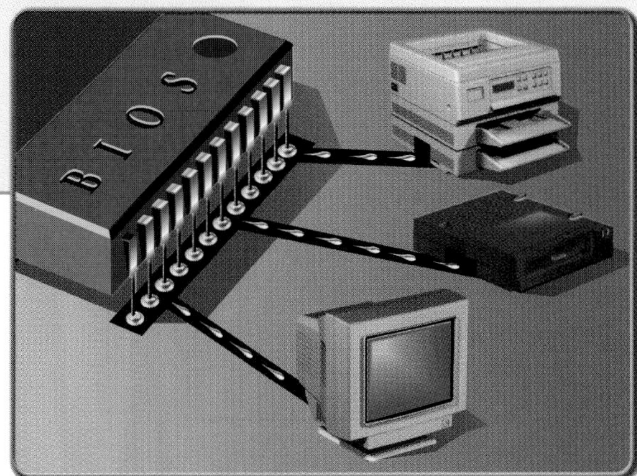

SYSTEM BOARD (CONTINUED)

TROUBLESHOOT AND MAINTAIN

My system board is not working properly. What should I do?

A problem with a system board is often caused by a malfunctioning component, such as a faulty memory module. To find the component causing the problem, remove a component not required for basic operation and then start the computer to determine if the problem still exists. Repeat this procedure with different components until you discover which component is causing the problem.

My system board and components are not faulty. Why am I experiencing problems?

Problems such as computer lockups may actually be caused by a loss of power or a computer virus. See page 38 for information about protecting your computer from a loss of power. See page 22 for information about computer virus protection.

Is there software I can use to test my system board?

Diagnostic software allows you to test your system board. For example, diagnostic software can help you determine if all the ports on the computer are working properly. You can purchase diagnostic software at most computer stores.

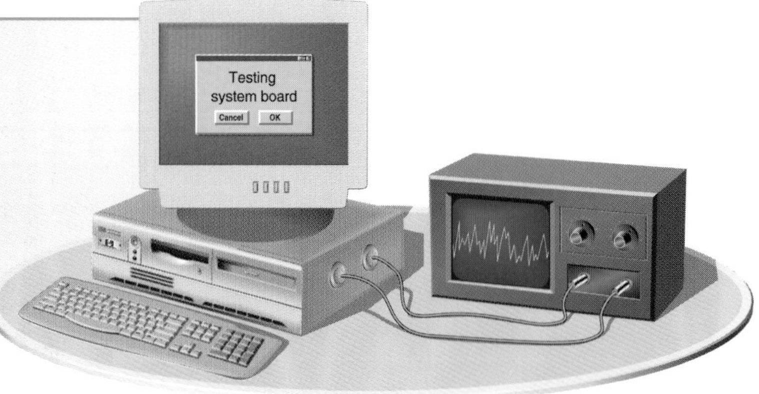

How can I determine if my system board's settings are correct?

Check the documentation included with your system board or computer to determine if the system board settings are correct. Incorrect system board settings, such as an incorrect bus speed, can cause problems with the computer such as a lockup or failure to start.

How do I prevent my computer from overheating?

The CPU and other components inside the computer case generate heat. Overheating may cause the computer to malfunction. To prevent overheating, make sure the fan inside the computer is working properly. Many system boards have a built-in thermometer that will shut down the computer before it overheats.

How do I clean my system board?

You can use a can of compressed air to blow away the dust and dirt on your system board. If the system board is extremely dusty, you may need to remove the cables and components from the system board before cleaning.

POWER SUPPLY

A power supply changes the alternating current (AC) that comes from an electrical outlet to the direct current (DC) that a computer can use.

REPLACE A POWER SUPPLY

Before replacing a power supply, turn off the computer, unplug the power cable and remove the cover from the computer case. Then ground yourself and the computer case. For information about grounding, see page 6.

1

Disconnect the power supply cables from the system board and other devices inside the computer.

2

If necessary, remove the front of the computer case and unfasten the power switch from the front of the computer.

3

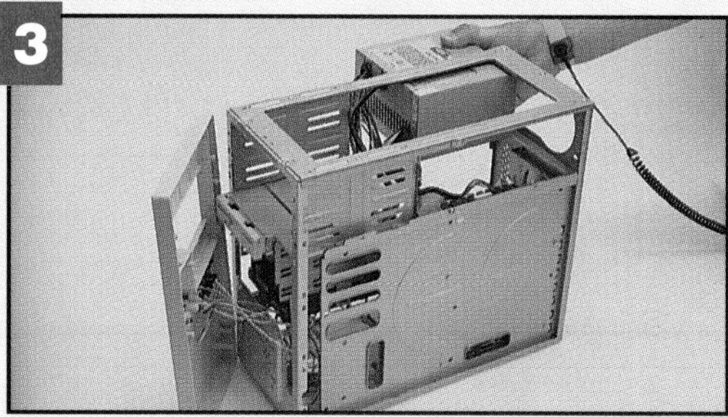

Remove the screws that secure the power supply in the computer case. Then slide the power supply out of the computer case.

4

Slide the new power supply into the computer case and use screws to secure it.

5

Reconnect all the cables. If necessary, reconnect the power switch and replace the front of the computer case. Then replace the cover on the computer case.

REPLACEMENT CONSIDERATIONS

Verify the Problem

Power supplies tend to be very reliable and usually work for many years without any problems. Symptoms of a faulty power supply can include the computer locking up repeatedly or other components failing to work consistently.

Before replacing a power supply, make sure the problems you are experiencing are not caused by another component, such as a malfunctioning hard drive.

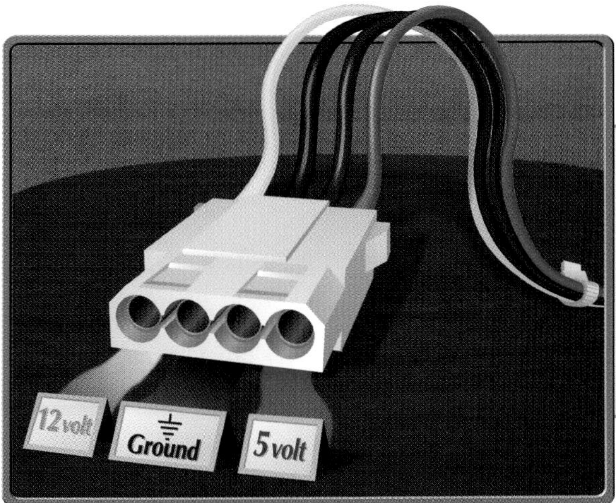

Test the Power Connector

One way to test for problems with a power supply is by checking the voltage in the power connector using a digital multimeter. The voltage will be 5 or 12 volts when the computer is running. If the power connector does not have the appropriate voltage, the problem is with the power supply.

Take Safety Precautions

In addition to unplugging the power supply from the electrical outlet on your wall, you should never take the cover off a power supply you are replacing. Even when the power supply is not plugged into an electrical outlet, it can still contain power.

CHOOSE A POWER SUPPLY

Wattage

The capacity of a power supply is measured in watts. A power supply with a capacity of 250 watts is more than enough for a typical computer.

Voltage Selector

Many power supplies allow you to switch between the 110-volt electrical system used in North America and the 220-volt electrical system used in other areas of the world. Some new power supplies can switch automatically.

Energy Efficiency

Some new power supplies are capable of turning themselves off after a period of inactivity to conserve energy. When the computer is needed again, this type of power supply uses a small electrical charge to "wake up" the computer.

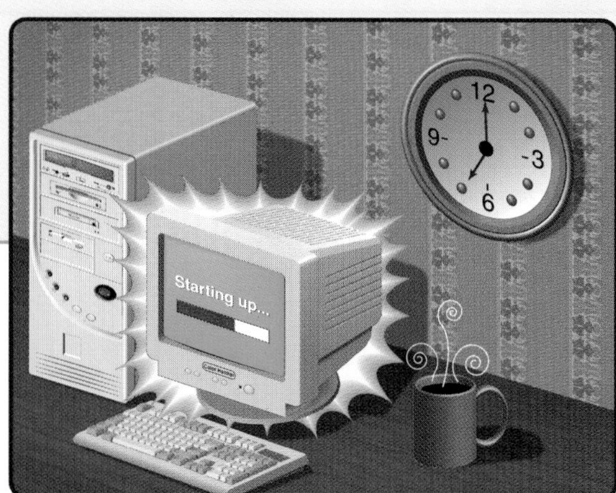

Form Factor

A form factor is a set of specifications that determines the general size and shape of a power supply. There are two main types of form factors—Baby AT and ATX. The power supply must use the same form factor as the computer case and system board.

The fan in a Baby AT power supply pushes air out of the computer. The fan in an ATX power supply draws air into the computer, which cools the power supply and other computer components more efficiently.

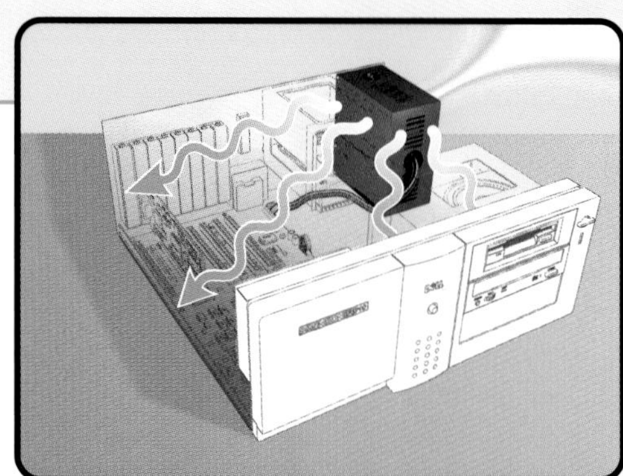

TROUBLESHOOT AND MAINTAIN

My computer does not turn on when I press the power button. Is my power supply failing?

A faulty power supply may not be the problem. Power supplies can be set up to work with the computer in different ways. For example, you may need to press and hold the power button for a specific number of seconds before the computer will turn on. See the documentation that came with the power supply or computer for more information.

How can I prolong the life of my power supply?

The location of your computer can influence the way the power supply performs. You should keep your computer in a cool, dust-free environment to help prolong the life of the power supply and ensure the fan has cool, clean air to move through the computer case.

Do I need to clean my power supply?

Over time, dust can accumulate on the fan opening and on the back of the power supply. You can remove this dust with a computer vacuum cleaner. You should never cover the fan opening to prevent dust from gathering, as this can cause the power supply to overheat and your computer to shut down.

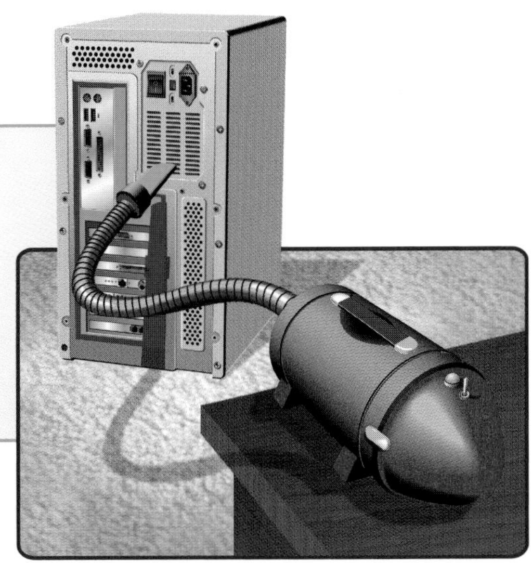

The Central Processing Unit (CPU) chip processes instructions, performs calculations and manages the flow of information through a computer system.

For upgrading, the two most popular types of CPU are the Pentium and Pentium II.

REPLACE A PENTIUM CPU

Before replacing a Pentium CPU, turn off the computer, unplug the power cable and remove the cover from the computer case. Then ground yourself and the computer case. For information about grounding, see page 6.

1

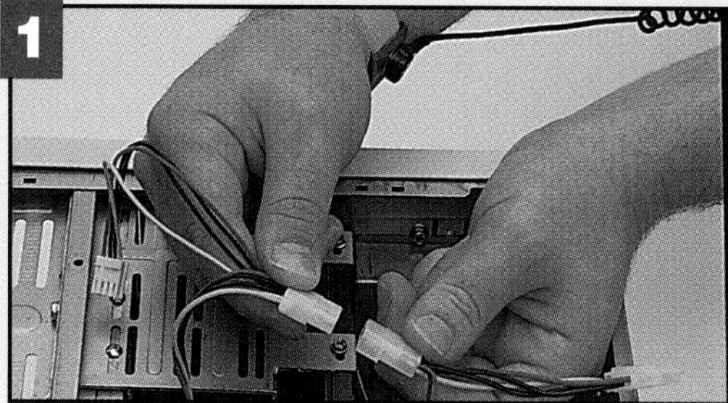

If necessary, disconnect the CPU fan's cable from the power supply.

2

If necessary, release the clip securing the CPU fan to the system board. Then lift the lever that secures the CPU in the socket.

3

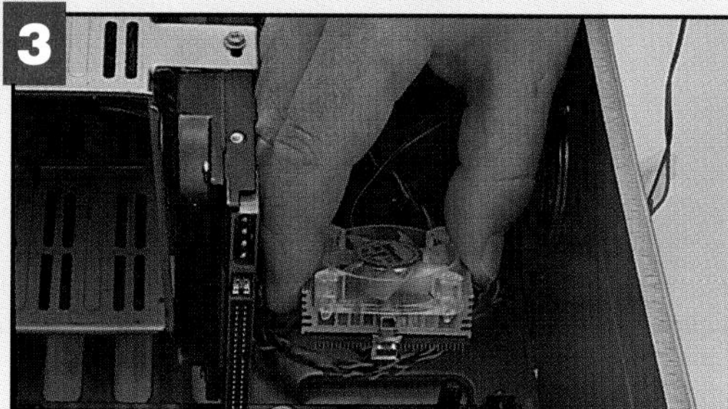

Lift the CPU out of the socket.

4

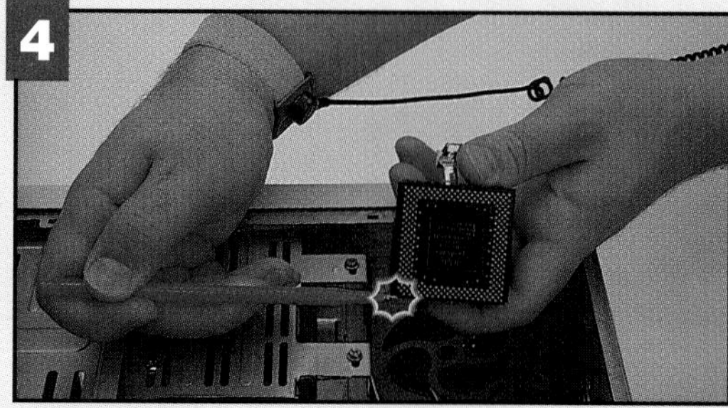

Align the beveled corner of the new CPU with the beveled corner on the socket. Then place the CPU in the socket.

5

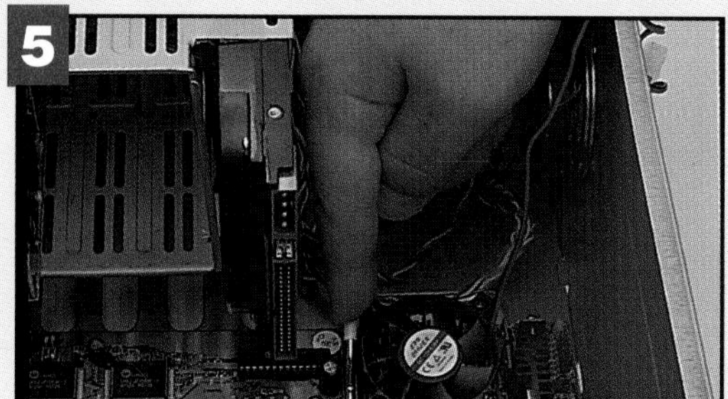

Push the lever down to secure the CPU in the socket. If necessary, use the clip to secure the CPU fan to the system board.

6

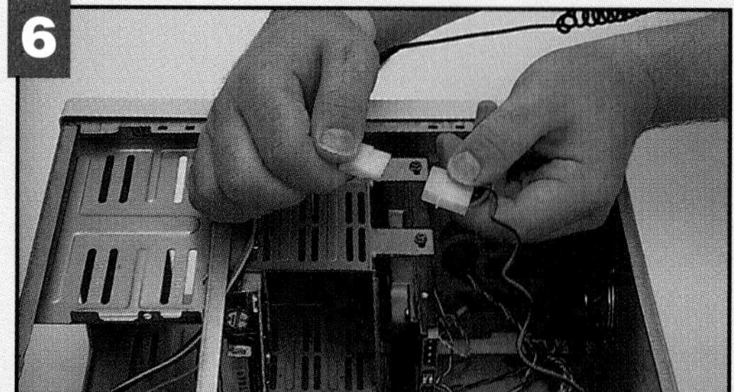

If necessary, connect the CPU fan's cable to the power supply. Then replace the cover on the computer case.

REPLACE A PENTIUM II CPU

Before replacing a Pentium II CPU, turn off the computer, unplug the power cable and remove the cover from the computer case. Then ground yourself and the computer case. For information about grounding, see page 6.

1

If necessary, disconnect the CPU fan's cable from the system board.

2

Push the clips on each end of the CPU inward and then lift the CPU out of the slot.

3

Place the new CPU in the guide rails for the slot and then press down firmly and evenly across the top of the CPU until it is securely inserted in the slot.

4

Push the clips on each end of the CPU outward until the clips snap into place.

5

If necessary, connect the CPU fan's cable to the system board. Then replace the cover on the computer case.

CHOOSE A CPU

Manufacturer

Pentium chips, the most popular type of CPU, are manufactured by Intel. There are several generations of Pentium CPUs, including Pentium, Pentium II/Celeron, Pentium III and Pentium 4.

Other popular CPUs include the Athlon, which is manufactured by AMD, and the Cyrix III, which is manufactured by VIA Technologies.

Speed

The speed of a CPU chip is usually measured in megahertz (MHz), although some newer CPUs have speeds measured in gigahertz (GHz). The faster the speed of a CPU chip, the faster the computer can operate.

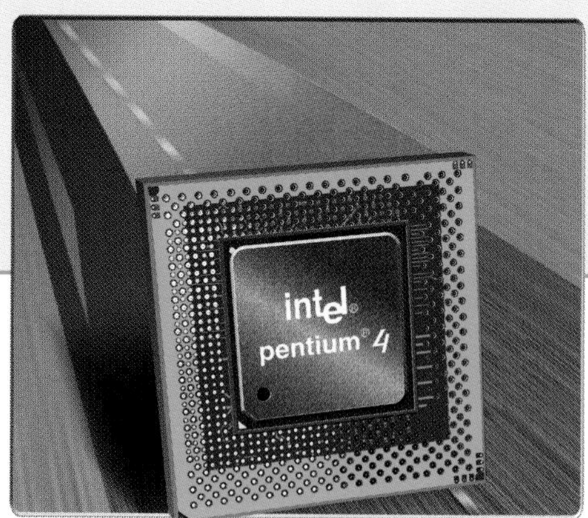

Socket Type

The type of socket on the system board determines the type of CPU you can install in the computer. A system board that has a square, two-inch socket, called Socket 7, can hold only a Pentium or comparable CPU chip. Intel's Pentium II and Pentium III chips can be installed only on a system board that has a slot similar in appearance to an expansion slot, called Slot 1.

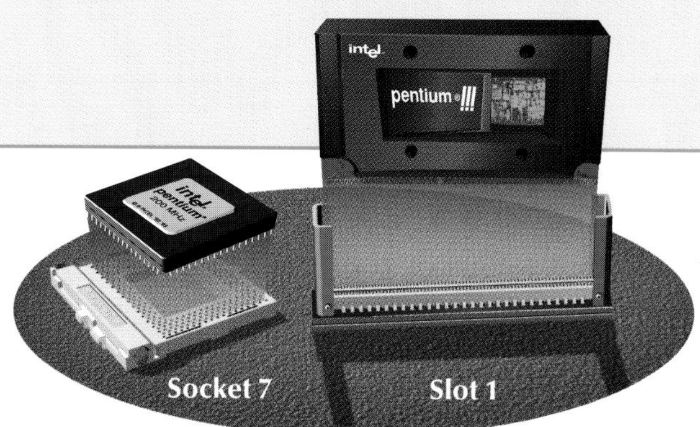

Fans

Some CPUs may have a large fan on the chip. Before upgrading to a different type of CPU, make sure you have enough space inside the computer to accommodate the new CPU's fan.

TROUBLESHOOT

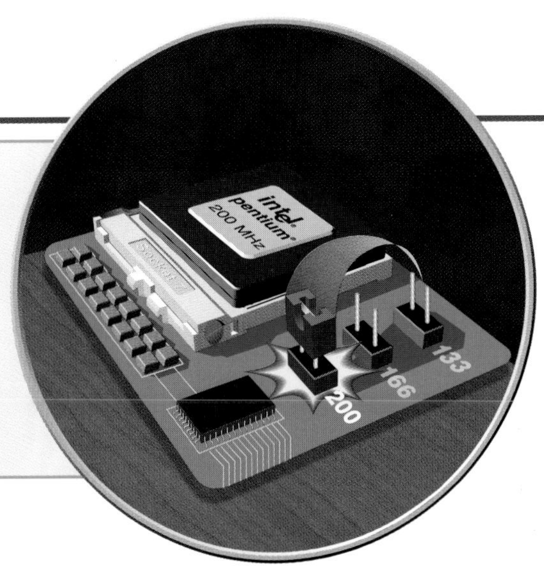

After installing my new CPU, do I need to adjust any settings on the system board?

You may need to adjust jumpers or switches on the system board to indicate the speed of your new CPU. If there are no jumpers or switches for the fastest speed of your CPU, your system board may not support that speed. To take advantage of the speed your new CPU offers, you may need to upgrade the system board.

I have installed a new CPU and now my computer freezes shortly after I turn it on. What is wrong?

The new CPU may be overheating. Try adjusting the jumpers or switches on the system board to reduce the speed of the CPU. If your computer operates properly at the reduced CPU speed, the CPU fan may not have been able to sufficiently cool the CPU. You should replace the CPU fan with a larger fan.

The CPU in my notebook computer is slow. How can I upgrade the CPU?

The mobile CPUs in notebook computers are not the same as the CPUs found in desktop computers. You should take the notebook computer to a repair service to determine if the CPU can be replaced. For information about repair services, see page 168.

MEMORY

Memory temporarily stores data in a computer. The main memory in a computer is called Random Access Memory (RAM).

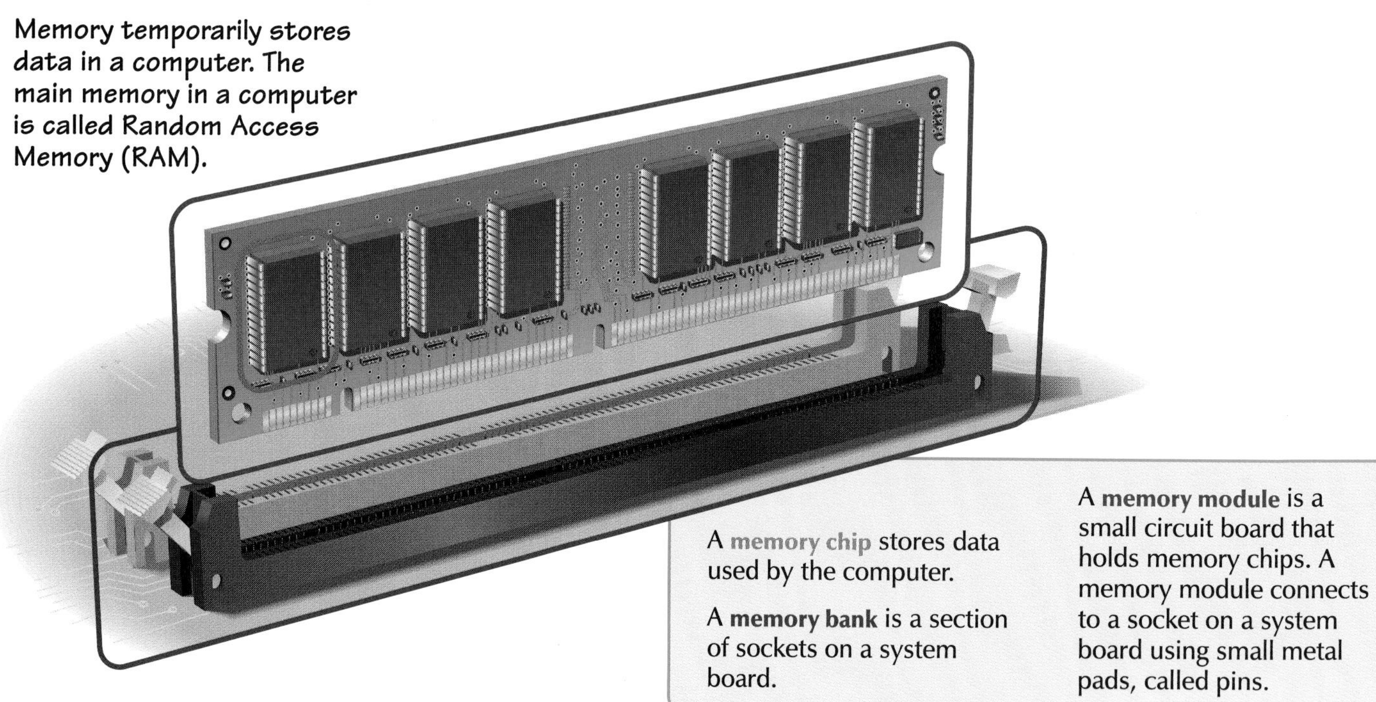

A **memory chip** stores data used by the computer.

A **memory bank** is a section of sockets on a system board.

A **memory module** is a small circuit board that holds memory chips. A memory module connects to a socket on a system board using small metal pads, called pins.

TYPES OF MEMORY MODULES

SIMM

A Single In-line Memory Module (SIMM) is an older type of memory module. SIMMs may have 30 or 72 pins.

A bank of SIMMs usually consists of two sockets, so you must install two SIMMs at a time.

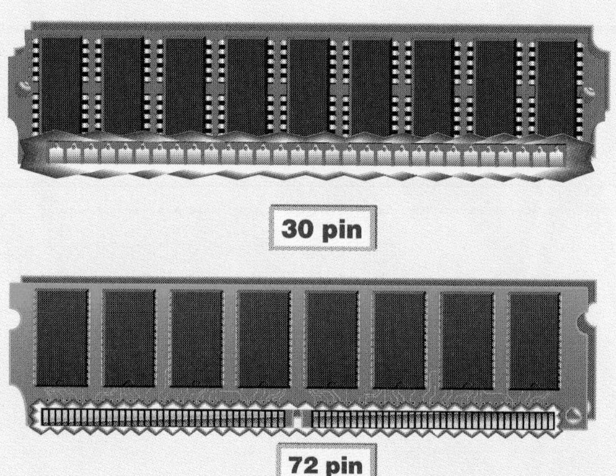

DIMM

A Dual In-line Memory Module (DIMM) is used in newer computers. A DIMM is similar to a SIMM, but has 168 pins.

A bank of DIMMs consists of only one socket, so you only need to install one DIMM at a time.

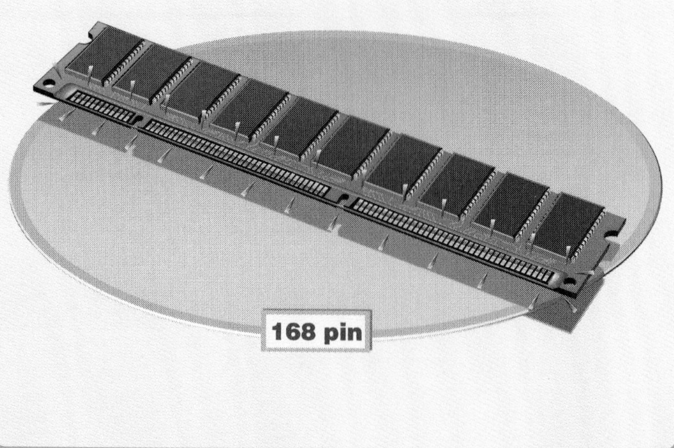

TYPES OF MEMORY

SRAM

Static RAM (SRAM) is efficient and fast, but is very expensive. SRAM is used in small amounts as cache memory in a computer. Cache memory improves the performance of a computer by storing data the computer frequently uses.

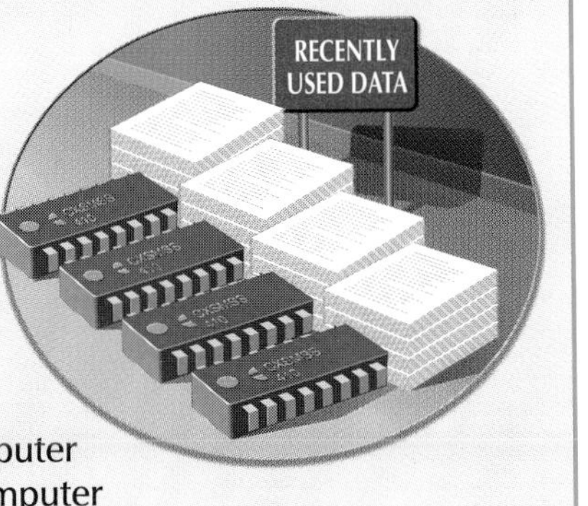

DRAM

Dynamic RAM (DRAM) was the first widely used type of main memory, but is no longer used in new computers.

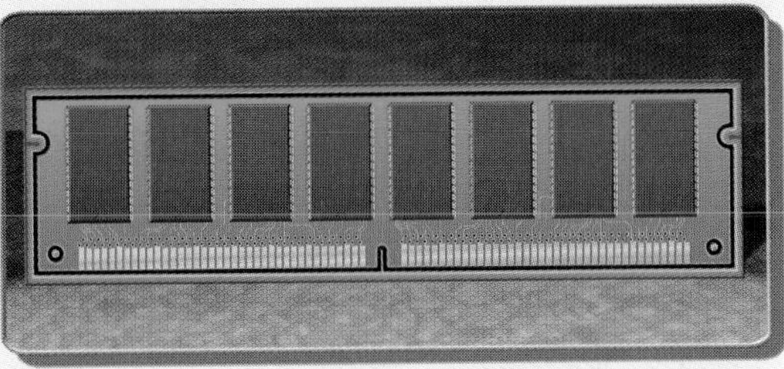

FPM DRAM

Fast Page Mode DRAM (FPM DRAM) is faster than conventional DRAM, but is now considered obsolete.

RDRAM

Rambus DRAM (RDRAM) is a new type of memory chip often found in high-performance computers.

EDO DRAM

Extended Data Out DRAM (EDO DRAM) is slightly faster than FPM DRAM and can be found on older Pentium computers.

SDRAM

Synchronous DRAM (SDRAM) is the most popular type of main memory used in newer computers. SDRAM is at least twice as fast as EDO RAM.

INSTALL SIMMS

Before installing SIMMs, turn off the computer, unplug the power cable and remove the cover from the computer case. Then ground yourself and the computer case. For information about grounding, see page 6.

1 Disconnect any cables inside the computer that restrict access to the memory sockets.

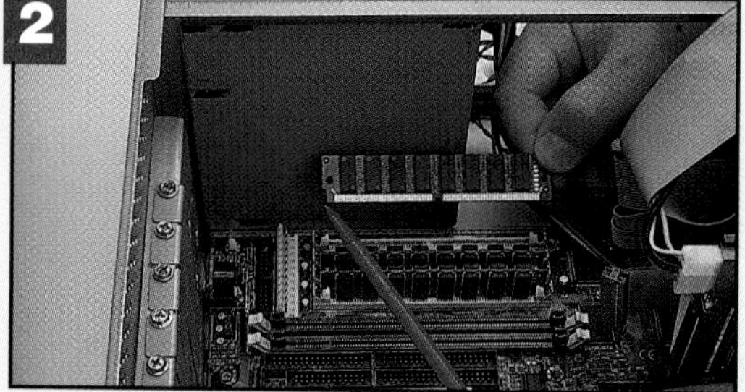

2 Locate the empty socket closest to the back of the bank where you want to install the SIMM. Then locate the key on the side of the socket and the notch on the side of the memory module. To ensure you install the memory module correctly, align the key with the notch.

3 Place the SIMM in the socket at a 45-degree angle.

4 Gently move the SIMM into an upright position until the clips on each end of the socket snap into place to secure the SIMM in the socket.

5 Repeat steps 2 to 4 to install the second SIMM.

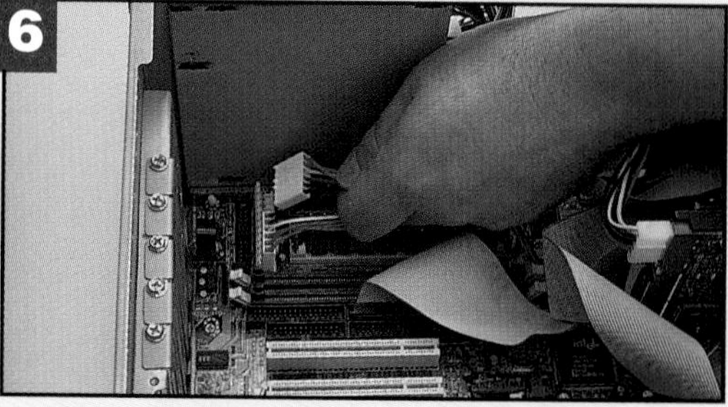

6 Reconnect any cables inside the computer. Then replace the cover on the computer case.

INSTALL A DIMM

Before installing a DIMM, turn off the computer, unplug the power cable and remove the cover from the computer case. Then ground yourself and the computer case. For information about grounding, see page 6.

1

Disconnect any cables inside the computer that restrict access to the memory sockets.

2

Push the clips on each end of the socket out of the way.

3

Locate the key on the side of the socket and the notch on the side of the memory module. To ensure you install the memory module correctly, align the key with the notch.

4

Push down firmly and evenly across the top of the memory module to insert it in the socket.

5

The clips snap into place to secure the DIMM in the socket.

6

Reconnect any cables inside the computer. Then replace the cover on the computer case.

CHOOSE MEMORY

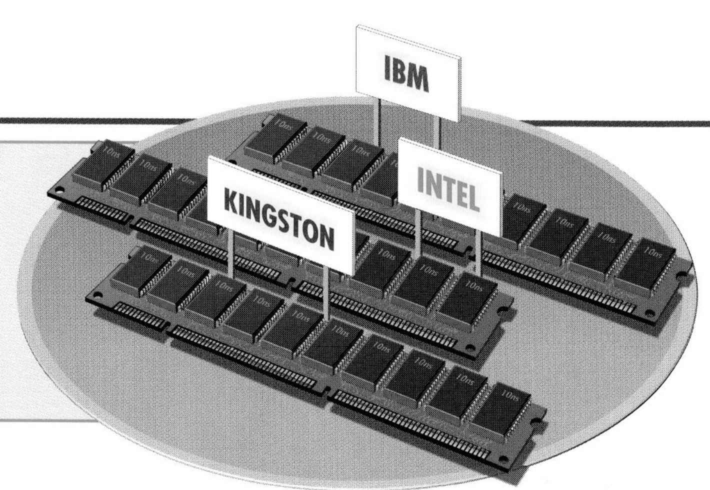

Identification

Most memory modules look very similar. This makes it difficult to identify the type of memory used in a computer. To determine the type of memory your computer uses, refer to the documentation included with your computer or system board.

Memory Size

Memory is measured in megabytes (MB). Computers are commonly sold with 32 or 64 MB of memory. You can improve the performance of a computer by adding more memory. Although most computers can hold at least 128 MB of memory, the capabilities of the system board may limit the amount of memory you can add.

System Board Compatibility

The system board in a computer determines the type of memory modules required. For example, you cannot install SIMMs in a system board that has only DIMM memory slots. You should also consider the type of metal used in the memory slots on the system board. Installing a memory module with tin connectors in a slot that uses gold, or vice versa, may lead to memory errors in the future.

Memory Speed

When purchasing memory, you must also ensure the speed of the memory is compatible with the system board. The speed at which information is accessed in SIMMs is measured in nanoseconds (ns). Many system boards can only use SIMMs that have memory speeds of 60 or 70 ns.

The speed at which information is accessed in DIMMs is measured in megahertz (MHz). Common memory speeds are 100 and 133 MHz.

Parity Checking

Parity checking is a system used to ensure information is stored properly in the computer's memory. Invalid data in the memory can result in errors such as a system failure.

New computers are much more reliable than older computers, so newer computers no longer support parity checking. If your computer supports SIMMs, you should determine whether your computer uses parity or non-parity SIMMs before purchasing memory.

Proprietary

Proprietary memory is designed for use with a specific type of computer. For example, you cannot use proprietary memory designed for a notebook computer in a desktop computer. Many notebook computers and high-end computers, such as servers, use proprietary memory.

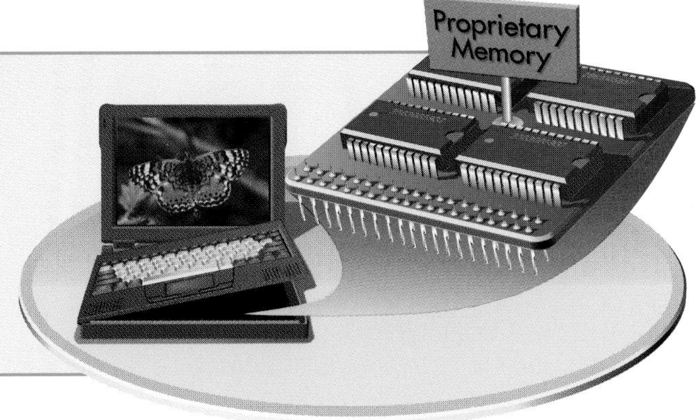

TROUBLESHOOT

Can I install memory modules made by different manufacturers?

Installing memory modules made by different manufacturers can cause problems such as memory read and write errors. Whenever possible, you should install memory modules made by the same manufacturer.

What happens if I break a clip when installing a memory module?

When installing a memory module, be careful not to break the clips that secure the memory module in place. If you break a clip, it may be impossible to install the memory module correctly, which could make the system board unusable.

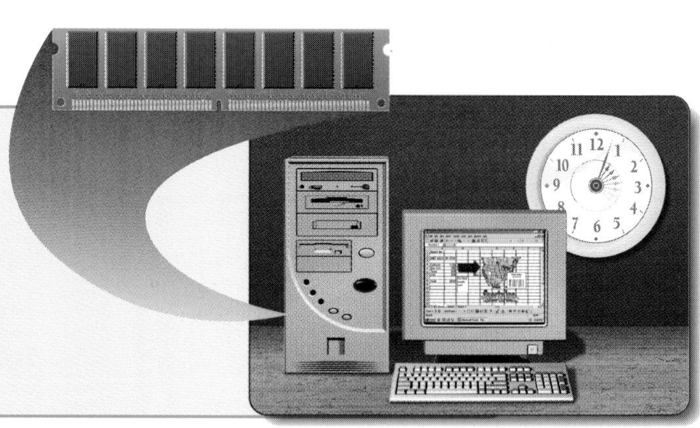

Should I test the new memory I installed?

After installing memory, you should perform a burn in for up to 48 hours. A burn in involves testing the memory for a long period of time to ensure it works properly. For example, you could set up your computer to repeatedly perform a memory-intensive task, such as a complicated spreadsheet calculation.

Is there a device I can use to verify that a memory module is working properly?

You can use a memory module tester to verify if a memory module is working properly. Although this device is very expensive to buy, some computer stores may have the device and will test a memory module for you.

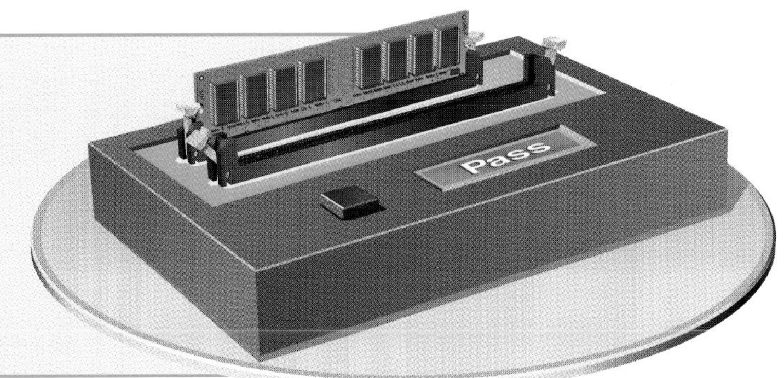

I just installed new memory. Why did I get a memory error message?

Memory chips are very susceptible to damage from static electricity. If you handled a memory module without properly grounding yourself, static electricity may have damaged the memory chips on the module. For information about protecting components from static electricity, see page 6.

How do I troubleshoot a memory error?

Memory errors are often difficult to troubleshoot because they are similar to problems caused by other components. You may be able to correct the problem by removing and then re-inserting a memory module in a socket.

EXPANSION CARD

An expansion card is a circuit board that provides improved or additional features to a computer.

REPLACE AN EXPANSION CARD

Before replacing an expansion card, turn off the computer, unplug the power cable and remove the computer case cover. Then ground yourself and the computer case. For information about grounding, see page 6.

1

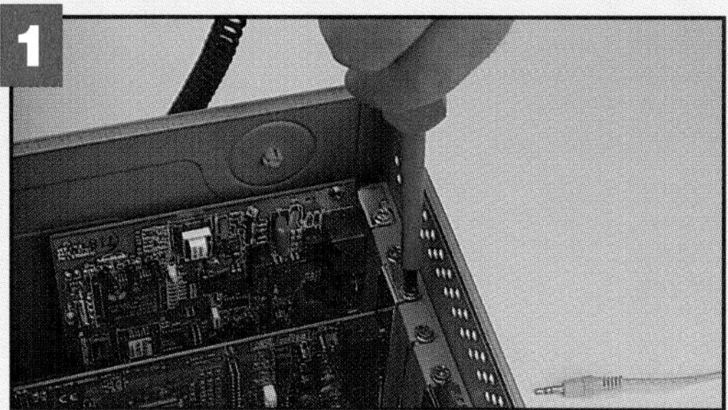

Disconnect any cables attached to the expansion card at the back of the computer and remove the screw securing the card to the computer case.

2

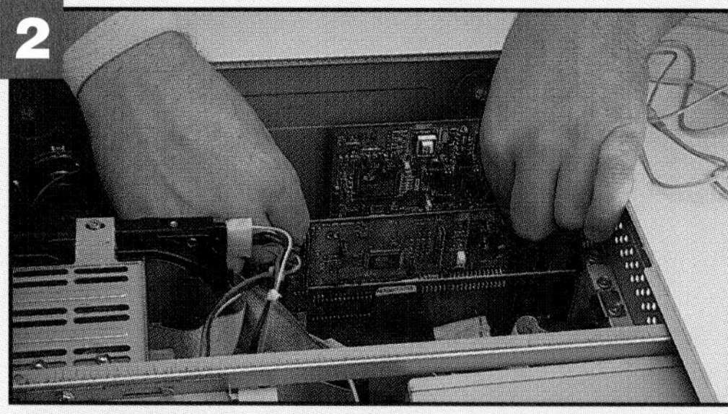

Grasp the top corners of the expansion card and pull straight up to remove the card from the slot.

3

Remove any cables connecting the card to other components inside the computer.

4

Use cables to attach other components to the new expansion card.

5

Place the expansion card in the slot. Press down firmly and evenly across the top of the card until it is securely inserted in the expansion slot.

6

Secure the expansion card to the computer case using a small screw. Then replace the cover on the computer case.

SET UP AN EXPANSION CARD

Adjust Settings

Expansion cards require several computer resources, such as Interrupt Request (IRQ) settings. Before installing an expansion card, make sure you have a list of the resources used by other devices. If the expansion card requires the same resources as another device, you may need to change the settings for the card. Most expansion cards come with an installation program you can use to change the settings. For information about resource settings, see page 144.

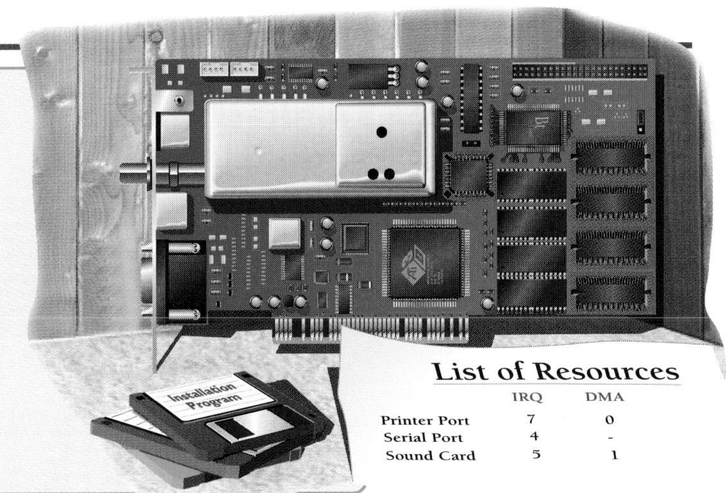

Installation Program
List of Resources
IRQ DMA
Printer Port 7 0
Serial Port 4 -
Sound Card 5 1

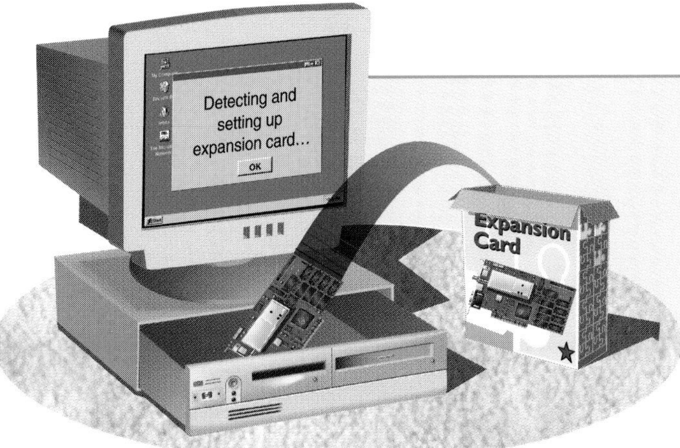

Plug and Play Technology

Most new computers and expansion cards use Plug and Play technology. When you install a Plug and Play expansion card, the computer may automatically detect and set up the card for you when you turn on the computer.

UPGRADE

If your computer does not have enough ports for all the devices you want to connect, you can install an expansion card to add an extra port. For example, you can install an expansion card to add an extra parallel port to the computer.

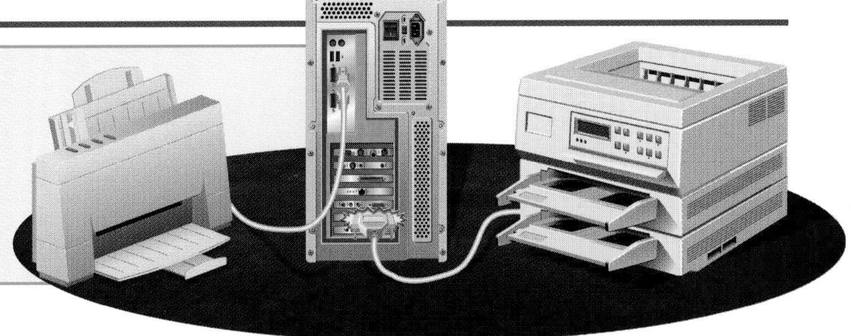

CHOOSE AN EXPANSION CARD

Expansion Slot Type

The type of expansion card you can use depends on the type of expansion slots in your computer. An expansion slot is a socket on the system board where you insert an expansion card. The most common types of expansion slots are Industry Standard Architecture (ISA) and Peripheral Component Interconnect (PCI). Most computers currently contain both types of expansion slots.

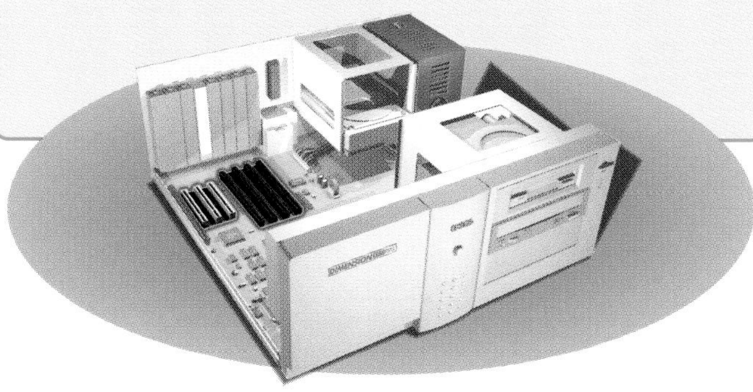

Cost

The cost of expansion cards varies, depending on the type and quality of the card. Although some expansion cards are expensive, adding or upgrading an expansion card can be one of the most economical ways to keep your computer up-to-date.

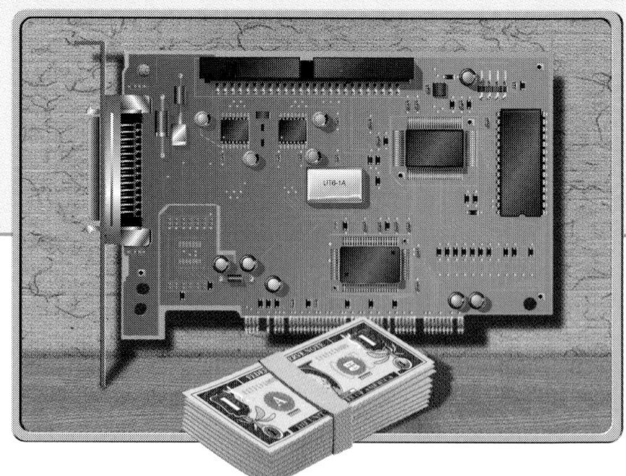

Length

Expansion cards vary in length. Complex expansion cards that contain many chips and components may take up the entire length of the computer. These long expansion cards are called full-length cards. Smaller cards, referred to as half-length cards, are more common.

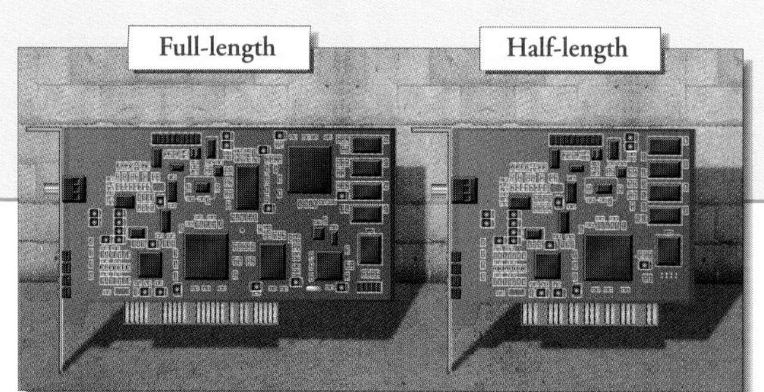

Forward Compatibility

Some types of expansion cards, such as SCSI cards, can be transferred to newer computers. Choosing forward-compatible expansion cards allows you to keep many of your existing devices when replacing your computer in the future.

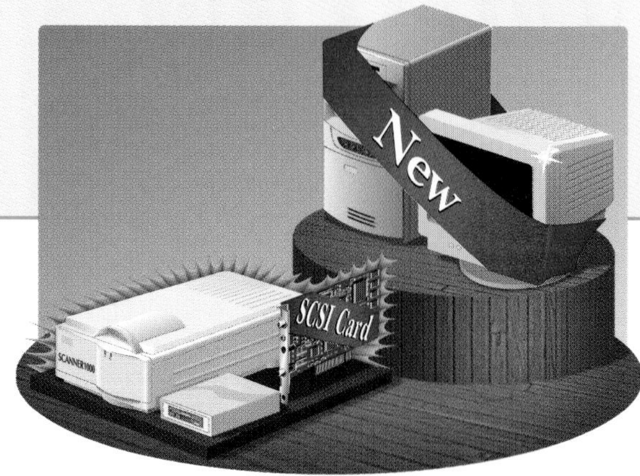

TROUBLESHOOT AND MAINTAIN

How can I test an expansion card?

Many expansion cards include testing software you can use to ensure the card is installed correctly. If an expansion card does not include testing software, you should use a simple procedure to test the device. For example, if you are installing a new parallel port, you can test the port by attaching a printer to the port and printing a text file.

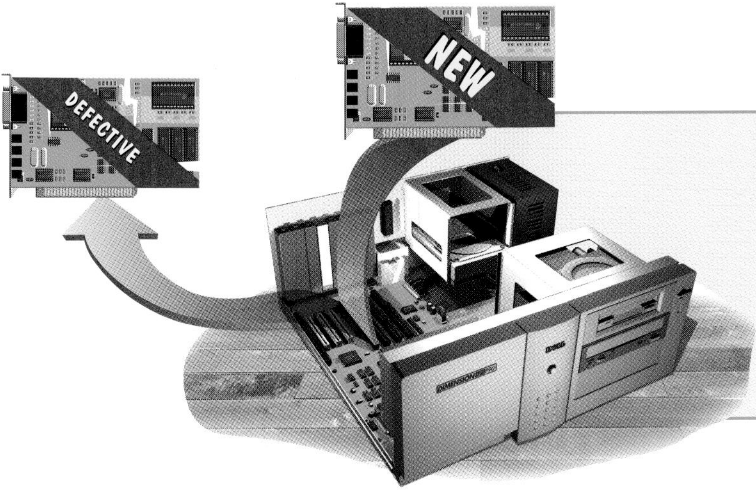

I think my expansion card is malfunctioning. How can I confirm this?

If an expansion card is not working, you can ensure the card is the cause of the problem by removing the card and replacing it with a card you know works properly.

How do I clean my expansion cards?

Expansion cards can become dusty and may require occasional cleaning. Remove the computer case cover and carefully use a computer vacuum cleaner or can of compressed air to remove dust from the card and expansion slot. For more information about cleaning a computer, see page 20.

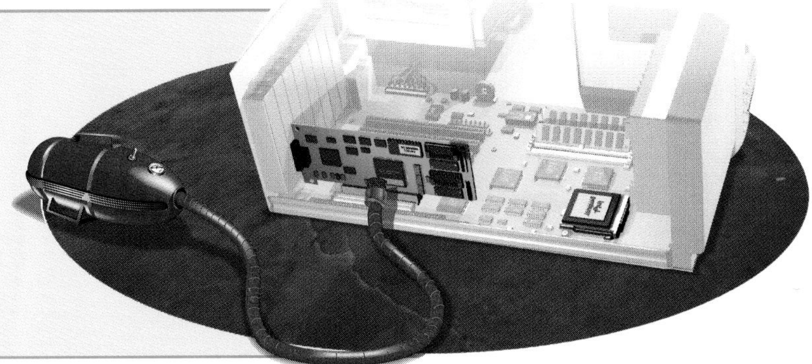

CHAPTER 3

INPUT AND OUTPUT DEVICES

Would you like to learn about keyboards, sound cards, digital cameras and USB and FireWire devices? This chapter introduces you to the input devices you use to communicate with your computer and the output devices your computer uses to communicate with you.

POINTING DEVICE

A pointing device allows you to select and move items on the screen. The mouse is the most common type of pointing device.

CONNECT A POINTING DEVICE

Before connecting a pointing device, turn off the computer.

1

Position the pointing device where you can use it comfortably.

2

Connect the cable from the pointing device to a port at the back of the computer. The mouse may connect to a mouse, serial or USB port.

MOUSE UPGRADES

Enhanced Capabilities

You can purchase a new mouse with improved capabilities, such as a button you can program to perform a specific action or a wheel between the left and right buttons that lets you quickly scroll through information.

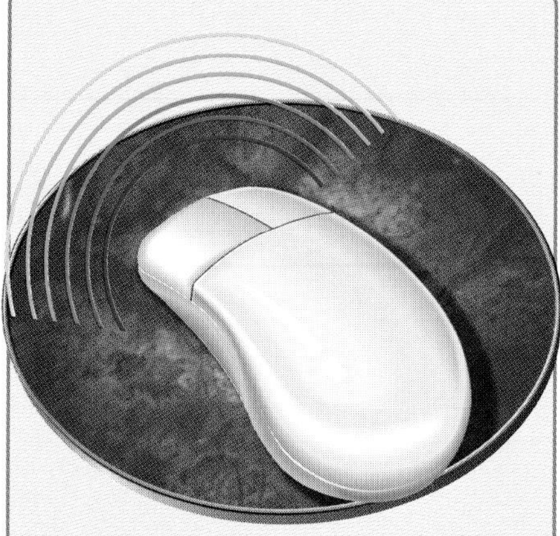

Cordless Mouse

You can purchase a cordless mouse that uses infrared or radio signals to send information to the computer.

Optical Mouse

An optical mouse works like a conventional mouse, but does not use a ball. An optical mouse uses an optical sensor to detect movement. Older optical mice require you to use a special reflective mouse pad.

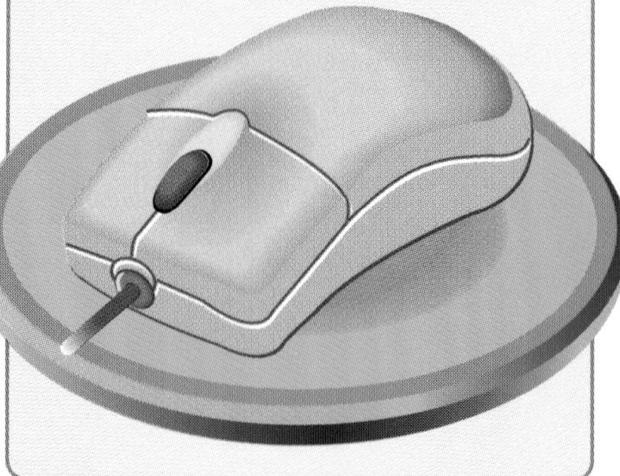

OTHER TYPES OF POINTING DEVICES

Trackball

A trackball is like an upside-down mouse that remains stationary on your desk. You can roll the ball with your thumb, fingers or palm to move the mouse pointer on the screen. A trackball is useful when you have limited desk space.

Touchpad

A touchpad is a surface that is sensitive to pressure and motion. You can tap the surface of the touchpad with your finger or press a button to perform an action such as a click.

Pointing Stick

A pointing stick resembles the eraser on the end of a pencil. The mouse pointer moves in the direction you push the pointing stick. Pointing sticks also have buttons, similar to mouse buttons, you can press to perform an action such as a click.

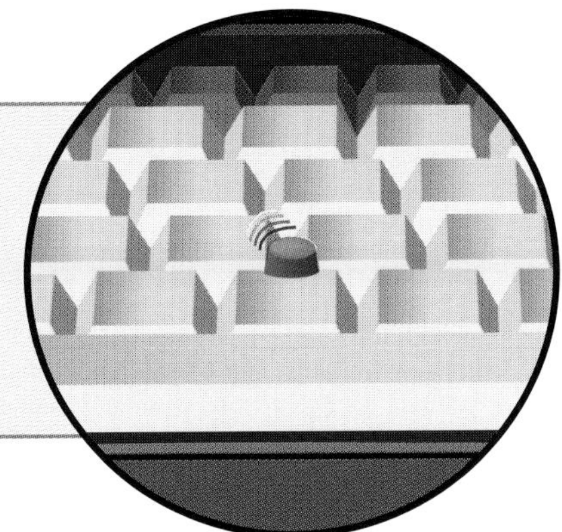

CLEANING

The ball inside a mouse collects dirt and debris from a desk or mouse pad. If your mouse pointer is hard to position and sticks on the screen, you may need to clean the mouse. Follow the manufacturer's instructions for cleaning the mouse.

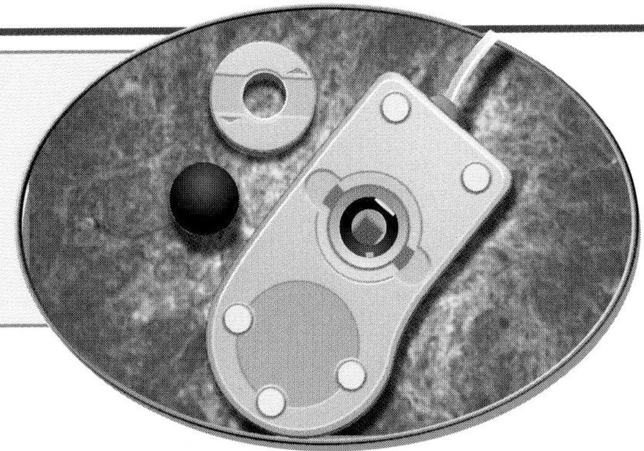

KEYBOARD

A keyboard allows you to enter information and instructions into a computer.

CONNECT A KEYBOARD

Before connecting a keyboard, turn off the computer.

1

Position the keyboard where you can use it comfortably.

2

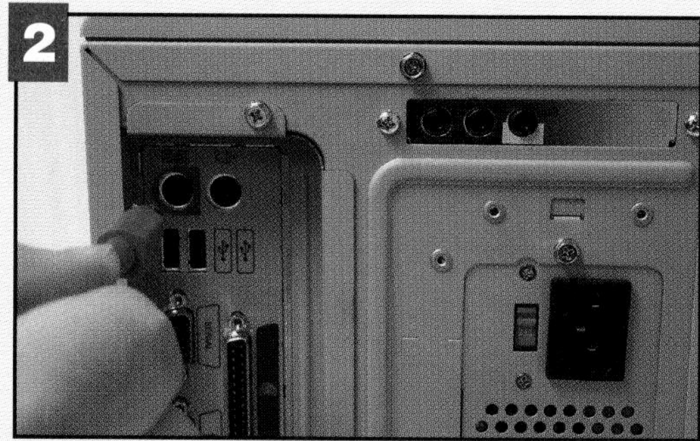

Connect the cable from the keyboard to the keyboard port at the back of the computer.

SET UP

Driver

All operating systems can automatically detect and set up a keyboard you connect. The operating system can also install the necessary driver for you. A driver is the software that allows the computer's operating system to communicate with and control the keyboard.

Keyboards that have built-in enhancements, such as trackballs, may require you to install additional drivers. The additional drivers are included with the keyboard.

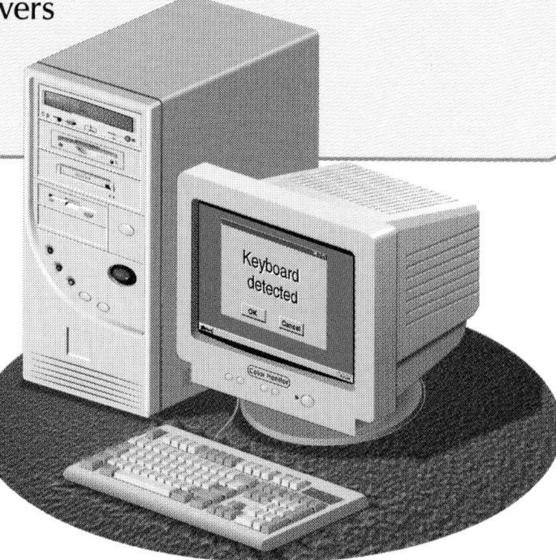

Connector

A keyboard connector may be a 5-pin DIN connector or a smaller 6-pin mini-DIN connector, also called a PS/2 connector. You can buy an adapter that will allow you to use either type of connector with your computer.

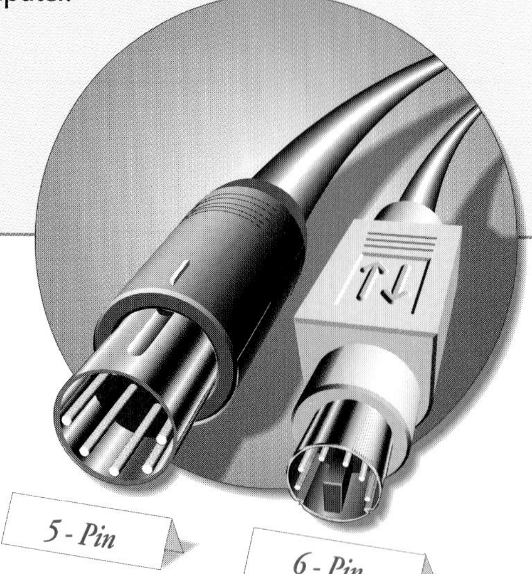

KEYBOARD UPGRADES

Cordless

Cordless keyboards do not use a cable to connect to a computer. A cordless keyboard may use an infrared transmitter and receiver or radio signals to communicate with a computer.

Ergonomic

Ergonomically designed keyboards position your hands naturally and support your wrists so you can work more comfortably.

Built-in Enhancements

Many new keyboards include built-in enhancements such as trackballs, microphones, speakers, volume controls and buttons you can program to perform tasks such as connecting to the Internet.

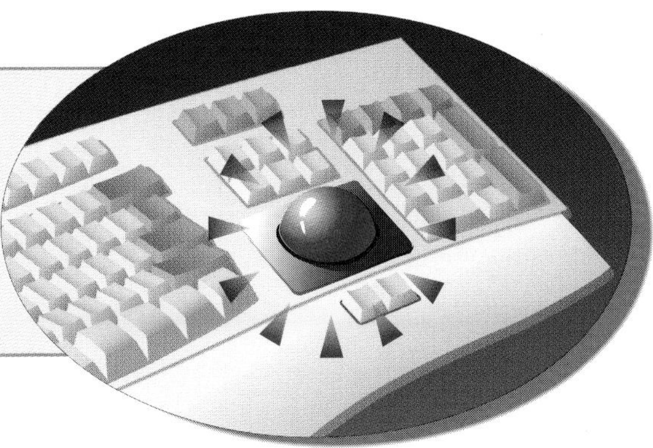

CLEAN

Over time, dust and dirt can accumulate on a keyboard, causing the keys to stick or not respond when pressed. To remove dust and dirt, you can run a computer vacuum cleaner over the keys. If vacuuming does not work, you can use a can of compressed air to blow out any dirt embedded in your keyboard.

The plastic outer surface of the keyboard can be cleaned with a damp cloth. You should not attempt to open your keyboard to clean the inside, as this can damage the keyboard.

PRINTER

A printer produces a paper copy of information generated by a computer.

CONNECT A PRINTER

Before connecting a printer, turn off the computer.

1

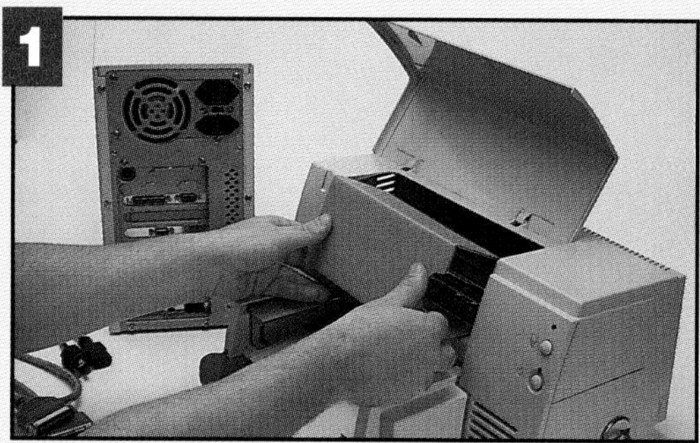

If necessary, remove any spacers or tape used to secure the printer's internal components during shipping. Then assemble the printer according to the instructions in the printer's documentation.

2

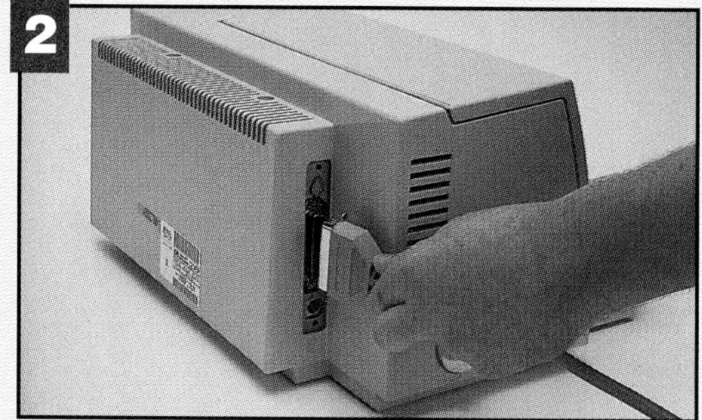

Connect the printer cable to the port on the printer.

3

Connect the printer cable to a parallel port at the back of the computer.

4

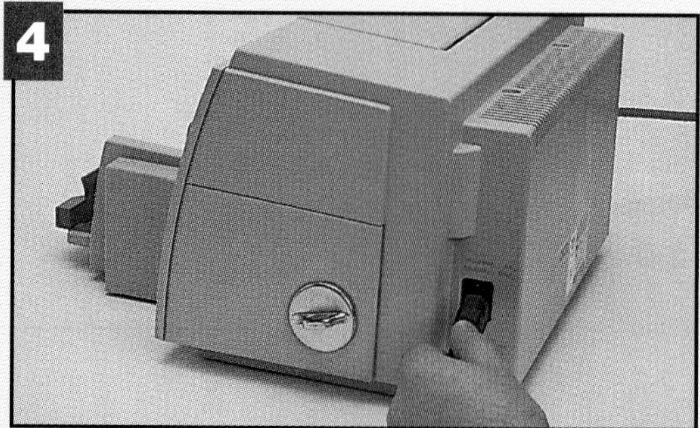

Connect the power cable to the power connector on the printer.

5

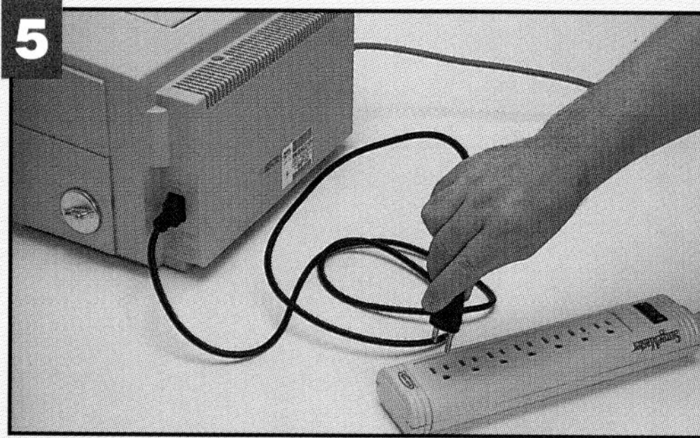

Plug the power cable into an electrical outlet.

TYPES OF PRINTERS

Ink-Jet Printer

An ink-jet printer produces high-quality documents at a relatively low price. You can use the documents produced by an ink-jet printer in most circumstances, except when only the highest quality is acceptable, such as for important business correspondence. An ink-jet printer sprays ink through small nozzles onto a page to produce images.

Laser Printer

A laser printer is a high-speed printer that is ideal for business documents and graphics. Laser printers produce the highest quality images, but are relatively expensive.

A laser printer works like a photocopier to produce images on a page. A laser beam draws images on a light-sensitive drum. The drum picks up a fine powdered ink, called toner, and then transfers the toner to the paper to create the images.

Dot-Matrix Printer

Dot-matrix printers were once very popular, but have been replaced in popularity by ink-jet printers. Dot-matrix printers typically use continuous form multipart paper and are commonly used for documents such as sales invoices and purchase orders. Inside a dot-matrix printer, a print head containing small blunt pins strikes an inked ribbon to stamp images on a page.

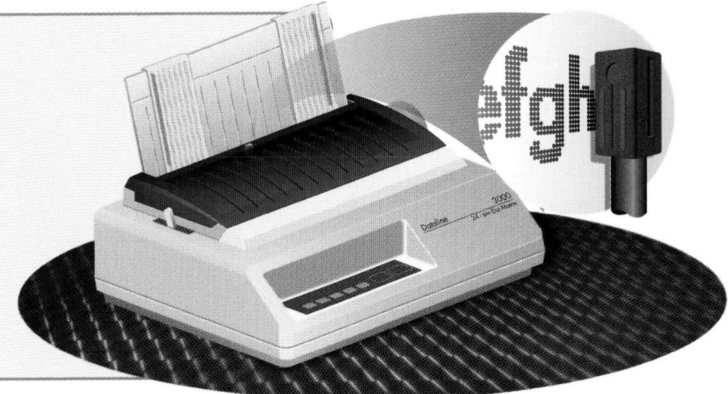

CHOOSE A PRINTER

Print Quality

The type of printer you should choose depends on the quality of the printed pages you require. Pages produced by a low-quality printer are suitable for draft copies of documents, but documents for correspondence or business use should be printed on a higher quality printer. The cost of a printer usually increases with the quality of the printed pages it can produce.

Speed

Printer speed is measured in pages per minute (ppm) and indicates how quickly a printer can produce printed pages. Most ink-jet printers produce images at a speed of 2 to 7 ppm. Most laser printers produce images at a speed of 4 to 24 ppm.

Resolution

Printer resolution is measured in dots per inch (dpi) and determines the quality of the images the printer can produce. The resolution of images produced by an ink-jet printer can range from 360 to 720 dpi. Most laser printers can produce images at a resolution of 600 dpi.

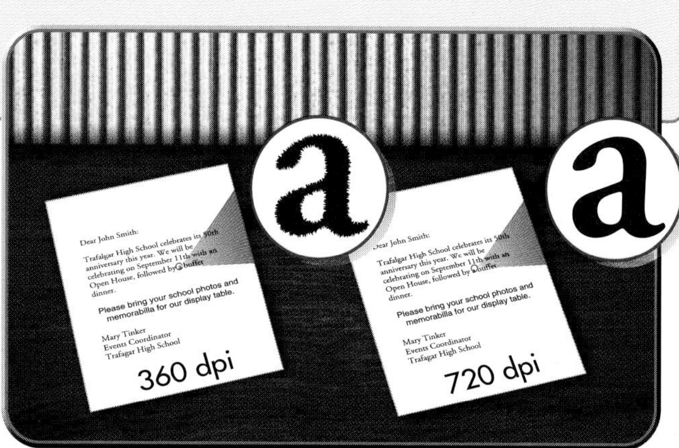

Software

Most printers intended for home use include software you can use to create special documents, such as greeting cards.

Consumables

All printers require items that have to be replaced on a regular basis, such as ink or toner. These items are called consumables. Before you purchase a printer, you should consider the number and cost of the consumables the printer requires.

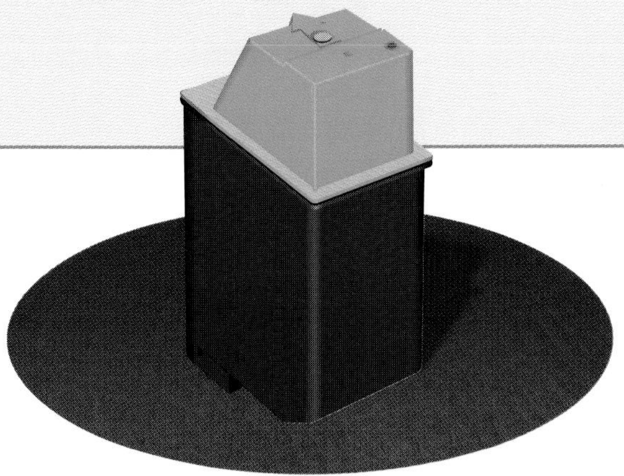

Print Media

When choosing a printer, you should check the size and type of paper the printer accepts. If you want to print on special printer media, such as envelopes, labels or transparencies, make sure the printer can accept these materials.

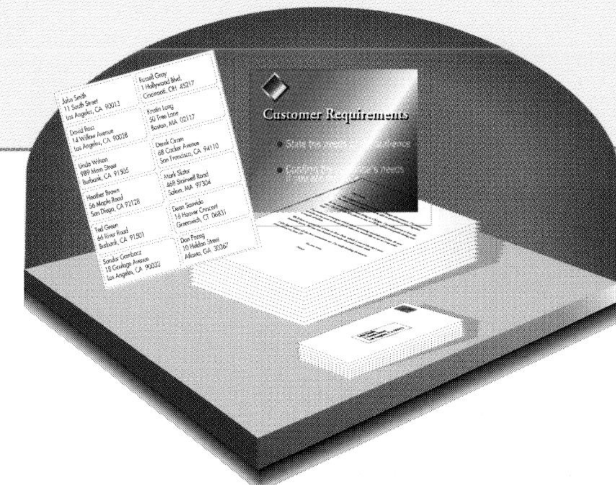

Color

Color printers usually use cyan, magenta, yellow and black ink to create color images on a page. Color ink-jet printers are the most popular because they are less expensive than other types of color printers and produce high-quality images.

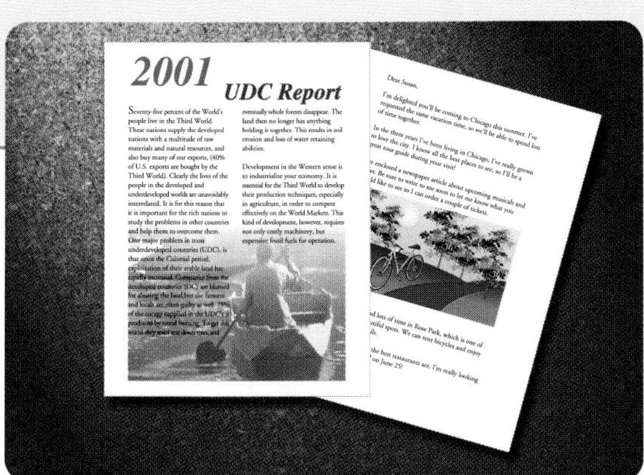

Warranty

The length of a printer warranty may range from 90 days to one year. Printers have many moving parts and are more prone to developing problems than other computer devices. You should consider purchasing an extended warranty or service contract for your printer.

SET UP

Change Settings

You can change settings such as the paper size or ink cartridge the printer uses. Instead of using switches or buttons on the printer, some printers include a software program so you can use your computer to change the printer's settings.

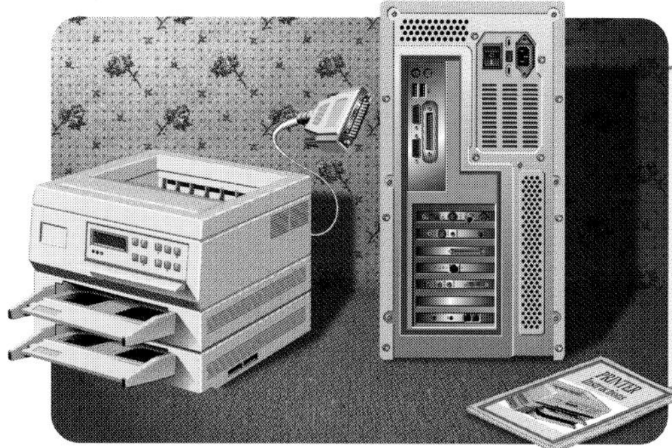

Connections

Most printers connect to a parallel port on a computer, but some printers connect to a serial or USB port. You can consult the printer's documentation to determine the type of port your printer uses.

Drivers

All printers require a driver to operate. A driver is the software that allows the computer's operating system to communicate with and control the printer. Most printers include an installation program you can use to install the necessary driver for the printer.

CLEANING

You should clean your printer on a regular basis. Over time, dust and dirt from print media can accumulate in the printer. You can use a computer vacuum cleaner or a can of compressed air to remove dust and dirt from most printers. In order to clean a large printer properly, you may need to disassemble the printer.

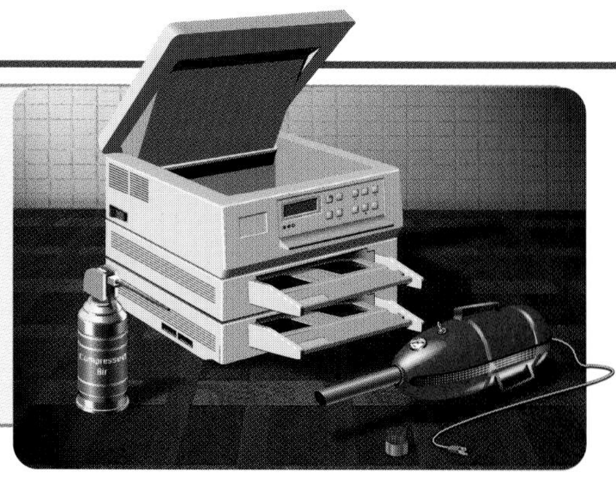

TROUBLESHOOT

Will my printer notify me if a problem occurs?

Printers often have built-in self-diagnostic features. Many printers, such as ink-jet printers, use a series of beeps to alert you of a problem. Most laser printers display a message that tells you a problem has occurred.

Why does paper keep getting jammed in my printer?

Paper jams are the most common type of printer problem. Some printers have panels you can open to access the inside of the printer and determine the cause of a paper jam. You should be careful when pulling out paper that has become jammed. Printers contain many small sensors that may be damaged by forcibly pulling on jammed paper.

How can I improve the quality of printed images?

When using an ink-jet printer, image quality improves when you use more expensive, coated paper. Some ink-jet printers can also use special glossy paper to produce photographic-quality images. Laser printers require a specific type of paper. For best results, check the printer's documentation to find the size, composition and weight of the paper the printer can use.

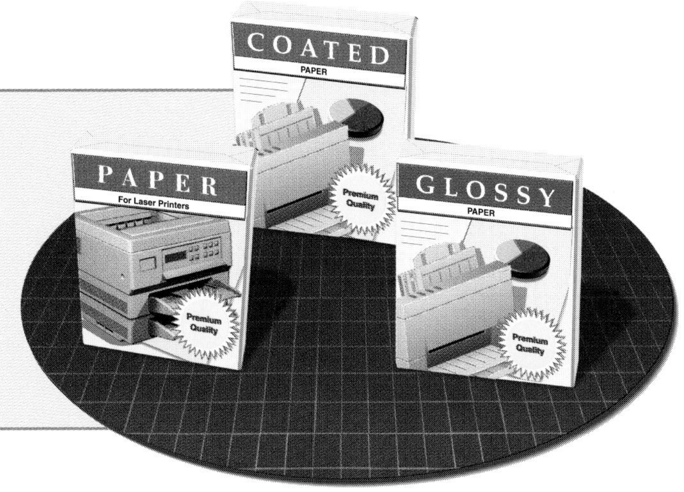

A video card generates the text and images that appear on the display area of the monitor.

INSTALL A VIDEO CARD

Before installing a video card, turn off the computer, unplug the power cable and remove the cover from the computer case. Then ground yourself and the computer case. For information about grounding, see page 6.

1

Select the expansion slot on the system board where you want to install the video card.

2

Remove the expansion slot cover from the computer case. The cover is usually held in place by a small screw.

3

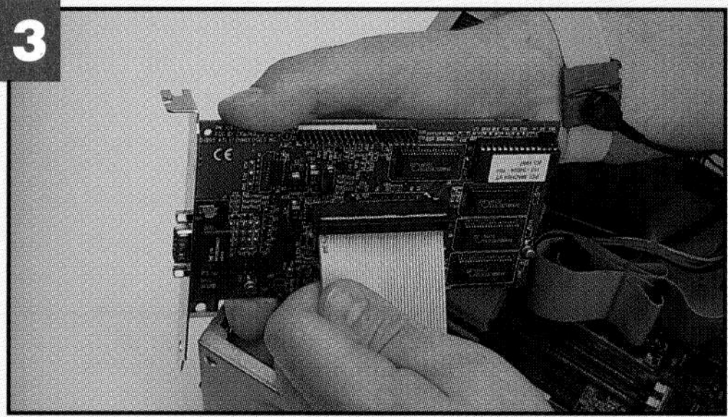

If necessary, use cables to connect the video card to other devices.

4

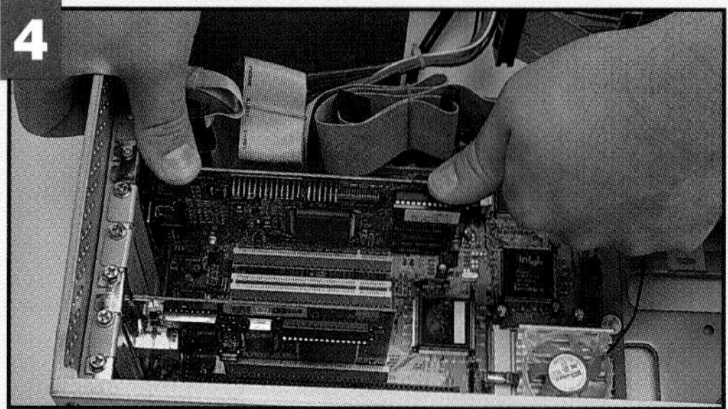

Place the video card in the expansion slot. Press down firmly and evenly across the top of the card until it is securely inserted in the expansion slot.

5

Secure the video card to the computer case using a small screw. Then replace the cover on the computer case.

SET UP AND TROUBLESHOOT

How do I set up a video card?

When you install a video card, your computer may automatically detect and set up the video card for you. The video card may include an installation program you can use if your computer does not automatically detect and set up the video card.

How do I set up my computer to use multiple monitors?

You must install a video card for each monitor you want to use and ensure that each video card supports the multiple-monitor feature. Your operating system's documentation should indicate which video cards you may use.

What should I do if my monitor stops displaying information or no longer displays information properly?

To determine if your monitor is not displaying information due to a malfunctioning video card, first test your monitor on another computer.

You should also ensure that the video card is installed in the correct expansion slot. Some computers require that the video card be plugged into a specific slot in the computer.

CHOOSE A VIDEO CARD

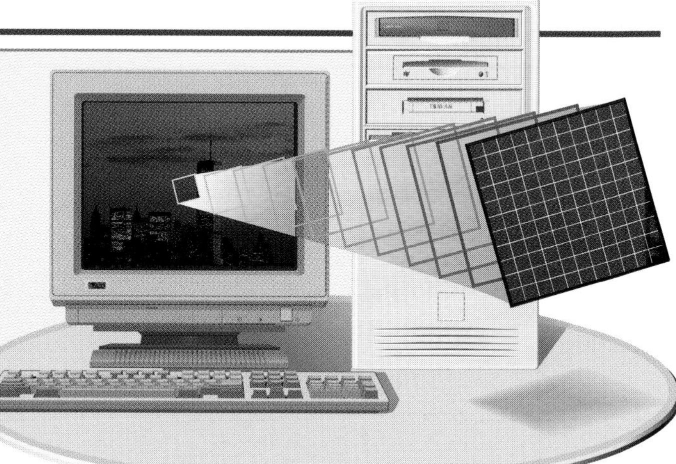

Resolution

Resolution determines the amount of information displayed on the screen and is measured by the number of horizontal and vertical pixels. A pixel is the smallest element on the screen. Basic video cards can display a resolution of 640 x 480 or 800 x 600. Most new video cards can display a resolution of up to 1600 x 1600. The video card and monitor must be able to use the same resolution.

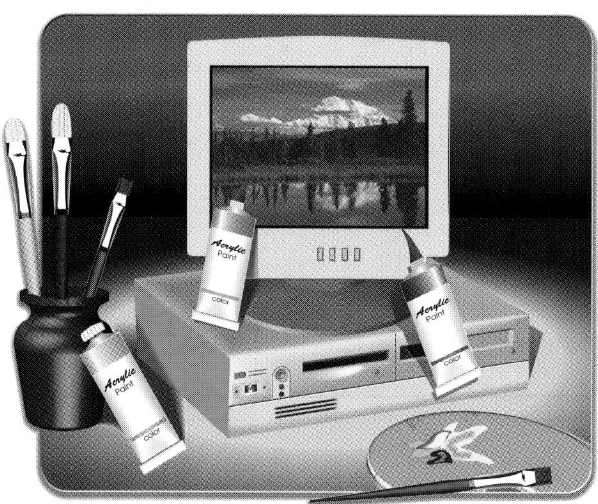

Color Depth

The video card determines the number of colors a monitor can display. Basic video cards can display 256 colors. Today, most video cards can display over 65,000 colors.

Refresh Rate

The refresh rate determines the speed that information is redrawn on the screen and is measured in hertz (Hz). The higher the refresh rate, the less flicker on the screen. This helps reduce eyestrain. 72 Hz is a common refresh rate. The video card and monitor must be able to use the same refresh rate.

UPGRADE

Driver

A driver is the software that allows the computer's operating system to communicate with and control the video card. All video cards require a driver. Video card drivers are frequently updated and improved. You should always ensure that you are using the correct and most up-to-date driver for your video card.

Memory

A video card uses memory chips to store the information it displays on the screen. You can add memory chips to a video card to increase the capabilities of the video card. Adding memory chips can increase the resolution and color depth the video card can display.

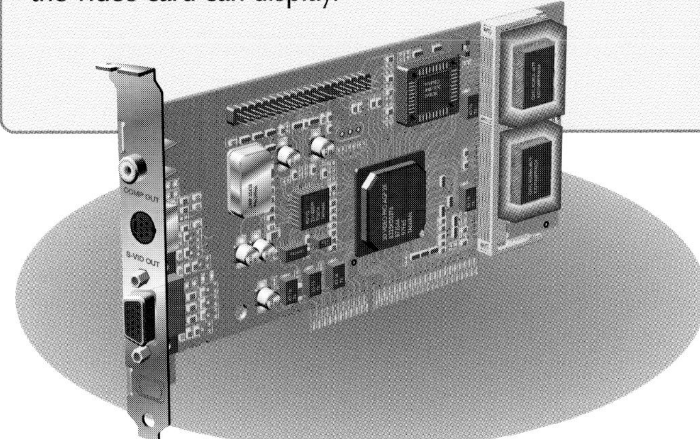

Graphics Processing Unit

You can purchase a video card that has a special chip, called a Graphics Processing Unit (GPU). The GPU allows the video card to display information on the screen without using the CPU, which can improve the computer's performance.

Built-in Video Port

Many system boards come with a built-in video port. To upgrade the video capabilities for a computer with a built-in port, you must disable the port on the system board and then install a new video card in an expansion slot.

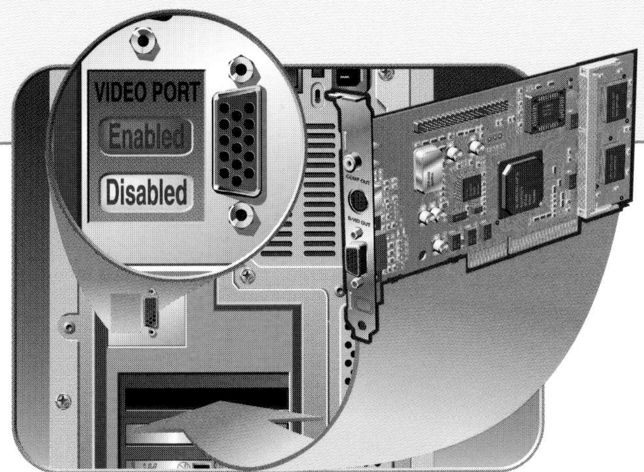

A monitor is a device that displays text and images generated by a computer.

CONNECT A MONITOR

Before connecting a monitor, turn off the computer.

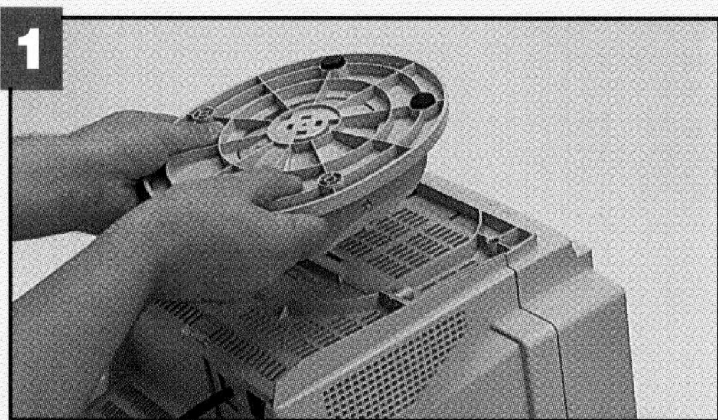

1 Most monitors come with a tilt-and-swivel base that lets you adjust the angle of the screen and reduce glare from overhead lighting. If necessary, attach the base to the monitor.

2 If necessary, connect the monitor cable to the back of the monitor. The monitor cable is permanently attached on some monitors.

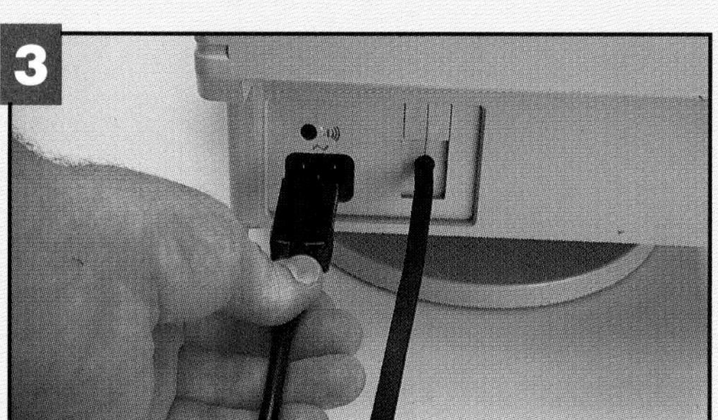

3 If necessary, connect the power cable to the back of the monitor. The power cable is permanently attached on some monitors.

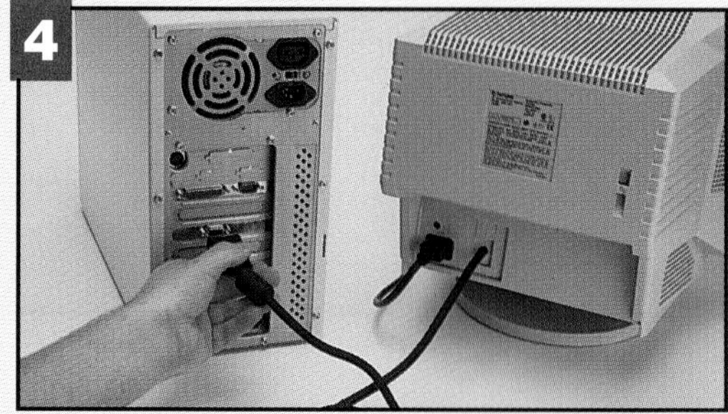

4 Connect the monitor cable to the monitor port at the back of the computer. The monitor port is usually located on the video card.

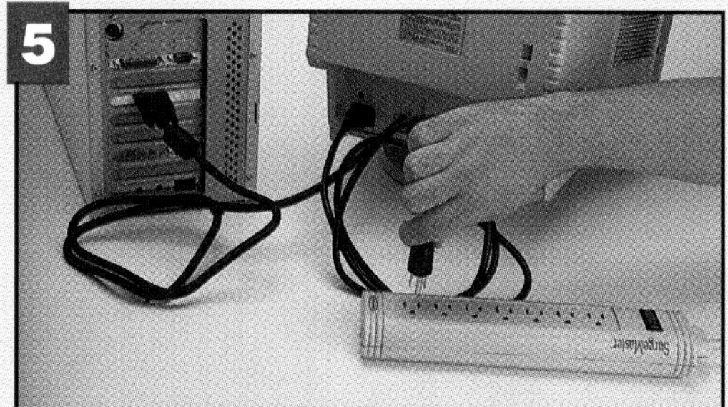

5 Plug the power cable from the monitor into an electrical outlet.

TYPES OF MONITORS

There are two types of monitors available—CRT and LCD.

CRT

Most monitors use Cathode Ray Tube (CRT) technology to display information. This is the same technology used in television sets. CRT technology uses a beam of high-speed electrons, called a cathode ray, to draw images on the end of a glass tube. The end of the glass tube is the screen.

LCD

Some monitors use Liquid Crystal Display (LCD) technology to display information. The screen of an LCD monitor is made up of liquid crystal between two pieces of specially treated glass. Electrical impulses cause the liquid crystal to change color. These colors make up the images on the screen.

In the past, LCD monitors were only used on portable computers, but are now available for desktop computers. LCD monitors are more expensive than CRT monitors, but are lighter, thinner and consume less electricity. LCD monitors are also called flat-panel monitors.

CHOOSE A MONITOR

Resolution

Resolution determines the amount of information a monitor can display and is measured by the number of horizontal and vertical pixels. A pixel is the smallest element on the screen. Most new monitors can display a resolution of up to 1600 x 1600. The monitor and video card must be able to display the same resolution.

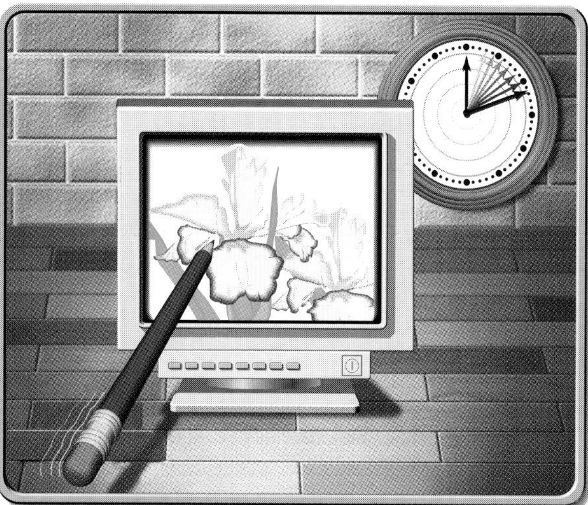

Refresh Rate

The refresh rate determines the speed that a monitor redraws, or updates, images. The higher the refresh rate, the less flicker on the screen, which helps reduce eyestrain.

The refresh rate is measured in hertz (Hz). The monitor and video card must be able to use the same refresh rate. A monitor with a refresh rate of 72 Hz or more is recommended.

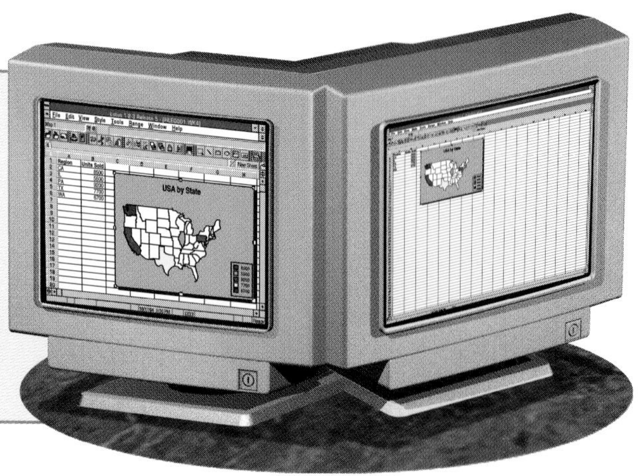

Multisync

Some monitors can display information using only one resolution and refresh rate. A multisync monitor can display information using different resolutions and refresh rates. A multisync monitor can detect which resolution and refresh rate the video card is using and then automatically switch to the appropriate settings. Most new monitors are multisync monitors.

Size

The size of a monitor is measured two ways. The nominal size is measured diagonally across the picture tube inside the monitor. The viewable size is measured diagonally across the screen. The nominal size is usually greater than the viewable size.

Some manufacturers advertise both sizes, but many advertise only the nominal size. A common nominal monitor size is 15 inches, although 17 and 21 inch monitors are gaining in popularity as prices fall.

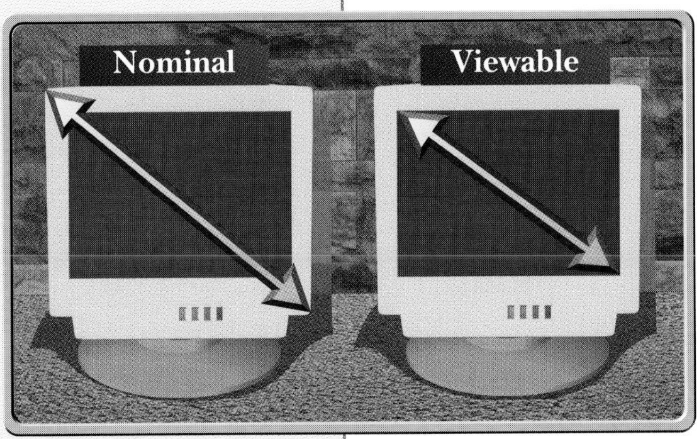

Dot Pitch

The dot pitch is the distance between pixels on a screen. The dot pitch determines the sharpness of images on the screen and is measured in millimeters (mm). The smaller the dot pitch, the clearer the images. For example, a monitor with a dot pitch of .26mm will display crisper images than a monitor with a dot pitch of .30mm.

ENERGY STAR

The Environmental Protection Agency (EPA) developed an energy-saving guideline called ENERGY STAR to reduce wasted energy and the pollution it causes. When you do not use an ENERGY STAR computer for a period of time, the monitor and computer enter an energy-saving sleep mode.

TROUBLESHOOT AND MAINTAIN

Why is my monitor not working properly?

Monitors tend to be one of the most reliable and robust components of a computer system. When a monitor fails to display information properly or does not display any information at all, the problem usually lies with the video card. A video card translates instructions from the computer to a form the monitor can understand. For information about troubleshooting a video card, see page 71.

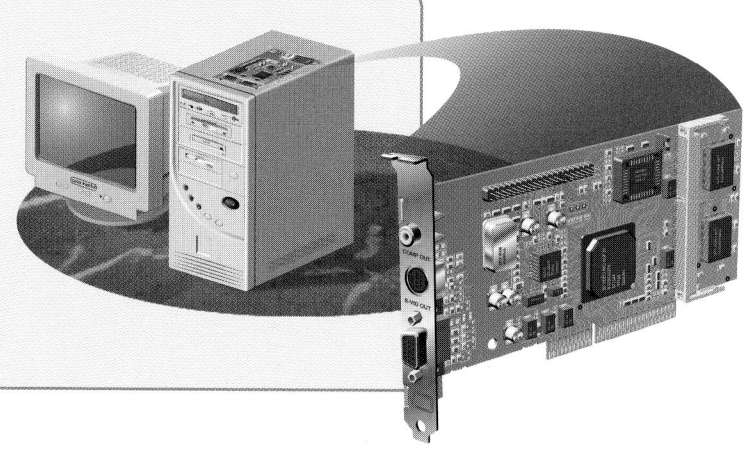

Why are the images on my screen discolored?

If images on your screen seem to display a blue, green or purple tinge, one of the primary colors may be missing. The cause of the problem may be a loose connection between the monitor and video card. Ensure that the screws on the monitor cable connector have been used to securely fasten the connector to the monitor port.

The images are not centered on my screen. How do I fix this problem?

Monitors have controls that allow you to adjust the position of the images displayed on the screen, as well as the brightness and contrast of the images. The controls are usually found on the front of the monitor.

Why is there a dark area on my screen?

If a monitor displays a dark or discolored area on the screen, it may have been exposed to strong magnetic fields. You should remove any devices that generate magnetic fields, such as heaters, from the area where the monitor is located and then degauss the screen to demagnetize it. Many monitors degauss automatically each time they are turned on. Some monitors also have a degauss button you can use.

My screen often goes blank. What is the problem?

Most new computers are ENERGY STAR-compliant. The screen on an ENERGY STAR-compliant monitor goes blank when the computer is not used for a period of time. You can move the mouse or press a key on the keyboard to wake the computer.

How do I clean my monitor?

Before cleaning a monitor, you should refer to the monitor's documentation for instructions. Many monitors have an anti-glare coating that helps to reduce the amount of light reflected off the screen. Some monitors also have an anti-static coating that repels dust. If you use the wrong substance to clean the screen, these coatings may be affected.

TV TUNER CARD

A TV tuner card allows you to watch television programs on your computer.

A TV tuner card may have built-in video capabilities or may need to be connected to the video card in your computer.

INSTALL A TV TUNER CARD

Before installing a TV tuner card, turn off the computer, unplug the power cable and remove the cover from the computer case. Then ground yourself and the computer case. For information about grounding, see page 6.

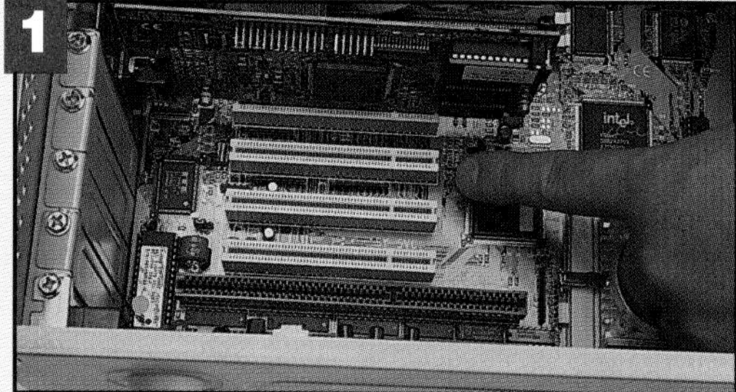

1 Select the expansion slot on the system board where you want to install the TV tuner card.

2 Remove the expansion slot cover from the computer case. The cover is usually held in place by a small screw.

3 If necessary, use a cable to connect the TV tuner card to other devices.

4 Place the TV tuner card in the expansion slot. Press down firmly and evenly across the top of the card until it is securely inserted in the expansion slot.

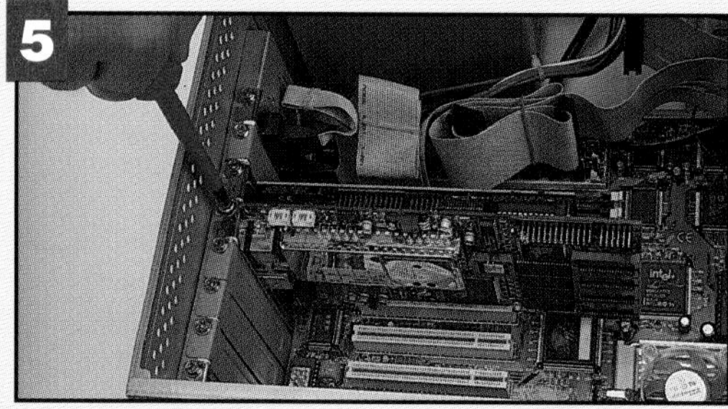

5 Secure the TV tuner card to the computer case using a small screw. Then replace the cover on the computer case.

6 Connect the television cable to the TV tuner card.

SET UP

Every TV tuner card comes with an installation program you can use to set up the TV tuner card to work with the computer.

CHOOSE A TV TUNER CARD

Video Capture

Most TV tuner cards allow you to save still images and full-motion video clips from a video source or television program as a file on your hard drive.

Intercast Technology

Some television channels use Intercast technology to broadcast additional information with their programs. This allows you to watch a television program and view text and graphics related to the program at the same time. Most TV tuner cards support Intercast technology.

Closed Captioning

Most TV tuner cards can scan the closed captioning text of a television channel for a keyword. When the keyword appears, the TV tuner card displays the television program on your monitor. Most cards also allow you to save the closed captioning text from a television program as a file on your hard drive.

SOUND CARD

A sound card allows a computer to play and record high-quality sound.

INSTALL A SOUND CARD

Before installing a sound card, turn off the computer, unplug the power cable and remove the cover from the computer case. Then ground yourself and the computer case. For information about grounding, see page 6.

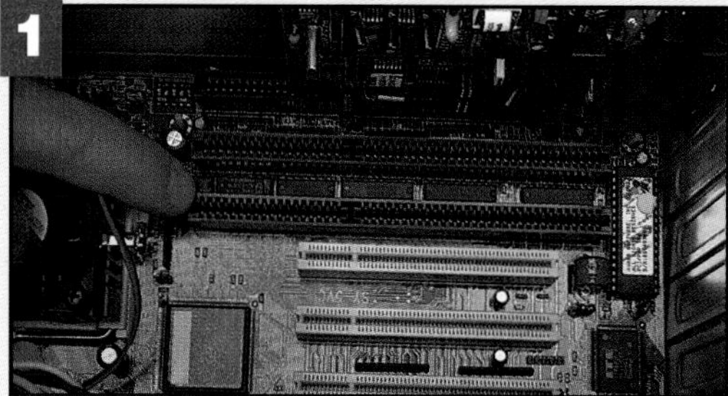

Select the expansion slot on the system board where you want to install the sound card.

Remove the expansion slot cover from the computer case. The cover is usually held in place by a small screw.

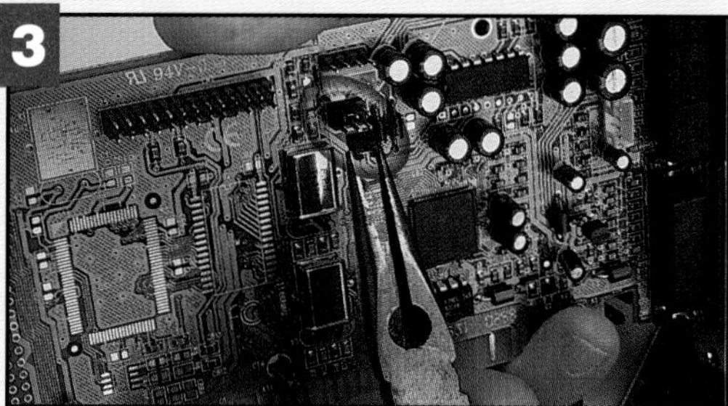

If necessary, use the jumpers or switches on the sound card to adjust the settings for the sound card.

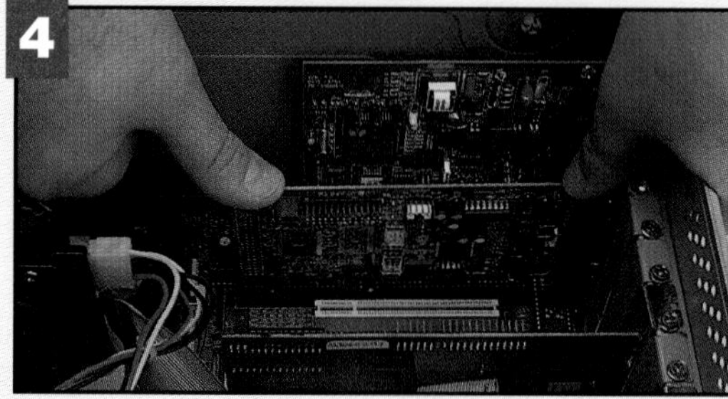

Place the sound card in the expansion slot. Press down firmly and evenly across the top of the card until it is securely inserted in the expansion slot.

If necessary, connect the audio cable to the sound card. Then connect the audio cable to the CD-ROM drive. This allows your computer's speakers to play sound from compact discs.

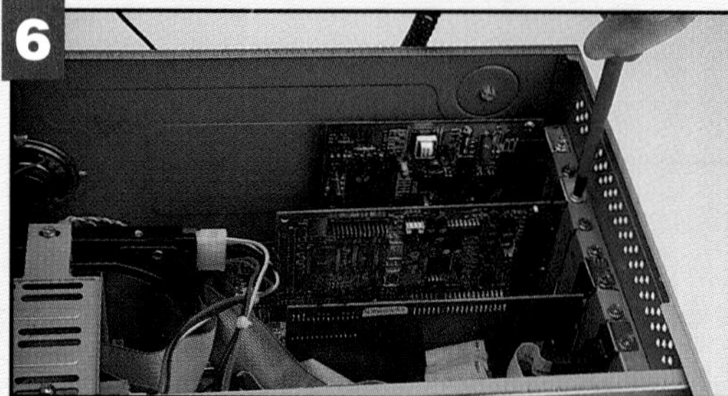

Secure the sound card to the computer case using a small screw. Then replace the cover on the computer case.

SET UP

Settings

When you install a sound card, your computer may automatically detect and set up the sound card for you. If your computer does not automatically set up the sound card, you can consult the sound card documentation for information about the resource settings, such as Interrupt Requests (IRQ) and Direct Memory Access (DMA) channels, the sound card requires.

Before setting up a sound card, make sure you have a list of the resources used by the other devices in the computer. If the sound card requires the same resources as another device, you may need to change the settings for the device. For more information about resource settings, see page 144.

Driver

Sound cards require one or more drivers. A driver is the software that allows the computer's operating system to communicate with and control the sound card. Most sound cards include an installation program that installs all the necessary drivers at once. If there is no installation program, you may have to install a separate driver for each port and jack on the sound card. Drivers are usually available at the sound card manufacturer's Web site.

CHOOSE A SOUND CARD

MIDI Support

Musical Instrument Digital Interface (MIDI) is a set of instructions that allows you to connect a musical instrument, such as a synthesizer, to a sound card. This lets you use a computer to play, record and edit music. Many musicians use MIDI to compose music on a computer.

A sound card that supports MIDI also ensures that a computer can generate the sounds often found in games and presentation packages.

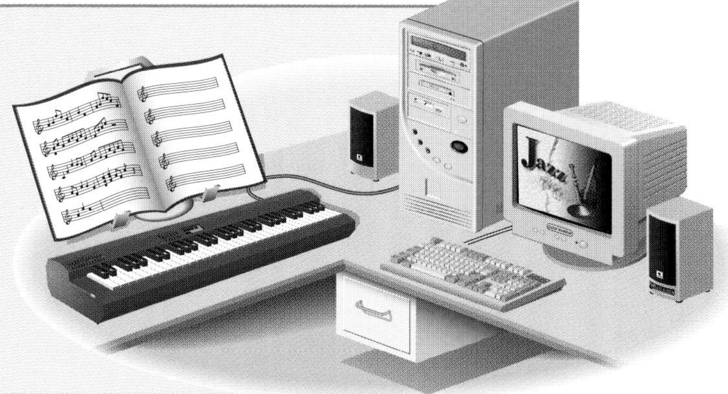

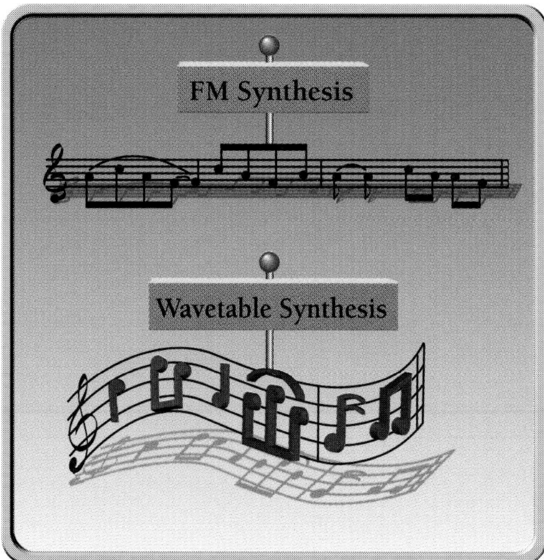

FM and Wavetable Synthesis

There are two ways a sound card can produce MIDI sound—FM synthesis and Wavetable synthesis. FM synthesis uses mathematical formulas to imitate the sounds of musical instruments. This results in less realistic sound.

Wavetable synthesis uses actual recordings of musical instruments. This results in rich, realistic sound. Sound cards that use Wavetable synthesis are more expensive, but produce higher quality sound than cards that use FM synthesis.

Sound Blaster Compatible

Sound Blaster is the accepted industry standard for sound cards. You should purchase a Sound Blaster compatible sound card to ensure that the sound card will work with most programs and operating systems.

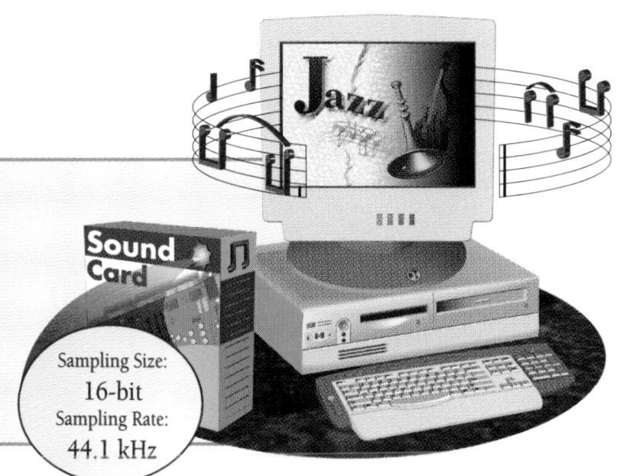

Sampling Size and Rate

The sampling size and rate of a sound card determines the quality of the sound produced. For good quality sound, buy a sound card with a least a 16-bit sampling size and a 44.1 kHz sampling rate.

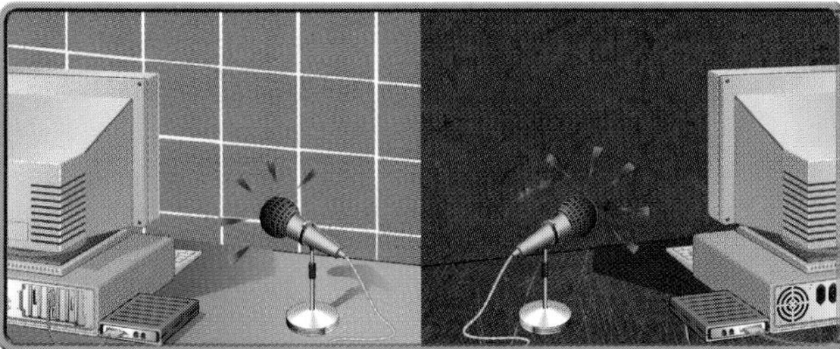

Full-Duplex

A full-duplex sound card can send and receive sounds at the same time. When using a computer to have a conversation over the Internet, a full-duplex sound card lets people talk at the same time. With a half-duplex card, people must take turns talking.

Multi-Speaker Capability

Some sound cards can support up to five speakers, which can further enhance the sound capabilities of the computer.

UPGRADE

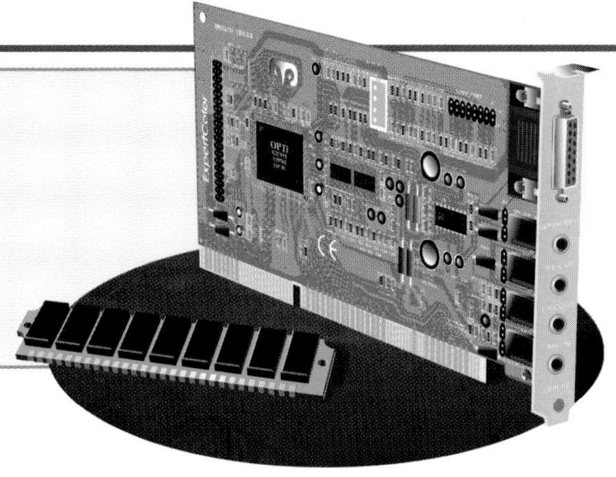

You may be able to add memory to your sound card. Adding memory allows you to increase the capabilities of the sound card. Sound cards usually contain more than enough memory for most programs, including games. In most cases, you will only need to add memory if you plan to use the computer to compose or sample music.

SPEAKERS

Speakers allow you to hear the sound generated by a sound card.

Most computers come equipped with low-quality speakers. You may want to upgrade to higher quality speakers if you use your computer to play games or listen to music CDs.

CONNECT A SET OF SPEAKERS

Before connecting a set of speakers, turn off the computer.

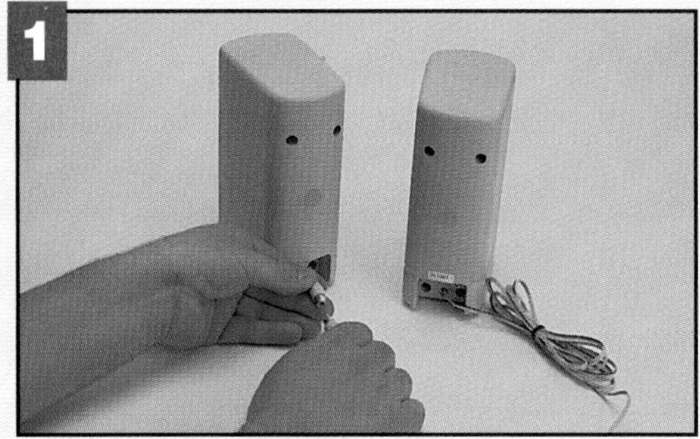

1 If necessary, connect the speakers together using the speaker cable.

2 Position the speakers in the desired location.

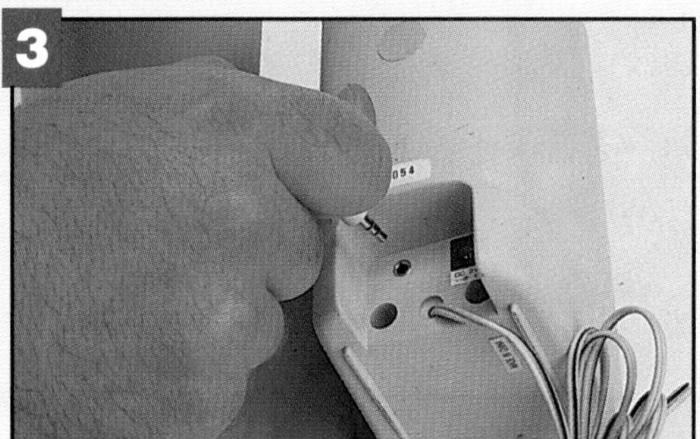

3 If necessary, connect the audio cable to the back of the main speaker. The main speaker often has a volume control and power switch.

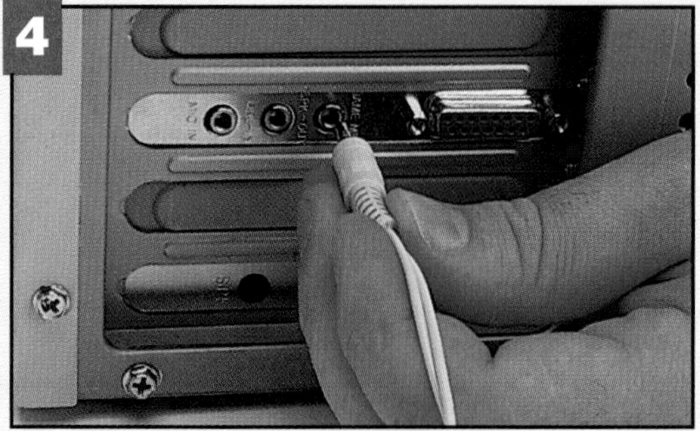

4 Connect the audio cable to the speaker jack at the back of the computer. The speaker jack is usually found on the sound card.

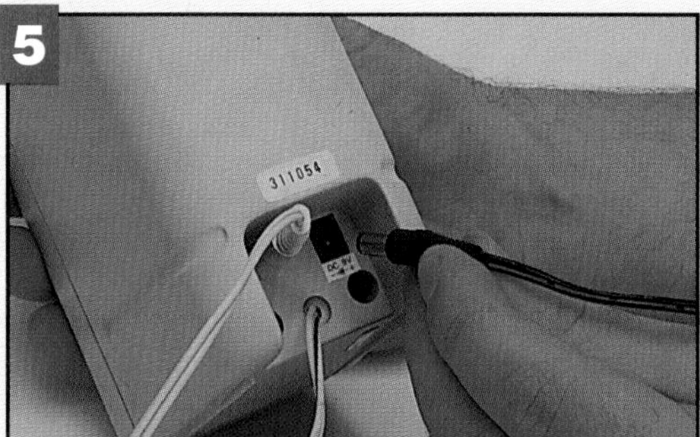

5 If necessary, connect the power cable to the back of the main speaker. Then plug the power cable into an electrical outlet

CHOOSE SPEAKERS

Shielded Speakers

You should choose shielded speakers. Shielded speakers prevent the magnets inside the speakers from distorting the images on a monitor or damaging hard drives and floppy disks.

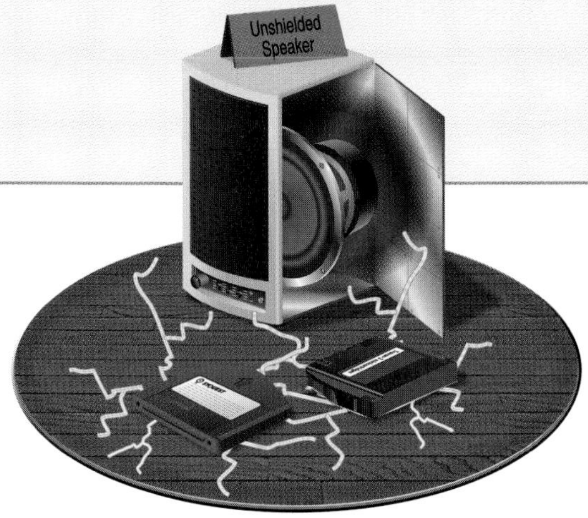

Frequency

Frequency is measured in hertz (Hz) and refers to the range of high and low sounds speakers can produce. The range of human hearing is 20 to 20,000 Hz. Some high-quality speakers have a frequency of 40 to 20,000 Hz.

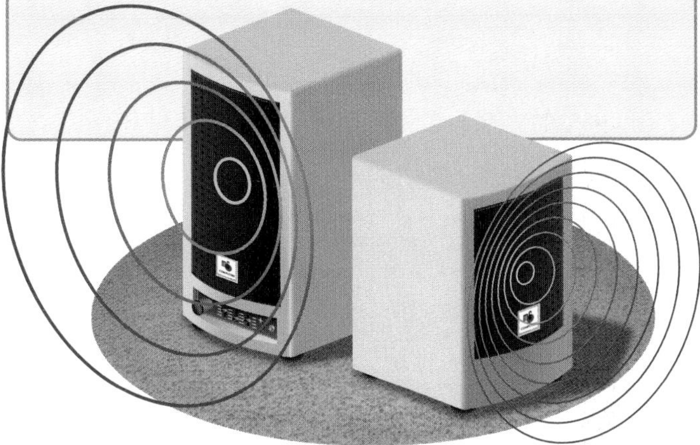

USB Speakers

Some speakers connect to USB ports. USB speakers add sound capabilities to a computer that does not have a sound card. If you use USB speakers, your CD-ROM drive must support Digital Audio Extraction to be able to play music CDs.

Features

Some speakers include features that can enhance the quality of sound the speakers produce. For example, a built-in amplifier can strengthen the signal from the sound card to improve speaker performance. Speakers that include 3-D sound enhancement technology seem to produce sound from a wider area. Some speaker systems also include a subwoofer, which produces low-frequency sounds and a richer sound.

MICROPHONE

You can use a microphone to record speech and other sounds.

CONNECT A MICROPHONE

Before connecting a microphone, turn off the computer.

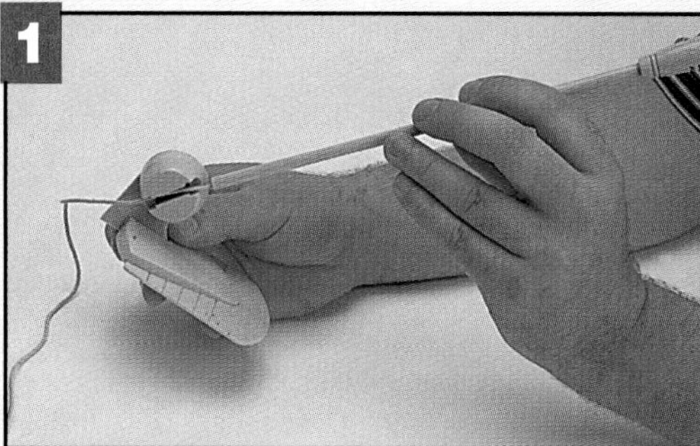

1 Some microphones come with a stand that lets you adjust the angle of the microphone to improve recording quality. If necessary, attach the stand to the microphone.

2 Position the microphone where you can use it comfortably.

3 Connect the cable from the microphone to the microphone jack at the back of the computer. The microphone jack is usually located on the sound card.

CHOOSE A MICROPHONE

The type of microphone you should choose depends on the way you want the microphone to record sound. A unidirectional microphone records sound from one direction, which helps reduce the amount of background noise that is recorded. This type of microphone is useful for recording an individual voice.

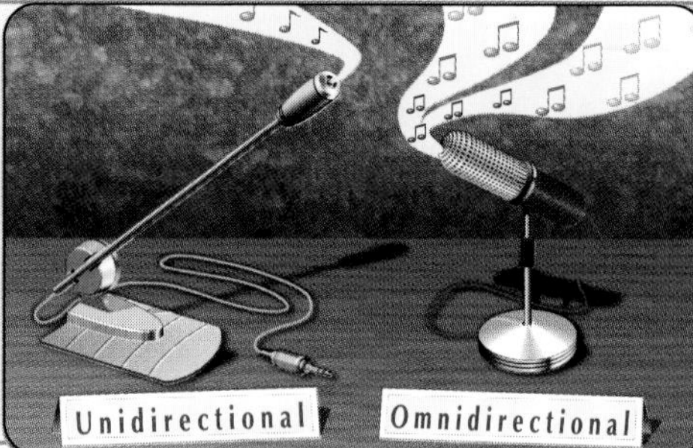

An omnidirectional microphone records sound from all directions. This type of microphone is useful for recording several voices in a group conversation.

PROGRAMS

There are many types of programs that require you to use a microphone. Conferencing programs allow you to use a microphone to communicate with others over the Internet. With voice control programs, you can speak into a microphone and use voice commands to control your computer. Speech recognition programs allow you to speak into a microphone to create documents, instead of typing text with your keyboard.

TROUBLESHOOT

How can I improve the quality of my recordings?

Make sure the microphone is positioned away from sources of unwanted background noise, such as appliances or open windows. You should also make sure the microphone is positioned close to, but not directly in front of, the person using the microphone.

You may also have to change the microphone's settings. Some operating systems allow you to adjust the balance and volume settings for the microphone.

How can I take full advantage of my high-quality microphone?

A high-quality microphone will not produce good quality recordings if connected to a less than adequate sound card. You may need to upgrade your sound card to get the best performance from the microphone.

JOYSTICK

A joystick is a device that allows you to interact with a computer game.

CONNECT A JOYSTICK

Before connecting a joystick, turn off the computer.

1

Position the joystick where you can use it comfortably. Most joysticks have suction cups that allow you to secure the joystick to your desk.

2

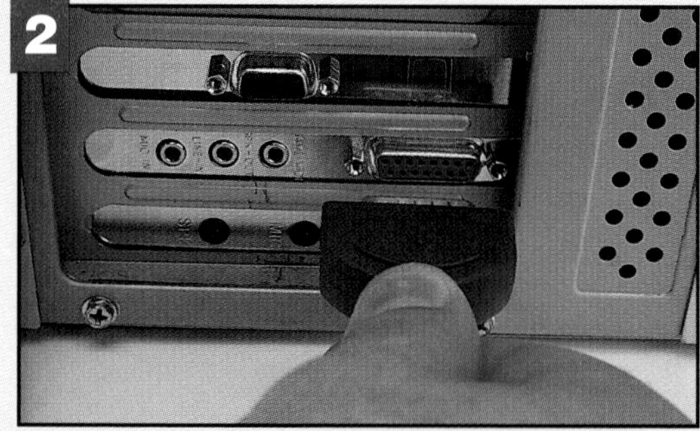

Connect the cable from the joystick to the joystick port at the back of the computer. The joystick port is usually located on the sound card.

JOYSTICK UPGRADES

Enhanced Joysticks

Some enhanced joysticks have extra controls to improve the way you play games. For example, enhanced joysticks that are designed specifically for driving games include a steering wheel and pedals. Other enhanced joysticks are programmed to move in response to actions in a game.

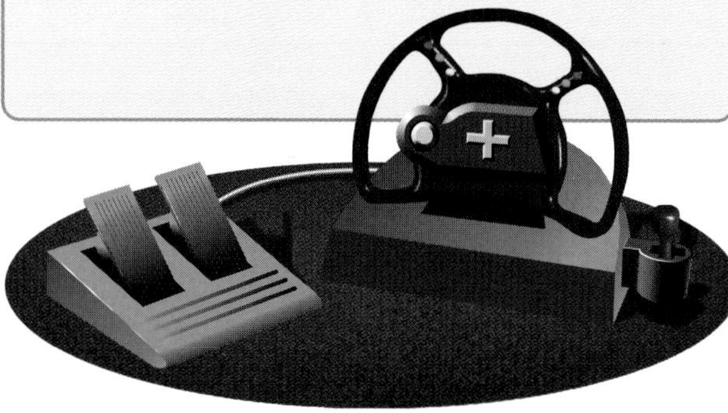

Gamepad

A gamepad is a small, handheld device that typically consists of a movement control on the left and function buttons on the right. Gamepads are useful for games that require rapid movement, such as fighting games.

SET UP

Driver

If you want to use your joystick to play a game designed for the Windows operating system, you may need to install a joystick driver included with Windows. You can consult your joystick's documentation to determine which driver you should install.

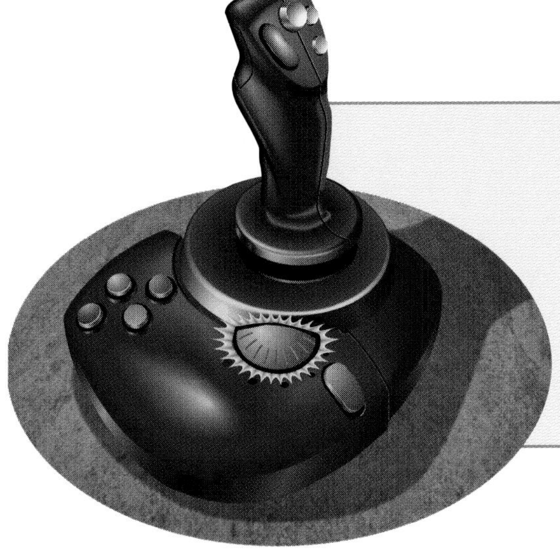

Calibration

You can calibrate your joystick to adjust and fine-tune the joystick's settings. Some joysticks have trim wheels you can use to help calibrate the joystick. Many operating systems, such as Windows, also allow you to calibrate a joystick. Some joysticks, such as enhanced joysticks, may need to be calibrated using the software that came with the joystick.

Game-Specific Settings

Some games require you to set up the joystick within the game. For example, you may need to specify the type of joystick you are using or assign specific functions to the buttons on the joystick. You can follow the directions in the game to set up the joystick.

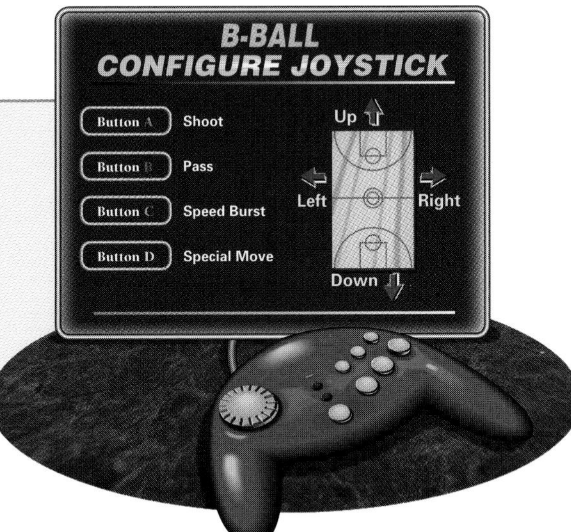

A scanner is a device that reads graphics and paper documents such as letters, forms and news clippings into a computer.

CONNECT A SCANNER

Before connecting a scanner, turn off the computer.

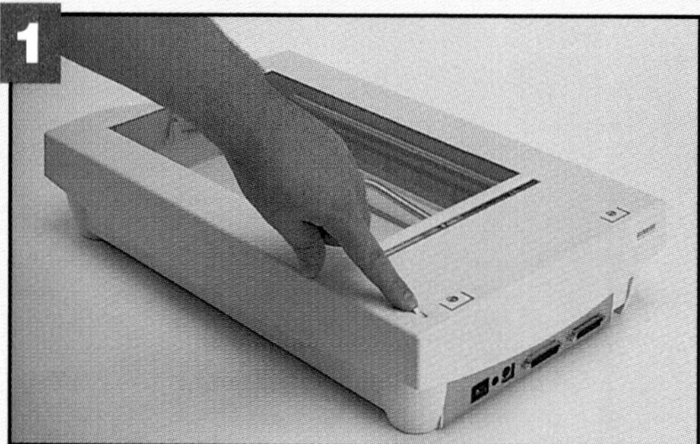

1 Many scanners have a transit lock, which secures the scanner's internal components during shipping. If necessary, release the transit lock.

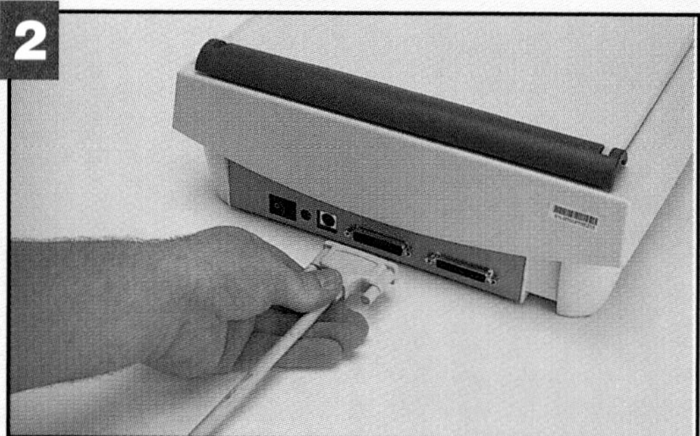

2 Connect the scanner cable to the port at the back of the scanner.

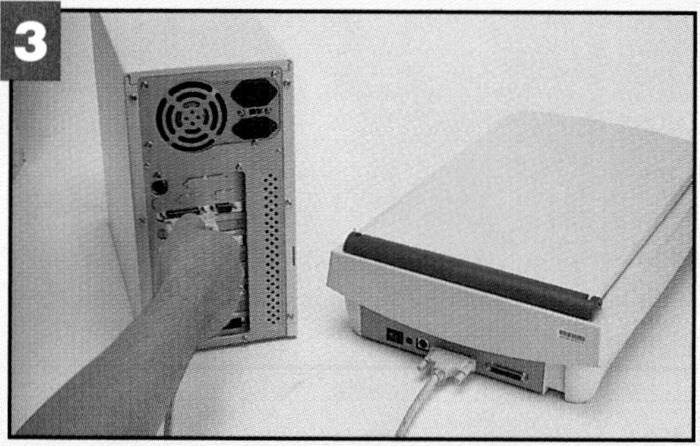

3 Connect the scanner cable to a port at the back of the computer. Scanners may connect to a parallel, SCSI or USB port.

4 If you connected the scanner to a parallel port in step 3, you can connect the cable from your printer to the printer port at the back of the scanner.

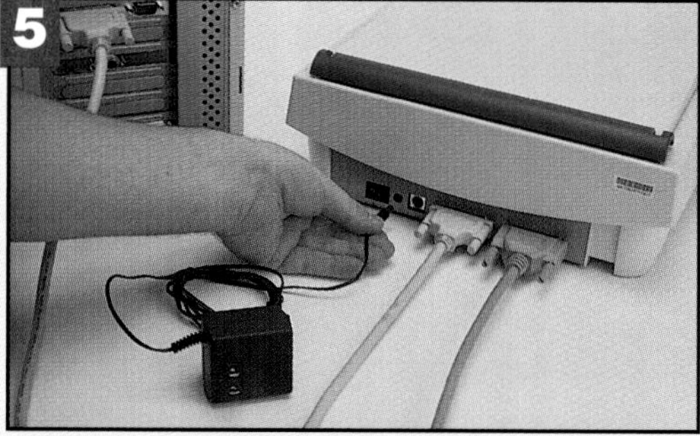

5 Connect the power cable to the power connector at the back of the scanner. Then plug the power cable into an electrical outlet.

TYPES OF SCANNERS

Flatbed

A flatbed scanner can scan single sheets of paper and pages in a book. Most flatbed scanners can scan documents up to 8.5 inches wide and 11 inches long. Some flatbed scanners can scan documents up to 8.5 inches wide and 14 inches long.

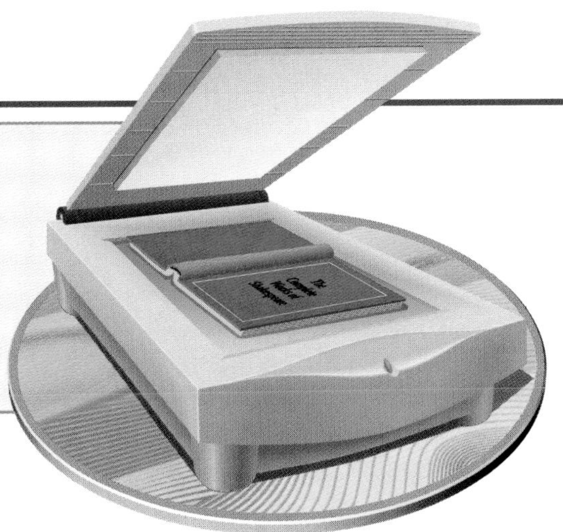

Sheet-Fed

A sheet-fed scanner can scan only single sheets of paper. If you want to scan a page in a book, you have to remove the page.

Sheet-fed scanners are less expensive and more compact than flatbed scanners.

Handheld

A handheld scanner can scan images up to four inches wide. You must manually move the scanner over the image you want to scan. This movement usually affects the quality of the scanned image. Smaller handheld scanners that resemble highlighter pens are also available. These scanners are useful for scanning lines of text.

Handheld scanners are inexpensive and portable, but the popularity of handheld scanners has decreased as the prices of flatbed and sheet-fed scanners have fallen.

SCANNER (CONTINUED)

CHOOSE A SCANNER

Resolution

The resolution of a scanner determines the amount of detail the scanner can detect. Scanner resolution is measured in dots per inch (dpi). Most scanners can detect 600 x 600 dpi, but some scanners can detect up to 2400 x 2400 dpi.

Color Depth

The color depth of a scanner is measured in bits and indicates the number of colors the scanner can detect. The more colors the scanner can detect, the higher the quality of the scan. Most scanners have a 24-bit color depth. A 24-bit scanner is capable of detecting over 16 million different colors.

TWAIN Compatible

All scanners include a driver that allows the operating system and programs, such as image editing software, to work with the scanner. TWAIN is the accepted industry standard for scanner drivers. A scanner that uses a TWAIN driver can be used by most operating systems and programs.

SOFTWARE

Image Editing Software

Image editing software allows you to change the appearance of a scanned graphic. You can adjust the brightness, contrast and color balance of a graphic. You can also make major changes to a graphic, such as removing an object. The image editing software included with most scanners is a limited version of commercial image editing software.

OCR Software

Optical Character Recognition (OCR) software places scanned text into a document that can be edited in a word processor. The OCR software included with most scanners is a limited version of commercial OCR software.

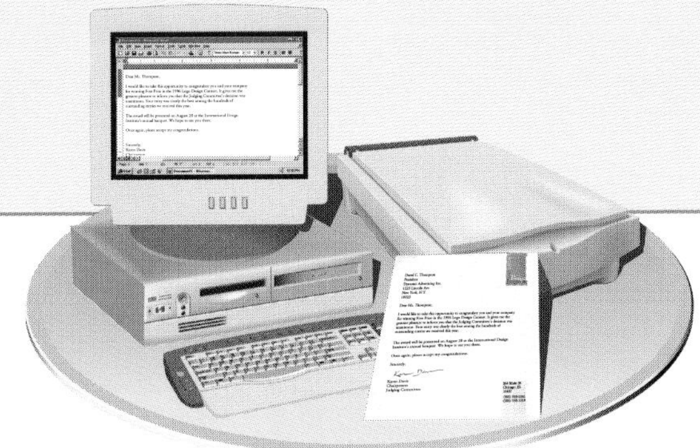

TROUBLESHOOT

Why is my scanner not working properly?

In most cases, if your scanner does not work properly, the cause of the problem is an incorrectly installed driver or software program. You should try re-installing the driver or software to correct the problem.

How can I improve the print quality of scanned images?

You should match the scanning resolution to your printer's resolution. For example, if you plan to print an image on a 600-dpi printer, you should scan the image at 600 x 600 dpi.

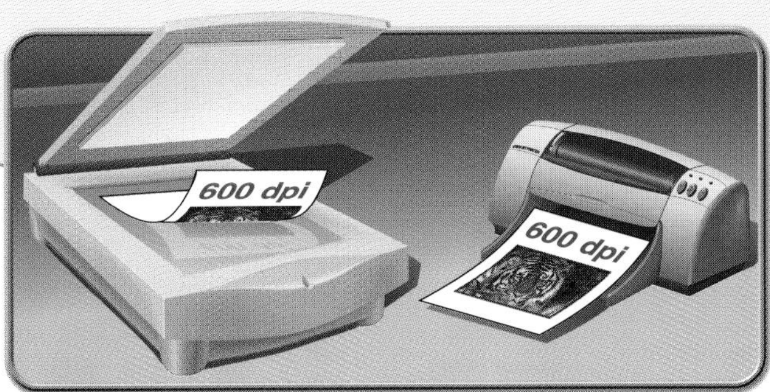

DIGITAL CAMERA

A digital camera lets you take photos that you can view and print using a computer.

You can use your photos in documents, on the World Wide Web or in e-mail messages.

CONNECT A DIGITAL CAMERA

Before connecting a digital camera, turn on the computer.

Connect the device cable to the port on the digital camera.

Connect the device cable to a port at the back of the computer. Digital cameras connect to a serial or USB port.

TROUBLESHOOT

My digital camera is not working properly. What should I do?

Digital cameras use batteries for power. If your digital camera is having problems such as a malfunctioning flash or is producing distorted images, you should check to see if the batteries in the camera are low on power. For best results, you should use fully charged batteries each time you begin using your digital camera.

How can I store more images on my digital camera?

Digital cameras allow you to adjust the quality of the images. Lower quality images take up less space in a camera's memory, so you can store more images.

CHOOSE A DIGITAL CAMERA

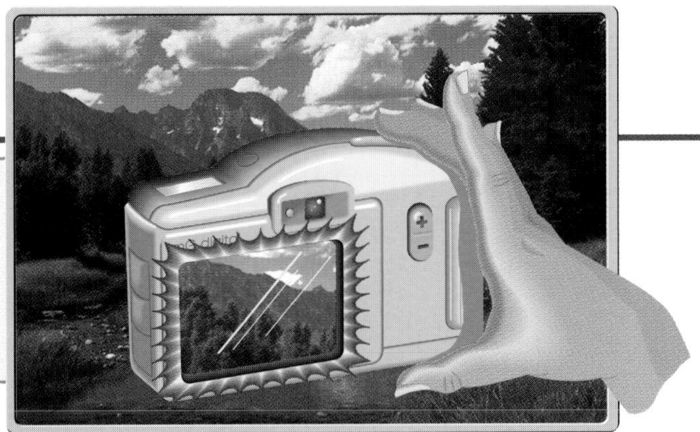

LCD Screen

Most digital cameras include a color Liquid Crystal Display (LCD) screen, which you can use to preview your shots and view photos you have taken.

Resolution

The quality of photos a digital camera can produce depends on the detail the camera can detect. Resolution is measured in megapixels. One megapixel is equivalent to a resolution of approximately 1000 x 1000 pixels. The higher the number of megapixels a camera can detect, the clearer and more detailed the photos. There are currently 1, 2 and 3-megapixel digital cameras available.

Memory

Digital cameras store photos in memory until you transfer the photos to a computer. Most digital cameras have either built-in or removable memory, but some cameras have both.

Removable
Most digital cameras with removable memory store photos on a memory card. Some digital cameras store photos on a regular floppy disk that fits inside the camera. You can replace a memory card or floppy disk when it is full.

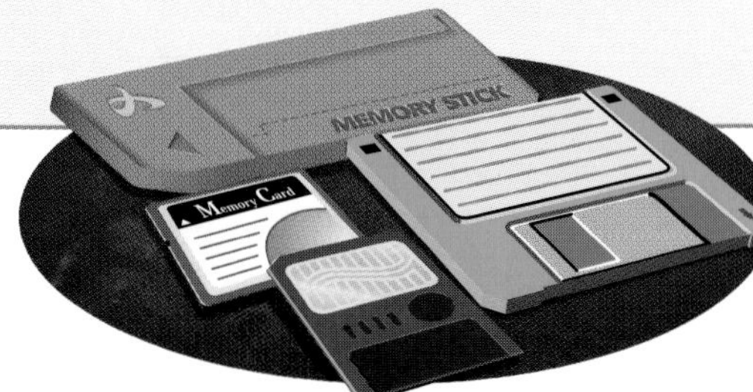

Built-in
The built-in memory in most digital cameras can store at least 15 high-quality photos. Once the built-in memory is full, you must transfer the photos to a computer before taking more photos.

USB HUB

The Universal Serial Bus (USB) hub allows you to connect multiple devices to your computer.

CONNECT A USB HUB

Before connecting a USB hub, turn on the computer.

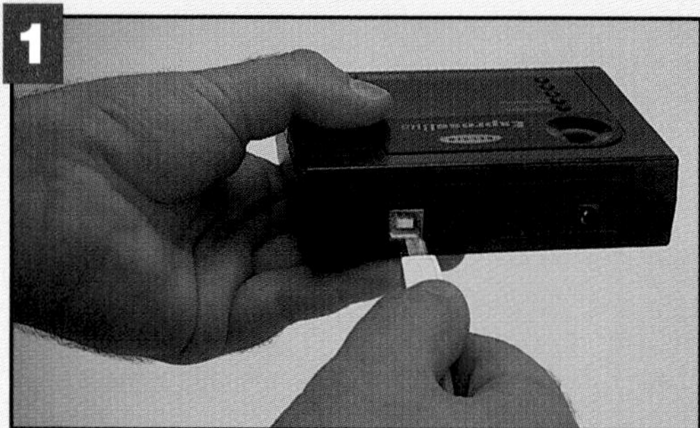

1 Connect the USB cable to the computer port on the USB hub.

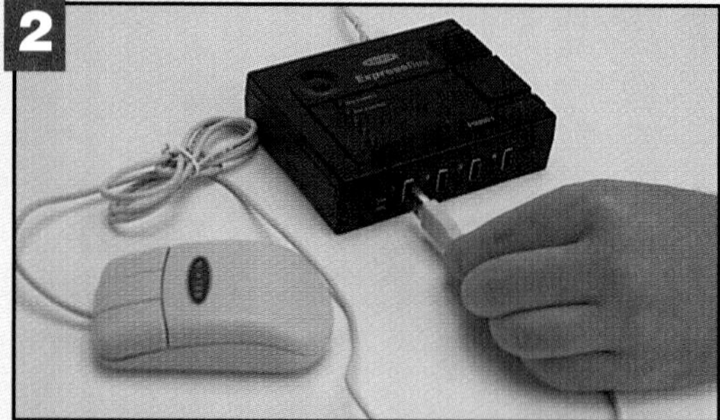

2 Connect your USB devices to the device ports on the USB hub.

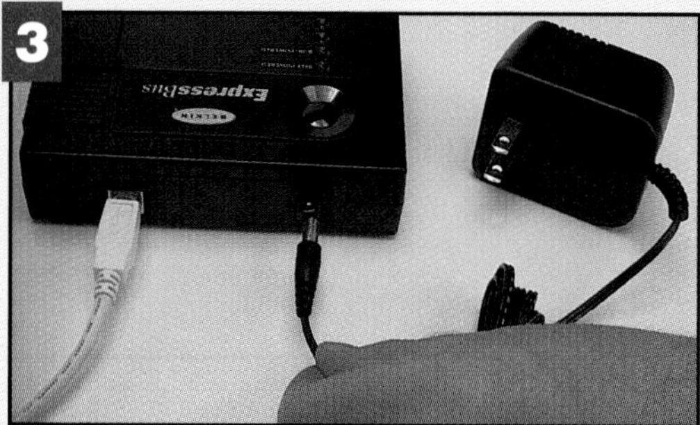

3 If necessary, connect the power cable to the USB hub. Then plug the power cable into an electrical outlet.

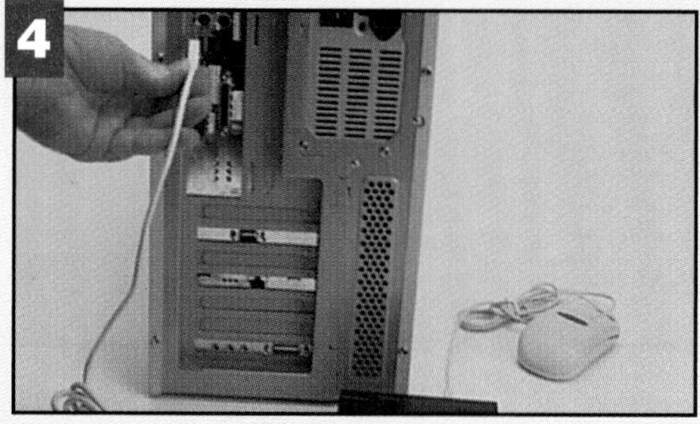

4 Connect the USB cable to the USB port at the back of the computer.

ADD A USB PORT

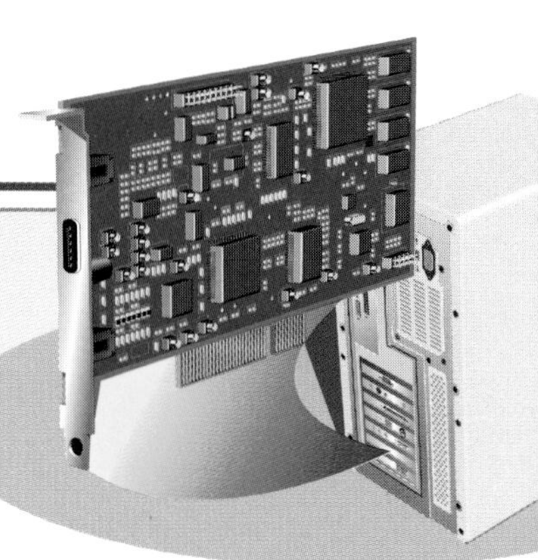

If your computer does not have a USB port, you can add a USB port by installing a USB expansion card. To install an expansion card, perform steps 4 to 6 on page 54.

CHOOSE A USB HUB

USB Devices

You can only connect devices that have a USB connector to a USB hub. Many devices are available with USB connectors, including tape drives, printers, modems and scanners.

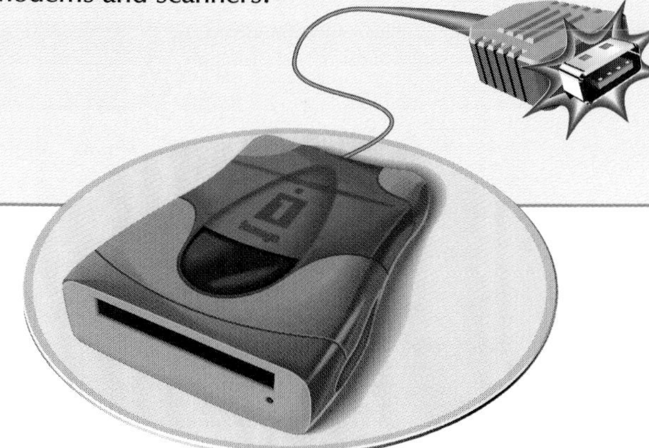

Device Support

You can only plug up to four devices into most USB hubs. A computer with a USB port can support up to 127 devices. To connect more devices to the computer, you can attach, or daisy chain, several hubs together. You can also purchase a USB device, such as a monitor, that has a built-in hub.

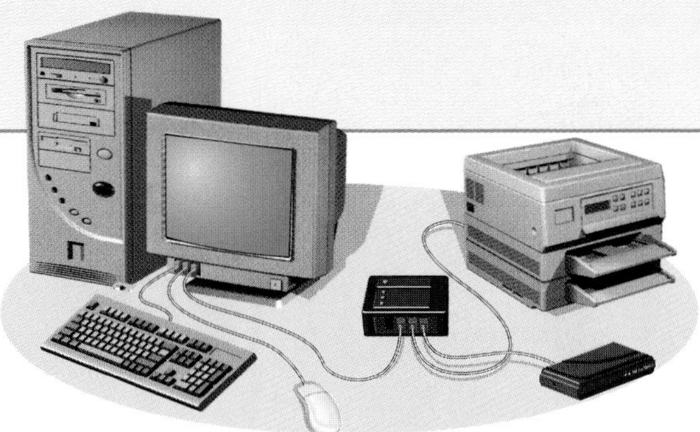

SET UP

Settings

When you connect a device, the USB hub usually detects the device and automatically adjusts the computer's settings to work with the device. You may not have to restart the computer.

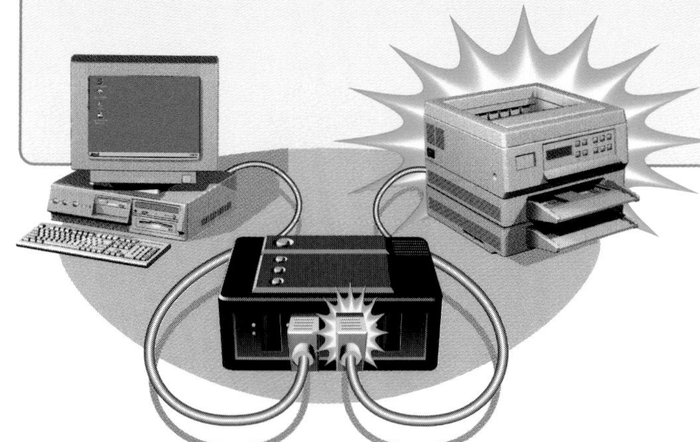

Cable Length

You can buy cable in many lengths, but your USB devices may not work properly if they are more than 15 feet from the USB port. You can extend the length of a connection by attaching several USB hubs together. This is useful if you need to connect a device far from your computer, such as a security camera.

FIREWIRE DEVICES

FireWire devices use the FireWire technology, which is a relatively new technology developed by Apple. FireWire is also referred to as IEEE 1394 or i.LINK.

A computer may support up to 63 FireWire devices.

CONNECT A FIREWIRE DEVICE

Before connecting a FireWire device, turn on the device and the computer.

1

Connect the device cable to the port on the FireWire device.

2

Connect the device cable to the FireWire port at the back of the computer.

ADD A FIREWIRE PORT

If your computer does not have a FireWire port, you can add a FireWire port by installing a FireWire expansion card. To install an expansion card, perform steps 4 to 6 on page 54.

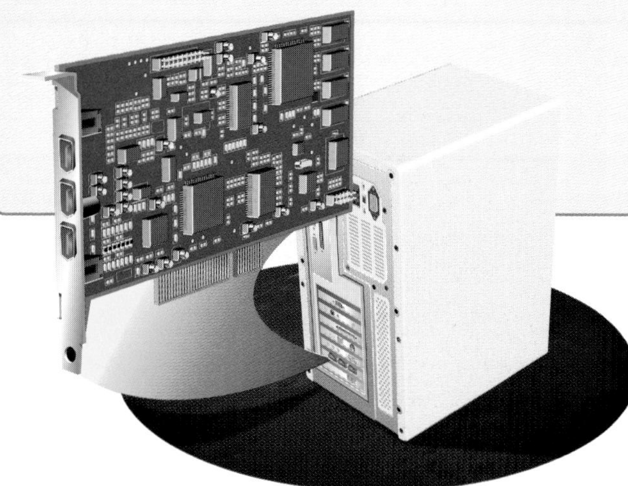

SPEED

The most exciting feature of FireWire technology is the speed at which FireWire devices can exchange information. FireWire devices can transfer data at speeds of up to 400 Mbps. This makes FireWire suitable for transferring large amounts of data, such as full-motion video.

SET UP

FireWire devices are easy to set up and configure. Unlike devices that use other technologies, such as SCSI, FireWire devices do not need any settings to be adjusted or switches to be set. You may have to install a driver for your FireWire device. A driver is the software that allows the operating system to communicate with and control the FireWire device. As FireWire devices become more common, more operating systems will automatically detect and install drivers for FireWire devices.

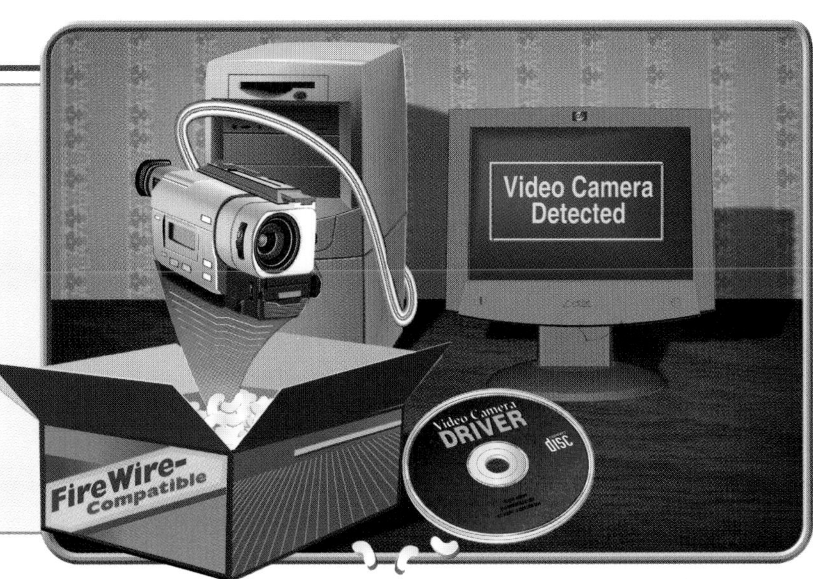

FIREWIRE CONSIDERATIONS

FireWire and USB

FireWire ports and devices are very similar to USB (Universal Serial Bus) ports and devices, but they are incompatible with each other. Currently, USB devices transfer information at a much slower speed than FireWire. USB is used for slower devices, such as mice and keyboards, while FireWire is more suitable for use with faster devices, such as external hard drives and full-motion video cameras.

Ports and Cables

FireWire ports are small rectangular ports with four contacts. FireWire cables are relatively thin compared to other cables and can be up to 14 feet long. Some devices may draw power from the computer through the FireWire cable, eliminating the need for a power cable.

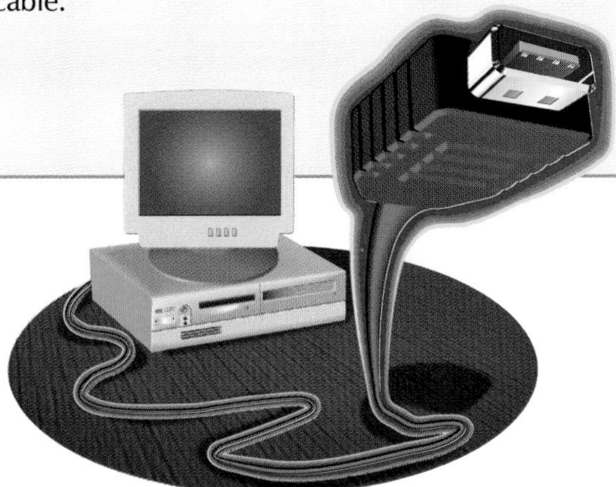

UPS

An Uninterruptible Power Supply (UPS) is a device that can provide temporary power in the event of a power failure.

Many UPSs include power conditioning features that prevent power fluctuations, such as spikes and surges, from reaching your computer.

CONNECT A UPS

Before connecting a UPS, turn off the computer and monitor.

1

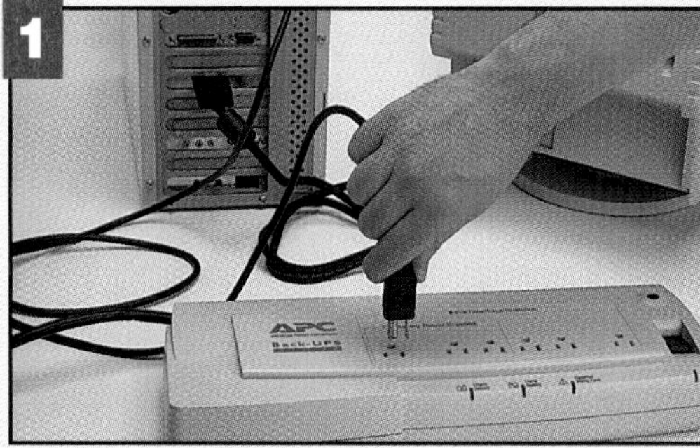

Unplug the computer's power cable from the electrical outlet and plug it into the outlet on the UPS.

2

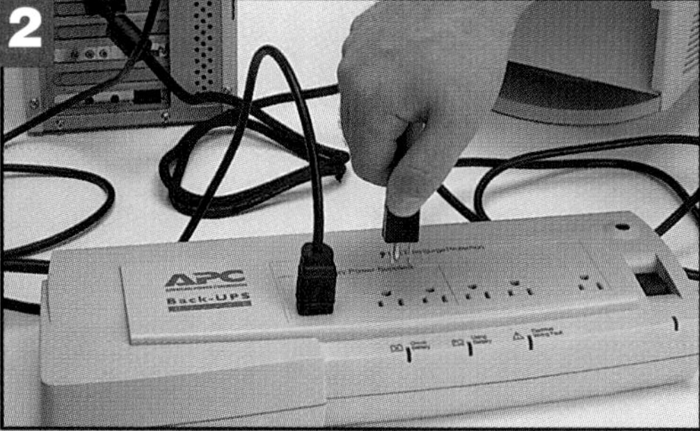

Unplug the monitor's power cable from the electrical outlet and plug it into the outlet on the UPS.

3

Plug the power cable from the UPS into an electrical outlet.

4

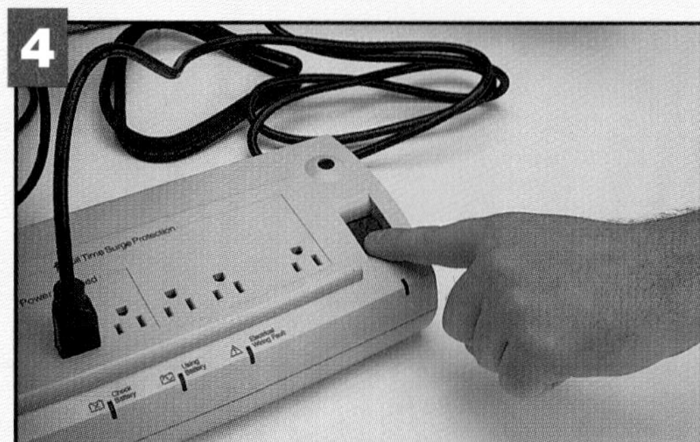

Turn on the UPS.

BATTERY

A battery inside a UPS stores electrical power. The battery in most UPSs requires 24 hours to charge completely. You do not have to wait for the battery to finish charging to use the computer, but the UPS will not work properly until the battery is completely charged. You should check your UPS's documentation for information about charging the battery.

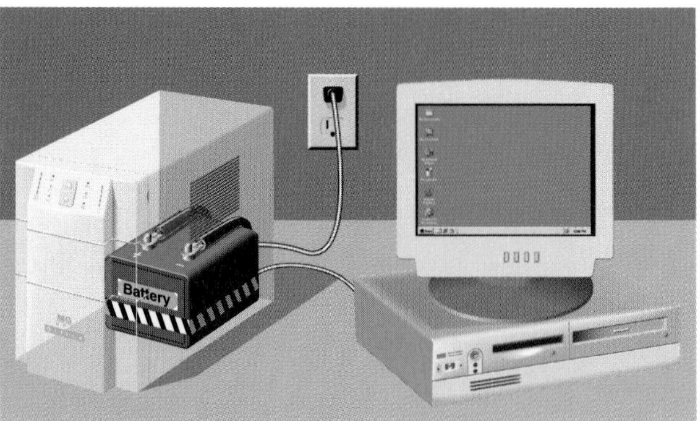

TYPES OF UPSs

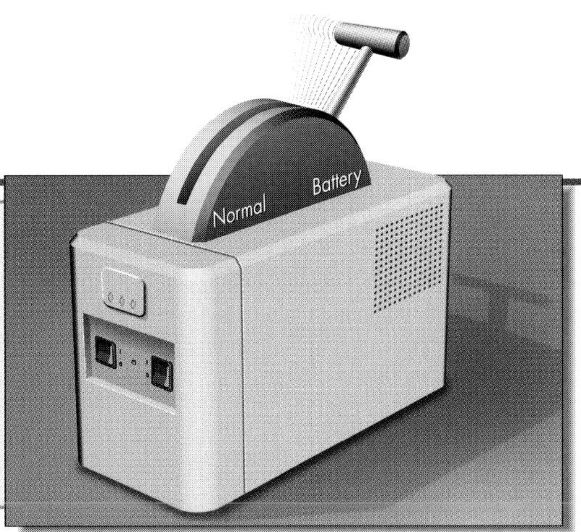

Standby

A standby UPS, also called an offline UPS, switches to battery power when it detects a power failure. There is usually a brief delay before the battery begins supplying power. Some standby UPSs also offer power conditioning features. This type of UPS is typically the least expensive.

Line-Interactive

A line-interactive UPS contains a transformer that continuously conditions the incoming power. This type of UPS switches to battery power only when the power level falls very low, such as when a power failure occurs.

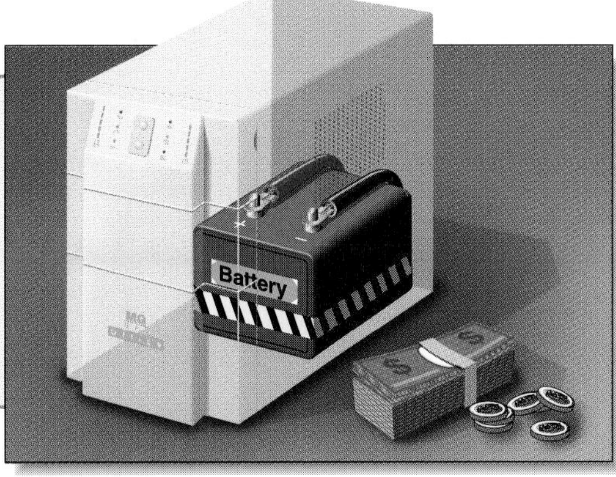

Online

An online UPS constantly uses the battery to condition the incoming power and therefore does not have to switch in the event of a power failure. This type of UPS provides the most protection from power fluctuations and is generally the most expensive.

GENERATORS

Most UPSs are not designed to keep your computer running for an extended period of time and provide power for only 5 to 20 minutes. If you want to be able to use your computer for long periods of time when there is a power failure, you should consider purchasing a generator.

CHOOSE A UPS

VA Rating

The VA rating determines how much power a UPS can deliver. The higher the VA rating, the more devices the UPS can support and the longer the battery can provide temporary power. A UPS with a 250 to 400 VA rating is sufficient for most home computers.

Telephone Socket

Many UPSs have a telephone socket where you can plug in the telephone cable from a modem. This protects the modem and computer from power surges transmitted over telephone lines.

Automatic Shutdown

Some UPSs include software that can automatically close programs and shut down a computer in the event of a power failure. This is useful if you are not at the computer when the power fails.

Large Devices

Most UPSs are not designed to support devices that require a lot of power to operate, such as a photocopier or laser printer. You should only plug these devices into a UPS specially designed for large devices.

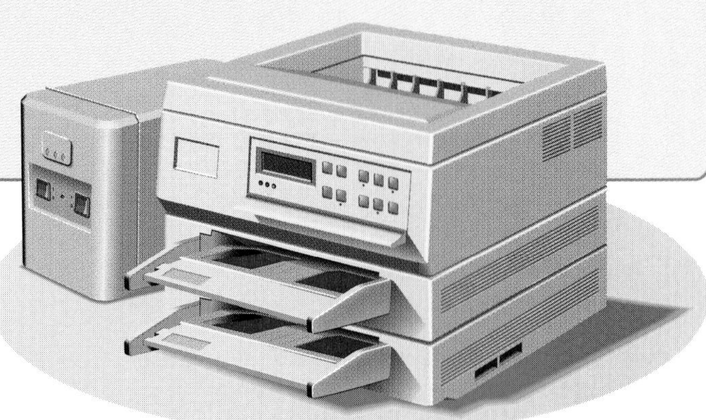

TEST AND TROUBLESHOOT

Should I test my UPS?

You should regularly test your UPS to make sure it is working properly. Many UPSs have a test button you can use to test the status of the UPS. You can also unplug your UPS from the electrical outlet on the wall to ensure the UPS is capable of providing temporary power if a power failure occurs.

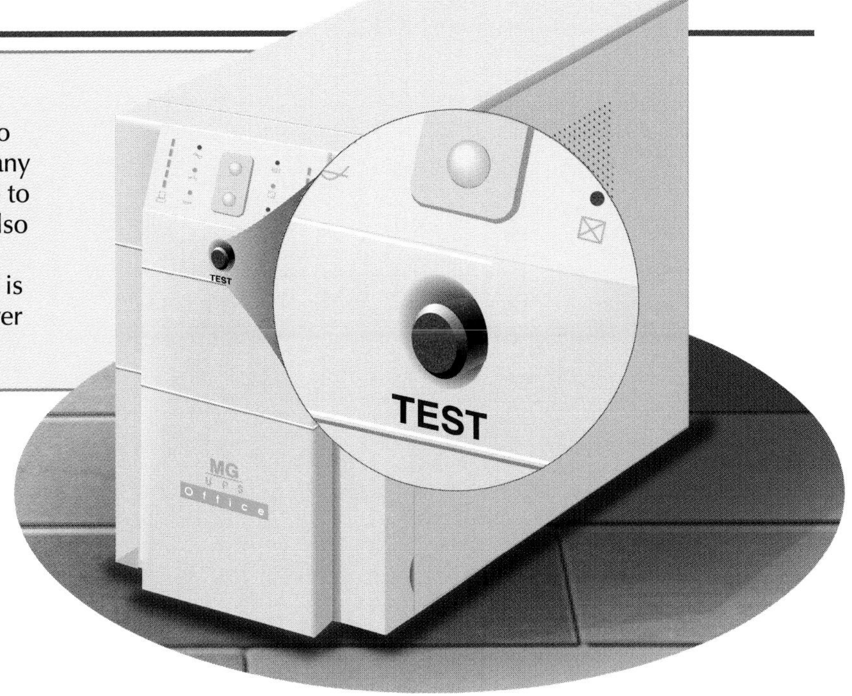

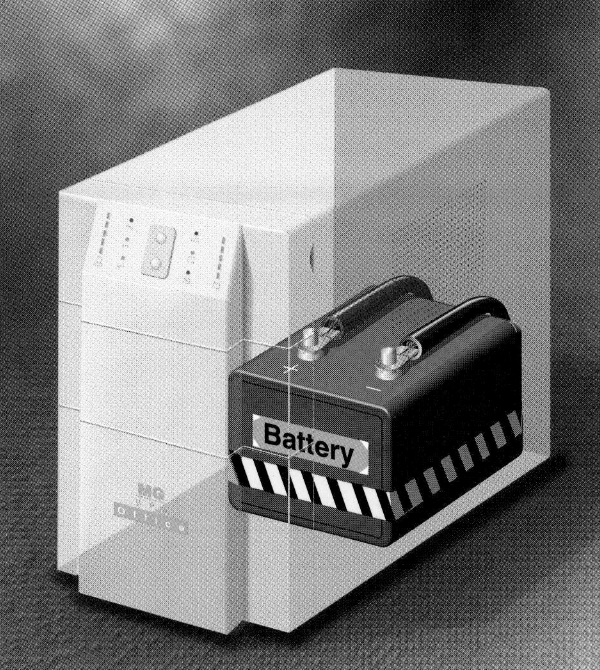

How can I tell if the battery needs to be replaced in my UPS?

UPSs tend to be very reliable and usually work for many years before you need to replace the battery. Problems associated with a faulty battery can include computer lockups, device failures and unexpected computer shutdowns.

Before replacing a battery, you should make sure the battery is the cause of the problems you are experiencing. Disconnect the computer from any devices, such as a printer, which are plugged into an electrical outlet on the wall. If the problems stop, the cause may have been power from an electrical outlet not protected by the UPS. If the problems persist, the battery is likely the cause.

Cable Modem

CHAPTER 4

COMMUNICATION DEVICES

Are you curious about the communication devices that allow you to send and receive information? This chapter explains how network interface cards and modems help your computer transmit information.

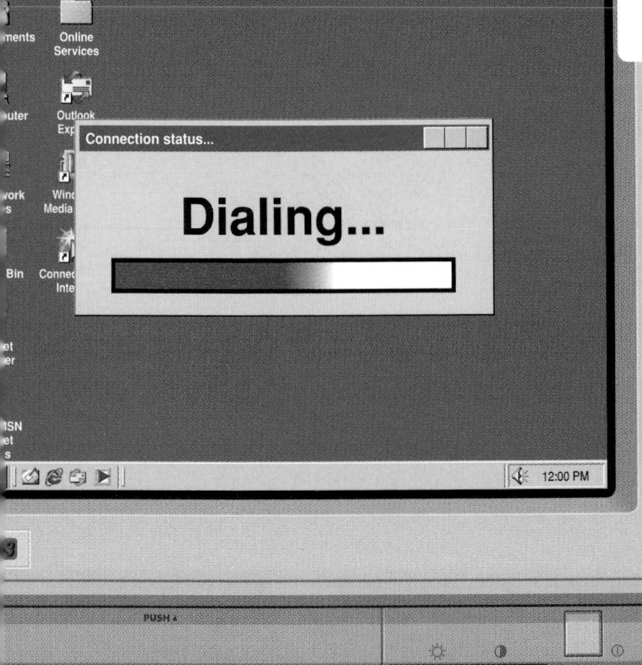

A Network Interface Card (NIC) physically connects a computer to a network and controls the flow of information between the computer and the network.

INSTALL A NETWORK INTERFACE CARD

Before installing a network interface card, turn off the computer, unplug the power cable and remove the cover from the computer case. Then ground yourself and the computer case. For information about grounding, see page 6.

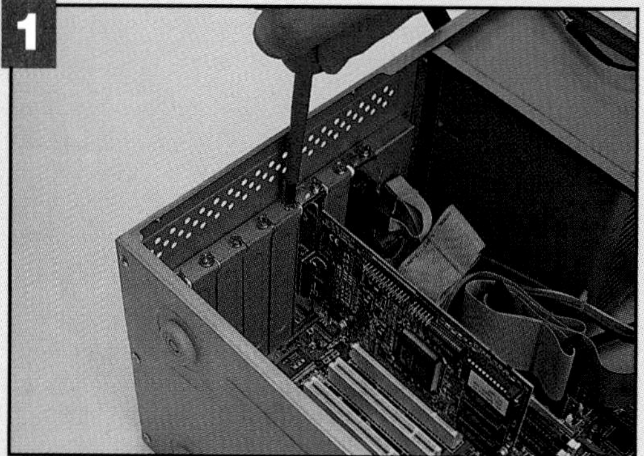

Remove the cover for the expansion slot where you want to install the card. The cover is usually held in place by a small screw.

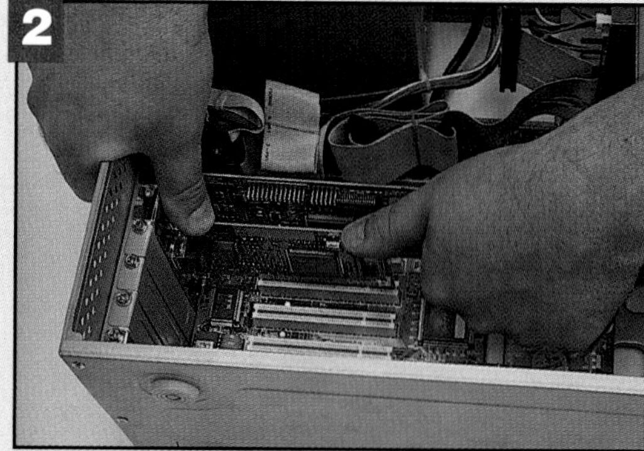

Place the network interface card in the expansion slot. Press down firmly and evenly across the top of the card until it is securely inserted.

Secure the network interface card to the computer case using a small screw. Then replace the cover on the computer case.

Plug the network cable into the network interface card at the back of the computer.

SET UP

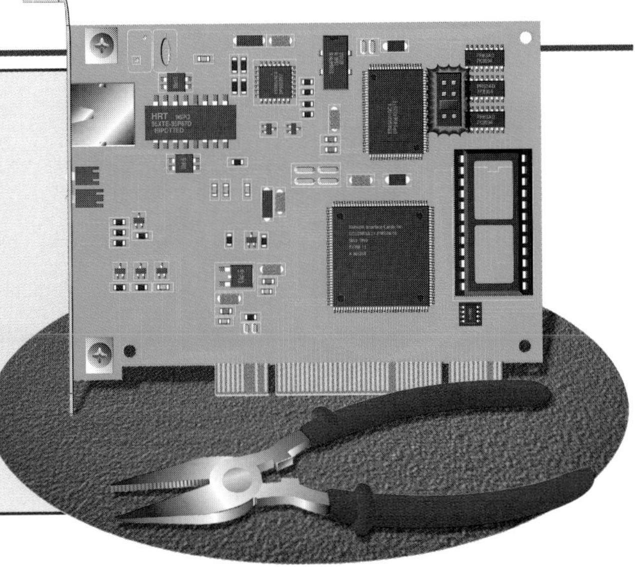

Change Settings

If your network interface card requires the same computer resources as another device, such as Interrupt Request (IRQ) settings, you may need to change the settings for the card. You may also need to change the settings for the card to specify which type of cable you are using.

Some network interface cards require you to use jumpers to adjust these settings, but most new cards include an installation program you can use. Consult the card's documentation for information about how to change the settings.

Install Driver

Network interface cards come with drivers for different types of operating systems. A driver is the software that allows the computer's operating system to communicate with and control the network interface card. To ensure the card performs at its best, you must install the correct driver.

Test Setup

Many network interface cards include testing software you can use to verify that the card is set up correctly and the computer can communicate with the card. Some testing software also lets you test the communication between your computer and other computers on the network.

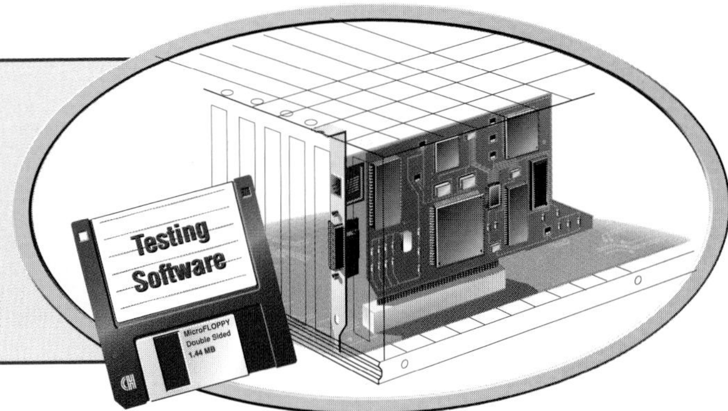

CHOOSE A NETWORK INTERFACE CARD

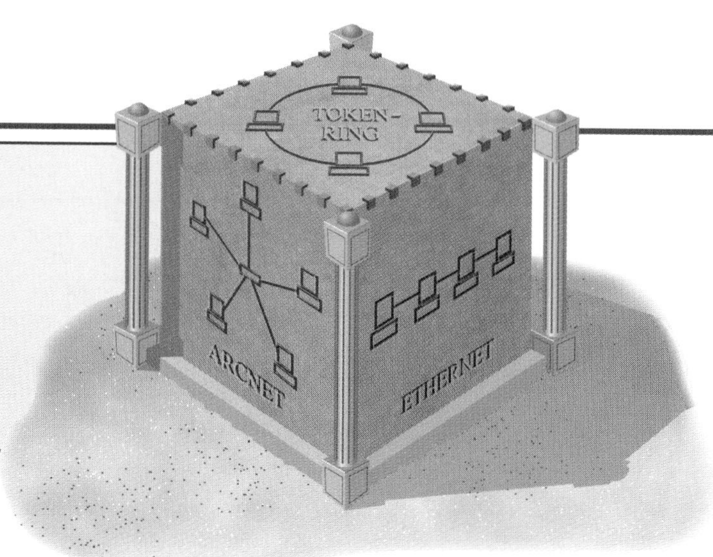

Network Type

Ethernet is the most popular type of network used when building new networks. Other types of networks include Token-Ring and ARCnet. A network interface card designed for one type of network cannot be used on another type of network.

Speed

The speed of a network is measured in megabits per second (Mbps) and indicates how fast information can transfer. Some Ethernet networks can transfer information at up to 1000 Mbps. Most commonly-used Ethernet network interface cards can transfer information at both 10 Mbps and 100 Mbps.

Cable

The two most popular types of network cable are coaxial and twisted pair. Coaxial cable, which is similar to television cable, is inexpensive and easy to work with. Twisted pair cable is similar to telephone cable and is less expensive than coaxial cable. If you are setting up a new network, you should consider using twisted pair cable.

The network interface card you choose must be compatible with the type of cable you want to use. Some network interface cards have two ports, allowing you to use either type of cable.

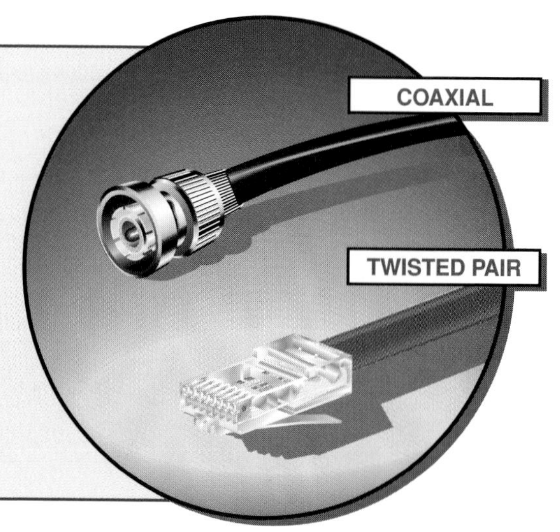

TROUBLESHOOT

How can I determine if my network interface card is communicating with the network?

Most network interface cards and other network devices include indicator lights to show the status of the connection. You should check the documentation that came with your network interface card for information about the indicator lights.

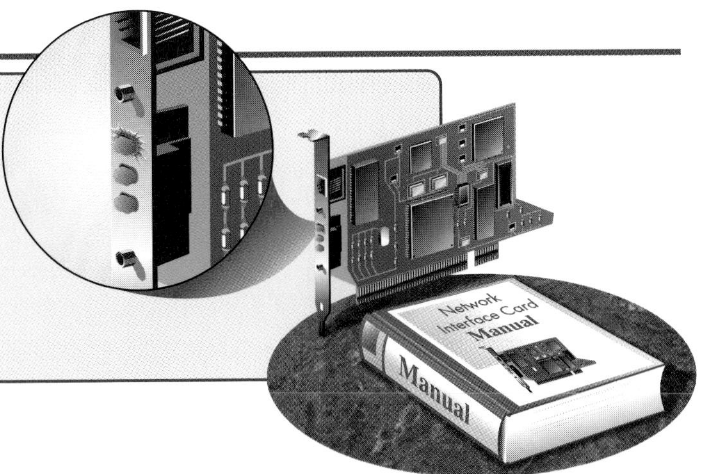

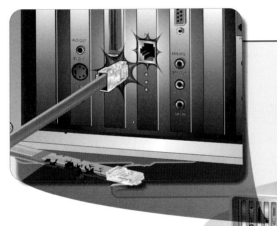

Why am I having problems accessing the network?

If you are experiencing problems transferring information on the network or you cannot access the network, the cable is usually the cause. To verify that a cable is the cause of a problem, replace the current cable with a cable you know works properly.

I think my network interface card is malfunctioning. How can I confirm this?

A malfunctioning network interface card can cause computer problems, such as corrupted data, and prevent you from accessing the network. You can easily confirm if a card is malfunctioning by replacing the current card with a card you know works properly.

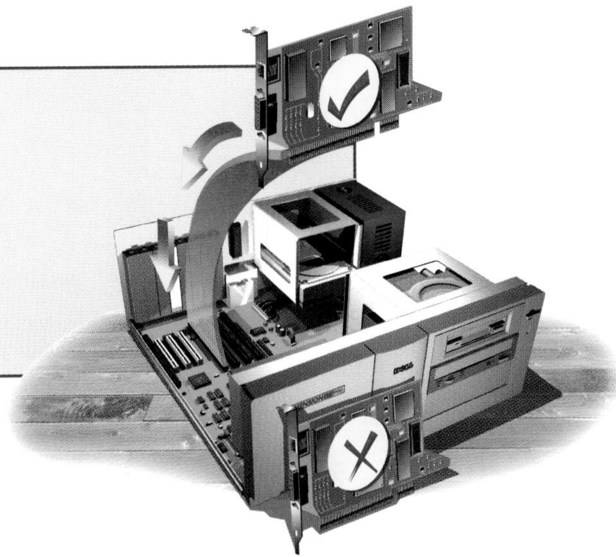

MODEM

A modem is a device that lets computers exchange information through telephone lines.

INSTALL A MODEM

Before installing a modem, turn off the computer.

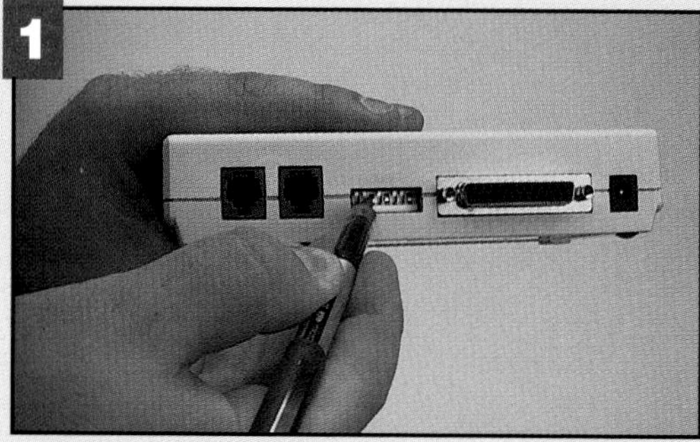

1 If necessary, use the switches on the back or bottom of the modem to adjust the settings for the modem. Consult the modem's documentation to determine if you need to adjust the settings.

2 If desired, connect the cable from your telephone to the back of the modem. This lets your telephone share the telephone line with your computer.

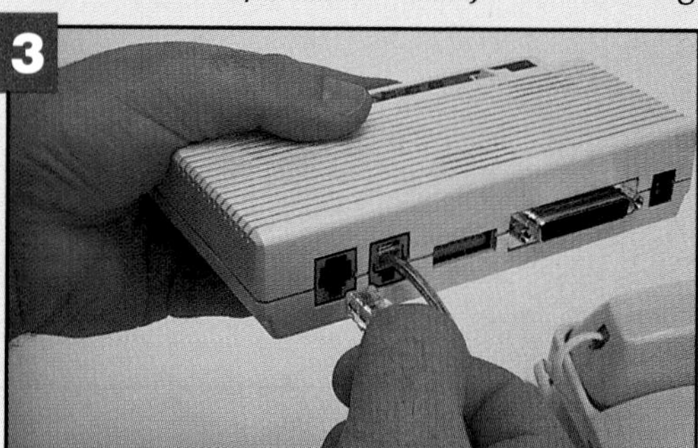

3 Connect the telephone line to the back of the modem. Then connect the telephone line to the telephone jack on the wall.

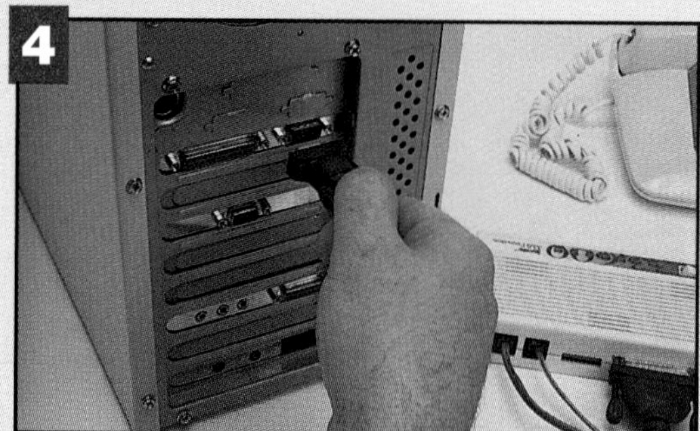

4 Connect the serial cable to the back of the modem. Then connect the serial cable to a serial port at the back of the computer.

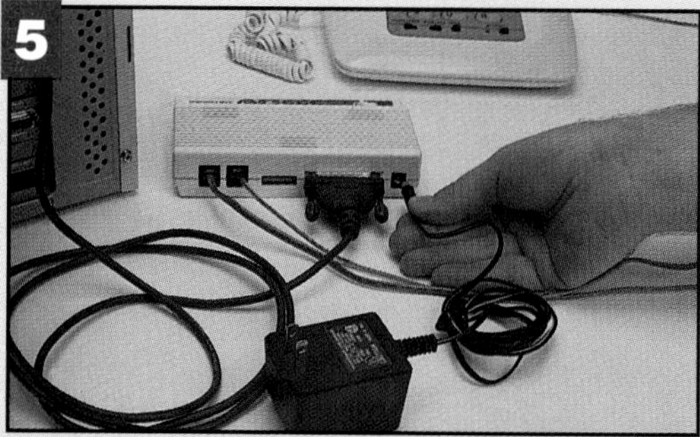

5 Connect the power cable to the back of the modem. Then plug the power cable into an electrical outlet.

INSTALL AN INTERNAL MODEM

An internal modem is an expansion card that plugs into an expansion slot inside a computer. To install an expansion card, perform steps 4 to 6 on page 54.

When you install an internal modem, your computer thinks another serial port has been added. If you want the modem to use one of the existing serial ports, you must adjust the jumpers on the modem. To avoid conflicts, you must then change the computer's settings to disable the existing serial port. For information about computer settings, see page 146.

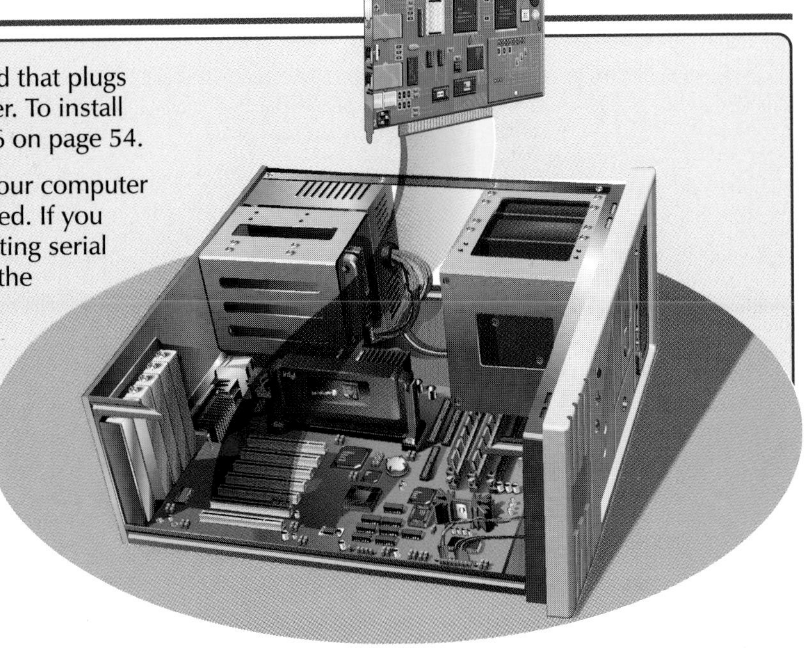

SET UP

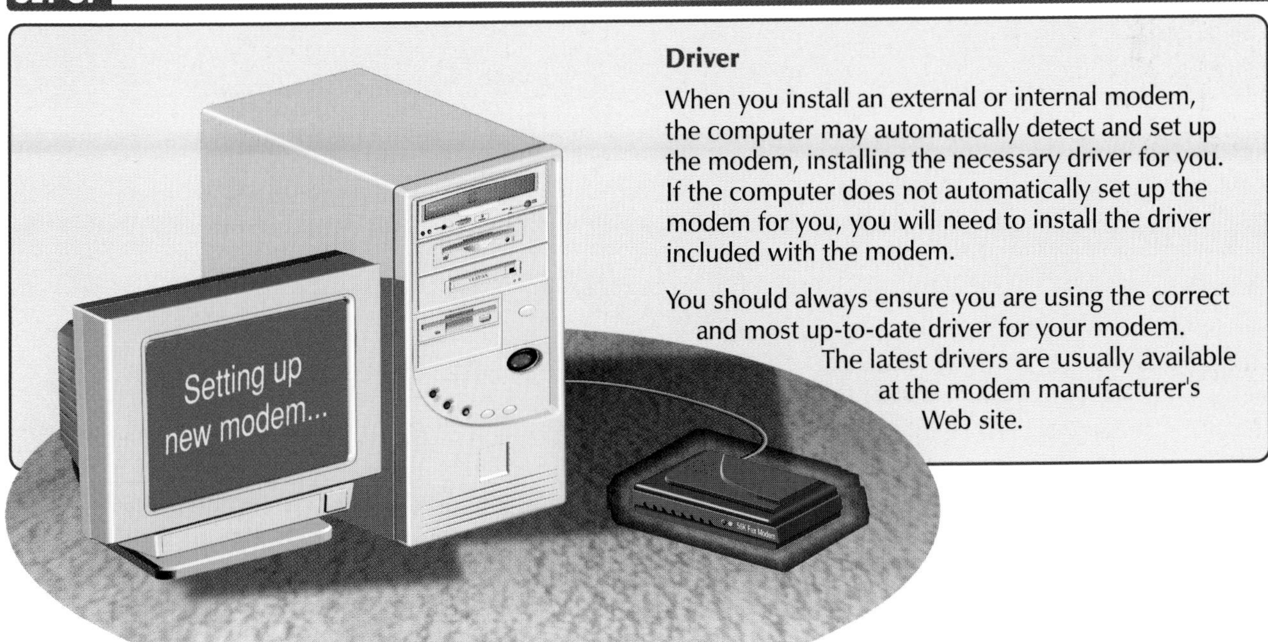

Driver

When you install an external or internal modem, the computer may automatically detect and set up the modem, installing the necessary driver for you. If the computer does not automatically set up the modem for you, you will need to install the driver included with the modem.

You should always ensure you are using the correct and most up-to-date driver for your modem. The latest drivers are usually available at the modem manufacturer's Web site.

CHOOSE A MODEM

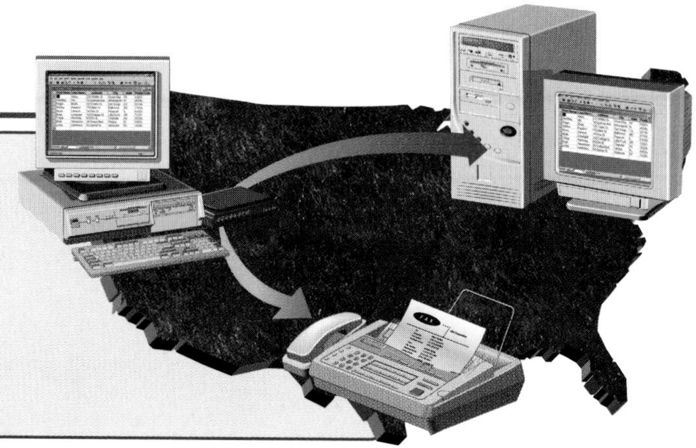

Fax and Voice Capabilities

Most modems can send and receive faxes. You can create a document on your computer and then fax the document to another computer or fax machine. Some modems also have voice capabilities that allow you to use the modem to send and receive voice telephone calls. This lets you use the modem as a hands-free telephone.

Speed

The speed of a modem is measured in kilobits per second (Kbps) and indicates the amount of information the modem can send and receive. Most modems can send information at 33.6 Kbps and receive information at 56 Kbps.

Communications Program

A communications program usually comes packaged with a modem. A communications program is software that manages the transmission of information between two modems. You should consider the features that the communications program offers.

UPGRADE

You may be able to upgrade your current modem to add capabilities, such as a faster speed, that were not available when the modem was produced. An upgrade may be a program you install on the computer or a chip you add to the modem.

TEST AND TROUBLESHOOT

Can I test the modem to make sure it is communicating properly with my computer?

Once a modem is installed and set up, you can use a program such as Phone Dialer, which is included with Windows, to test the modem. Try to make a telephone call using Phone Dialer. If the modem and computer are communicating properly, the modem will make a dialing noise.

Why is my modem having problems establishing a connection?

Features on your telephone line, such as voice-mail or call-waiting, may cause connection problems. The voice-mail feature changes the tone of the telephone line to indicate a message is waiting. This change in tone may prevent the modem from establishing a connection.

The call-waiting feature generates a beep to indicate an incoming call, which may cause some modems to lose the connection. You should disable the call-waiting feature before using a modem.

Why is my modem operating slowly?

If the speed at which your modem transfers information seems slow, the problem may be with the quality of the telephone line. If you frequently get slow transfer speeds, you should contact your local telephone company.

CABLE MODEM

A cable modem is a device that lets computers access the Internet using television cable.

Most cable companies will install and set up a cable modem for you.

CONNECT A CABLE MODEM

To connect a cable modem, you must first install a network interface card. To install a network interface card, see page 108. Before connecting the cable modem, turn off the computer.

1 Connect the television cable to the back of the cable modem.

2 Connect the network cable to the back of the cable modem.

3 Connect the network cable to the network interface card at the back of the computer.

4 Attach the power cable to the back of the cable modem. Then plug the cable into an electrical outlet.

SET UP

Before you can use a cable modem, you must adjust your computer's settings so the computer can work on a network. Most operating systems include software you can use to adjust your computer's settings to work on a network. The cable modem will include any additional software you need.

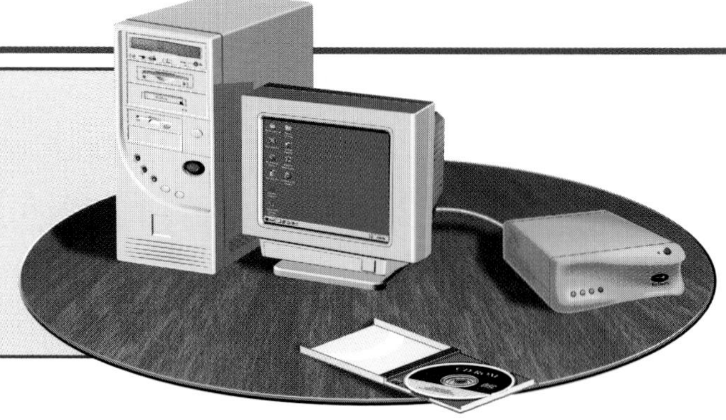

BENEFITS

Speed

Since cable modems transfer information through television cable, which is much faster than telephone lines, cable modems can transfer information at speeds of up to 4,000 Kbps.

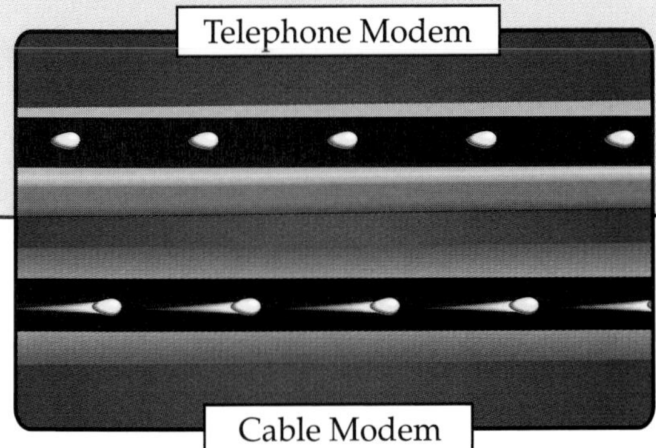

Convenience

A cable modem supplies a permanent connection to the Internet so you do not have to dial into an Internet service provider each time you want to access the Internet. A cable modem also does not tie up your phone line the way a telephone modem does when you are accessing the Internet.

OTHER TYPES OF HIGH-SPEED CONNECTIONS

DSL

Digital Subscriber Line (DSL) is a high-speed digital phone line service offered by telephone companies in most cities. DSL can transfer information at speeds from 1,000 Kbps to 9,000 Kbps.

Satellite

A satellite dish can transmit information to your computer at speeds of up to 400 Kbps. You need a telephone connection to transmit information to the Internet.

Wireless Cable Modem

A wireless cable modem connects to a wireless cable antenna and transfers information between the Internet and your computer at speeds of up to 10,000 Kbps.

zip
disc
DVD
CD
DVD
BUSY
CDR 2000
PHONES
WRITING
DISC IN
OPEN
CLOSE
Travan
Travan-3 minicartridges

CHAPTER 5

STORAGE DEVICES

Do you want to find out how to upgrade or repair the storage devices your computer uses to read and record information on storage media? This chapter discusses hard and floppy drives, removable storage devices and more.

HARD DRIVE

A hard drive is the primary device that a computer uses to store data.

A hard drive with a capacity of 10 to 20 GB (gigabytes) will suit most home and business users.

REPLACE A HARD DRIVE

Before replacing a hard drive, turn off the computer, unplug the power cable and remove the cover from the computer case. Then ground yourself and the computer case. For information about grounding, see page 6.

Remove the screws that secure the hard drive in the drive bay.

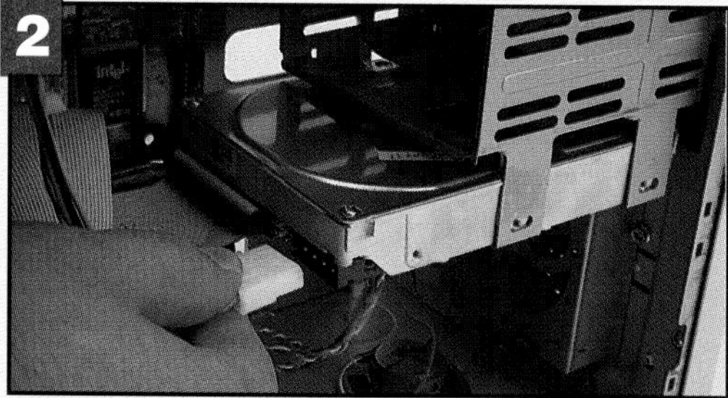

Disconnect the power supply cable from the back of the hard drive.

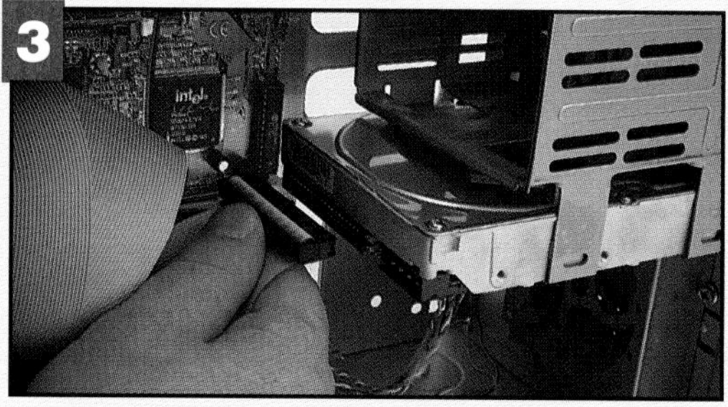

Disconnect the ribbon cable from the back of the hard drive. Then slide the drive out of the drive bay.

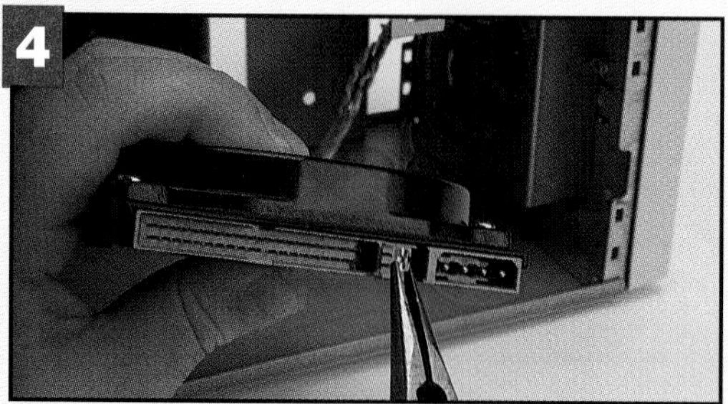

If necessary, adjust the jumpers on the new hard drive. Then slide the drive into the drive bay.

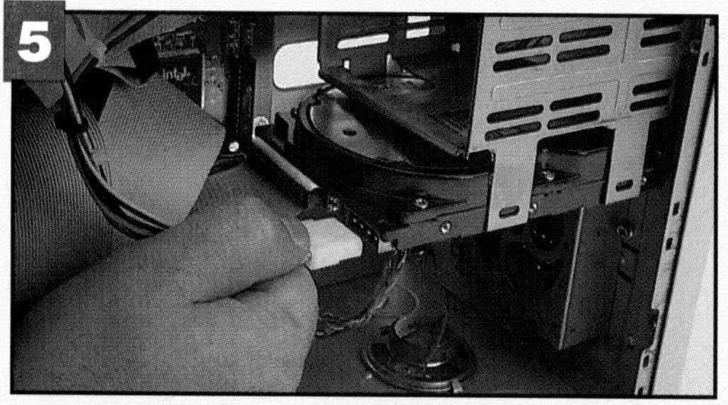

Connect the power supply cable and the ribbon cable to the back of the hard drive.

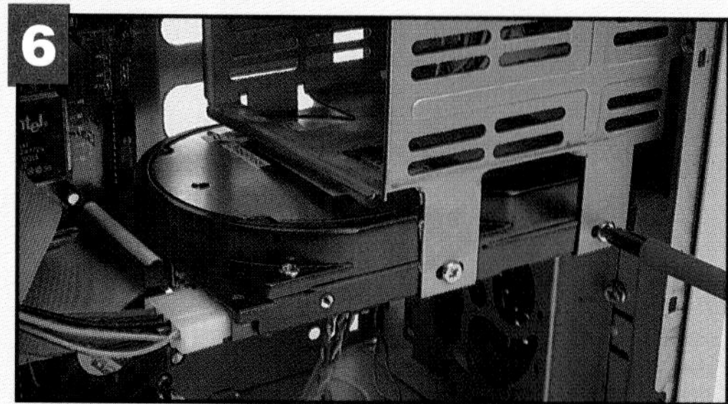

Using small screws, secure the hard drive in the drive bay. Then replace the cover on the computer case.

SET UP

Jumpers

If you use an Enhanced Integrated Drive Electronics (EIDE) ribbon cable to connect the hard drive and another device to the computer, you may have to change the jumpers on the devices. One device must be set as the master, while the other is set as the slave.

You may also need to adjust the jumpers on the hard drive if you are using a Small Computer System Interface (SCSI) ribbon cable to connect multiple devices. Each device must be assigned a unique number from zero to seven. Consult the drive's documentation for information on adjusting the jumpers.

Computer Settings

Your computer may automatically detect and set up a hard drive you install. If your computer does not set up the hard drive, you may need to change the computer's settings manually. For information about computer settings, see page 146.

INSIDE A HARD DRIVE

A hard drive magnetically stores data on a stack of disks, called platters. The disks spin at a high speed inside the drive. The drive has several read/write heads that move across the spinning disks to read and record data.

FORMAT A HARD DRIVE

Low-Level Format

A hard drive must be formatted before you can use the drive to store data. The low-level format is the first step in formatting a hard drive and is performed by the manufacturer. During a low-level format, the surface of each disk in the hard drive is divided into circles, called tracks. The tracks are then divided into sections, called sectors. The hard drive will store data on the tracks and sectors.

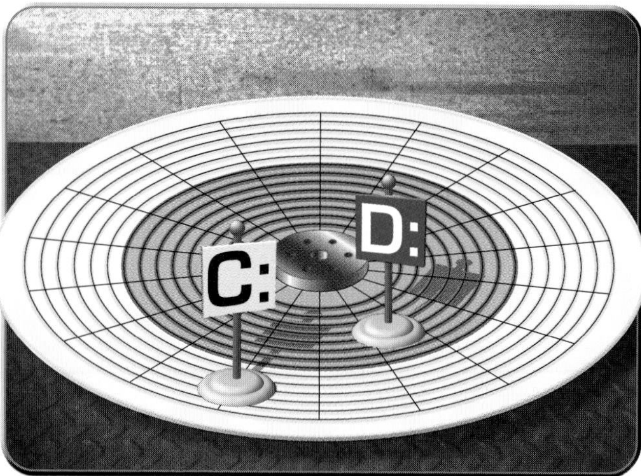

Partitioning

The second step in formatting a hard drive involves creating partitions. During partitioning, the operating system assigns a drive letter to all or part of a hard drive. You must create at least one partition before you can use a new hard drive. If you create multiple partitions, each partition acts as a separate hard drive and can have its own operating system.

High-Level Format

The last step in preparing a hard drive to store data is the high-level format. During a high-level format, the operating system prepares the hard drive to store and manage data. If the hard drive has multiple partitions, you will have to perform a high-level format on each partition.

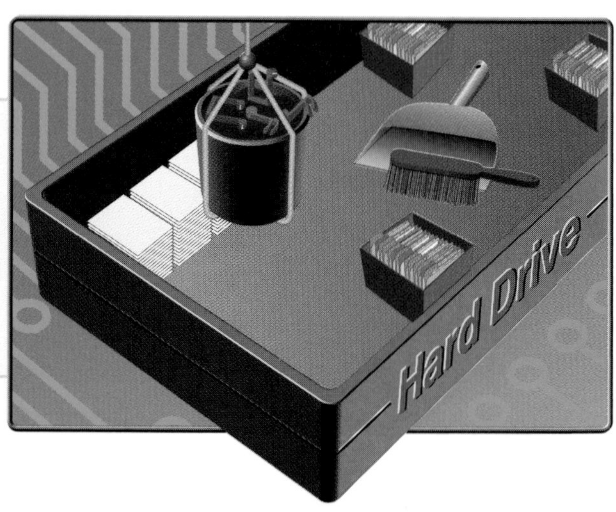

TROUBLESHOOT AND REPAIR

Can I improve the performance of my hard drive?

If your hard drive operates slowly, you may be able to improve performance by defragmenting the drive. A fragmented hard drive stores parts of a file in many different locations. To retrieve a file, the computer must access many areas of the drive. You can use a defragmentation program to place all parts of a file in one location. This reduces the time the hard drive spends locating the file. Most operating systems have a defragmentation program you can use.

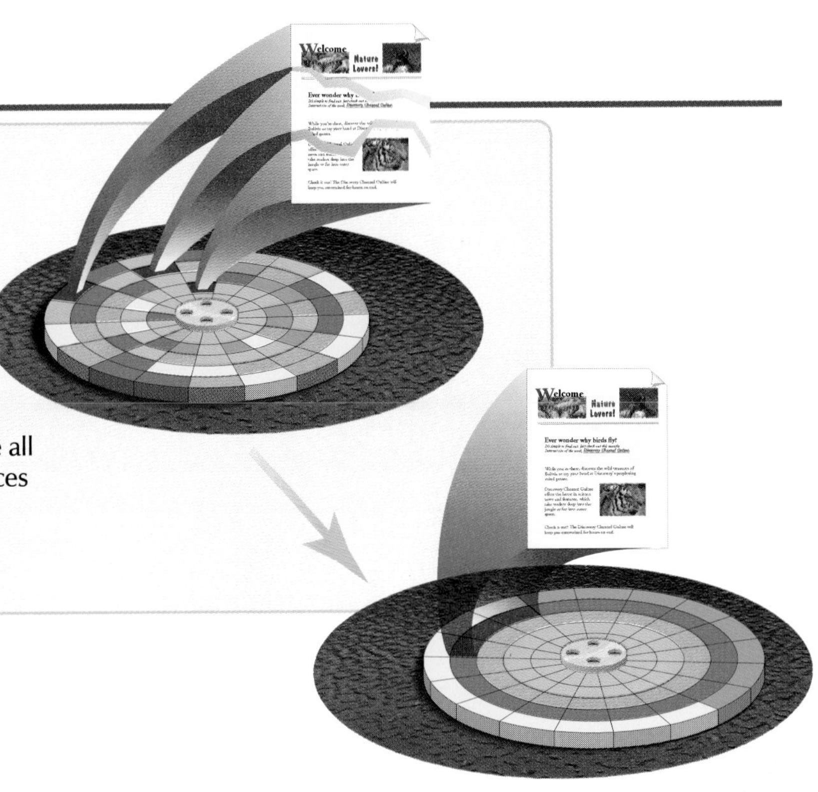

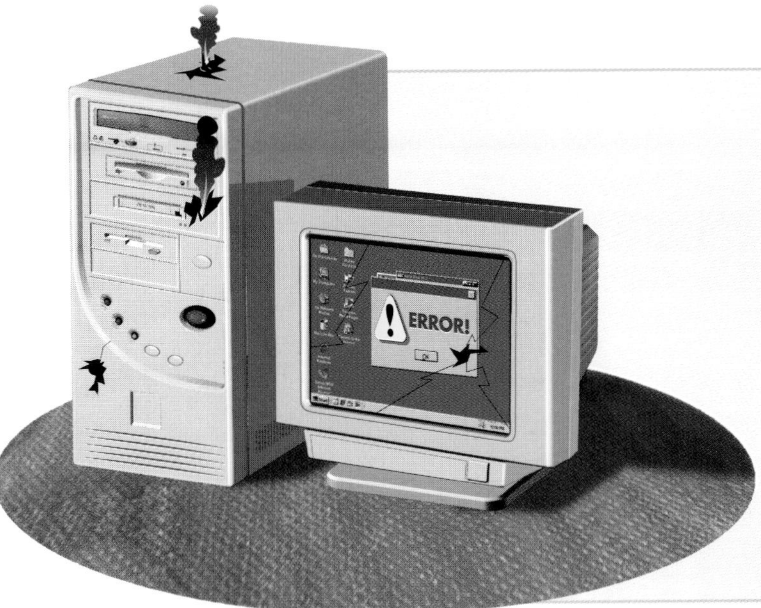

Can I correct errors on my hard drive?

As the disks in a hard drive deteriorate, errors become more frequent when you try to access or store data on the drive. While the occasional error is normal, repeated errors may be an indication that the hard drive is about to fail.

You may be able to correct these errors by performing a high-level format to erase all the data on the drive. If the high-level format does not correct the problem, you can perform a low-level format. Check the documentation that came with the hard drive for more information about performing a low-level format.

FLOPPY DRIVE

A floppy drive stores and retrieves data on floppy disks.

A floppy disk, also called a diskette, is a removable device that magnetically stores data.

REPLACE A FLOPPY DRIVE

Before replacing a floppy drive, turn off the computer, unplug the power cable and remove the cover from the computer case. Then ground yourself and the computer case. For information about grounding, see page 6.

1 Remove the screws that secure the floppy drive in the drive bay.

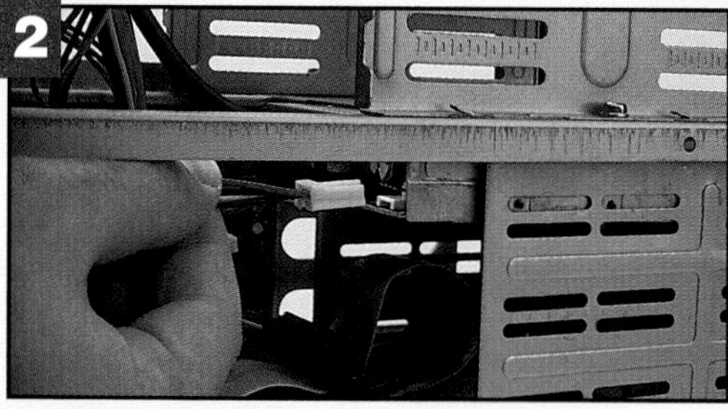

2 Disconnect the power supply cable from the back of the floppy drive.

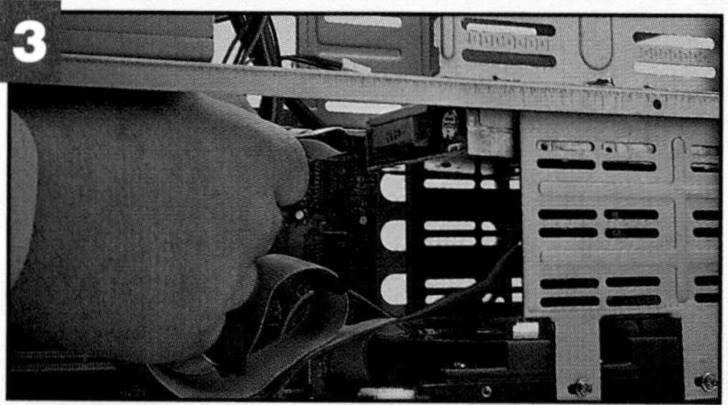

3 Disconnect the ribbon cable from the back of the floppy drive. Then slide the drive out of the drive bay.

4 If necessary, attach a mounting bracket to the new floppy drive. Then slide the drive into the drive bay.

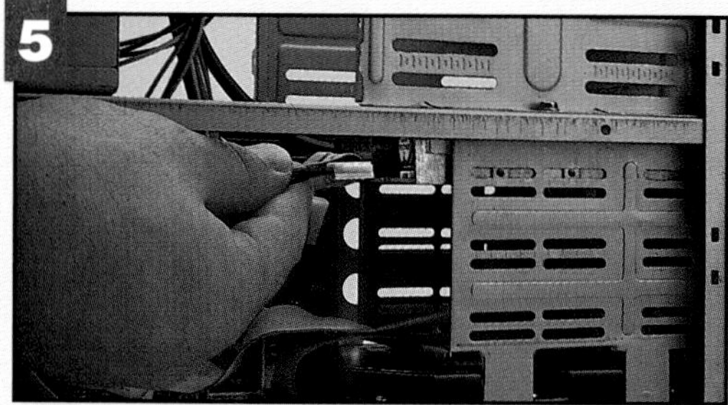

5 Connect the power supply cable and the ribbon cable to the back of the floppy drive.

6 Using small screws, secure the floppy drive in the drive bay. Then replace the cover on the computer case.

SET UP

Computer Settings

When you install a floppy drive, the computer may automatically detect and set up the drive for you. If the computer does not automatically detect and set up the floppy drive, you may need to change the computer's settings so it can work with the drive. For information about computer settings, see page 146.

Multiple Floppy Drives

Many floppy drive ribbon cables have two connectors separated by a twist in the cable. If you install a single floppy drive on your computer, the drive is called drive A and must be attached to the connector after the twist in the cable. If you install another floppy drive, the second drive is called drive B and must be attached to the connector before the twist in the cable.

INSIDE A FLOPPY DRIVE

Inside a floppy disk is a thin, plastic, flexible disk that magnetically stores data. The word floppy refers to this flexible disk. When you insert a floppy disk into a floppy drive, the flexible disk inside the floppy disk spins. The floppy drive has read/write heads that move across the flexible disk to read and record data on the disk.

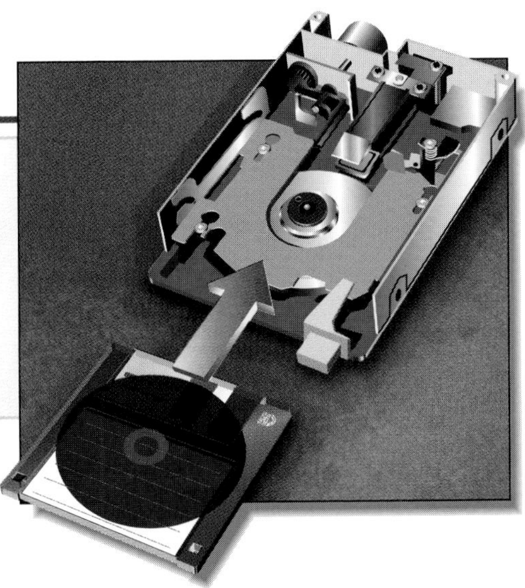

CHOOSE A FLOPPY DRIVE

You should choose a floppy drive that can use disks with at least the same storage capacity as the floppy disks used by the people you want to exchange data with.

Most floppy drives use 3.5-inch floppy disks that can store up to 1.44 MB of data. Some newer types of floppy drives use 3.5-inch floppy disks that can store up to 200 MB of data.

A floppy drive designed for disks with a storage capacity of 1.44 MB cannot use disks with a higher capacity. However, a floppy drive designed for higher capacity disks can also use disks with a capacity of 1.44 MB.

PROTECT FLOPPY DISKS

You can prevent data from being accidentally erased or replaced on a floppy disk by using the write-protect tab on the disk.

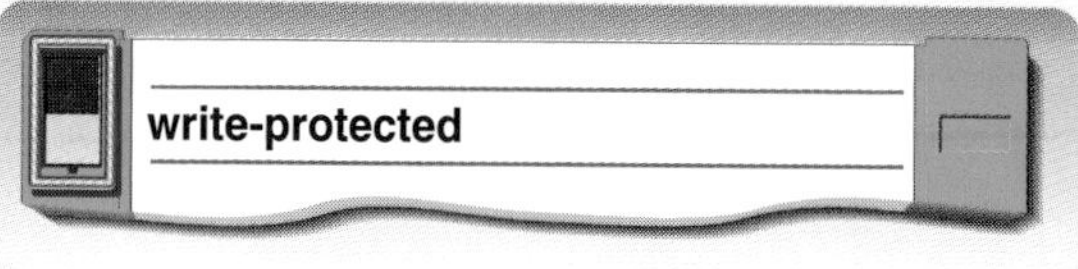

The data on a floppy disk can be damaged if the disk is exposed to magnetic fields such as the magnetic fields generated by your monitor and speakers. You should also make sure you do not store floppy disks in extremely hot or cold locations and do not spill liquids on the disks.

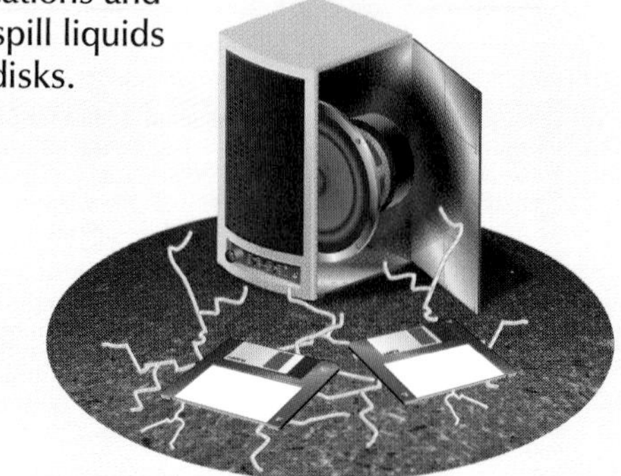

TROUBLESHOOT

The floppy drive light is on continuously. What is wrong?

The floppy drive light is normally on only when a floppy disk is being accessed. You should make sure the drive is properly connected to the computer. The red colored edge of the floppy drive cable should be aligned to pin 1 on the connectors on the system board and on the back of the floppy drive.

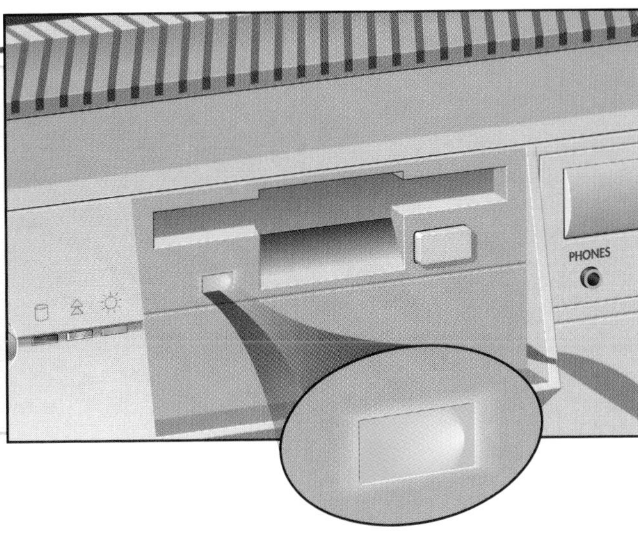

Why do I get an error message when my floppy drive tries to access a floppy disk?

The floppy disk may be defective. To determine if errors are due to a defective disk, try using another disk. If your floppy drive cannot access or store data on the second disk, you may need to clean the floppy drive. Cleaning kits are available at most computer stores.

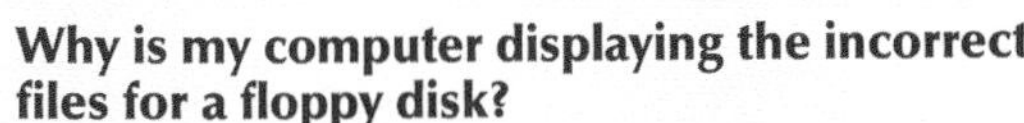

Why is my computer displaying the incorrect files for a floppy disk?

If your computer displays files that you know are not on the floppy disk, you may be using a defective cable. To verify that the cable is the cause of the problem, replace the current cable with a cable you know works properly.

REMOVABLE STORAGE DEVICE

A removable storage device allows you to store large amounts of data on removable disks. A removable disk is similar in size and shape to a floppy disk, but can store much more data.

INSTALL A REMOVABLE STORAGE DEVICE

Before installing a removable storage device, turn off the computer.

1

Connect the device cable to the port at the back of the removable storage device.

2

Connect the device cable to a parallel port at the back of the computer. Some removable storage devices connect to a SCSI, USB or FireWire port instead of a parallel port.

3

If you connected the device to a parallel port in step 2, you can connect the cable from your printer to the printer port on the back of the removable storage device.

4

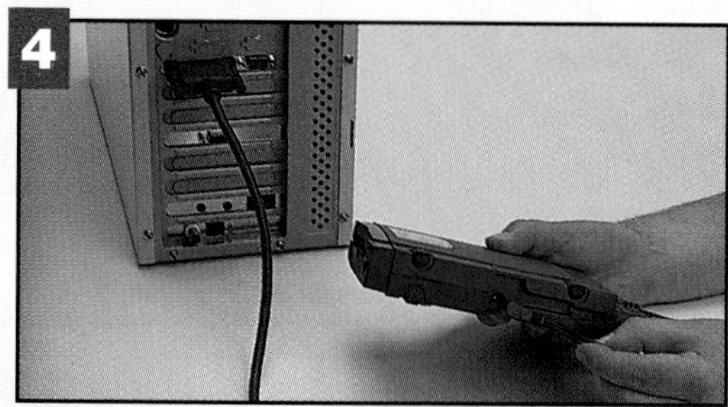

Connect the power cable to the power connector on the removable storage device. Then plug the power cable into an electrical outlet.

SET UP

When you install a removable storage device, the computer may detect and set up the device, installing the necessary driver for you. If the computer does not install the driver, you may need to install the driver yourself.

INSTALL AN INTERNAL REMOVABLE STORAGE DEVICE

You can install an internal removable storage device the same way you install a CD-ROM or DVD-ROM drive. For more information, see page 136.

You may have to adjust the jumpers on an internal removable storage device so the device can work with the computer. Some internal removable storage devices use an Enhanced Integrated Drive Electronics (EIDE) ribbon cable to connect to a computer, while others use a Small Computer System Interface (SCSI) ribbon cable. If there are devices already attached to the ribbon cable, you may need to adjust the jumpers on the internal removable storage device. Consult the device's documentation for information about adjusting the jumpers.

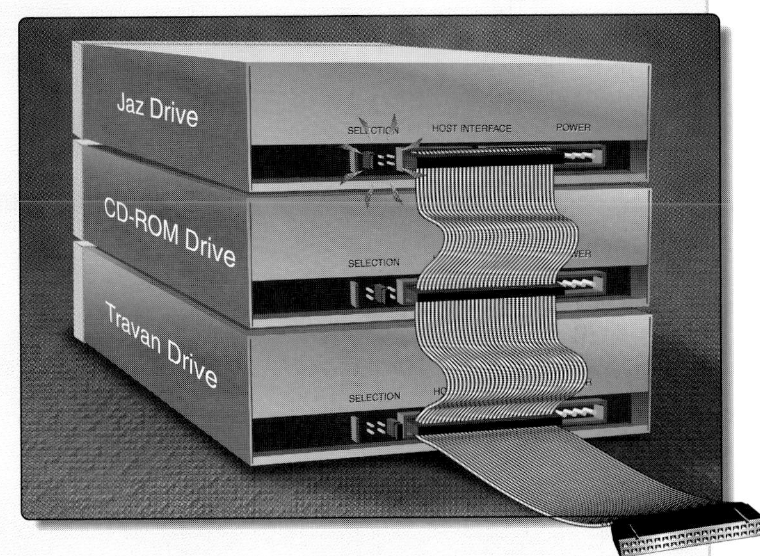

TYPE AND STORAGE CAPACITY

There are several types of removable storage devices available. Some types of devices are capable of storing a great deal more data than other types.

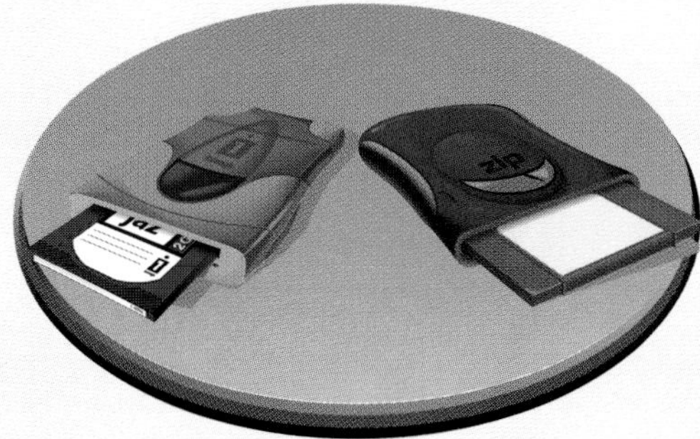

TYPE	STORAGE CAPACITY
LS-120 Drive	up to 120 MB
Zip Drive	up to 250 MB
Jaz Drive	up to 2 GB
Orb Drive	up to 2.2 GB

CHOOSE A REMOVABLE STORAGE DEVICE

Speed

Each removable storage device stores and accesses data at a specific speed. The type of device and how the device connects to the computer determine the speed.

Media Type

Some removable disks contain a thin, flexible disk, similar to the media used in floppy disks. Other removable disks contain hard platters, similar to the media used in hard drives. Disks containing hard platters are usually faster and store more data than disks containing flexible media.

Cost

Before purchasing a removable storage device, you should consider how much data you need to store and the cost per megabyte of storing the data. Inexpensive devices often use disks that cost more per megabyte than more expensive devices.

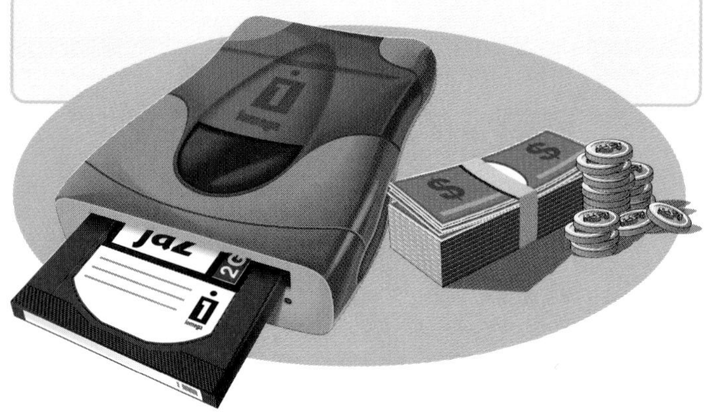

Software

Removable storage devices usually include a variety of software that lets you use the device. For example, a removable storage device may come with software that allows you to back up data on your computer, copy the contents of disks or restore data after a computer crash.

MAINTAIN AND TROUBLESHOOT

How can I protect the data on my removable disks?

The data on a removable disk can be damaged if the disk is mishandled or exposed to strong magnetic fields. To avoid damage, store disks in a cool, dry, clean environment, away from the magnetic fields generated by a monitor or speakers.

How do I clean my removable storage device?

Most removable storage devices require only an occasional external cleaning with a damp cloth. Refer to the manufacturer's instructions for more information about cleaning the device.

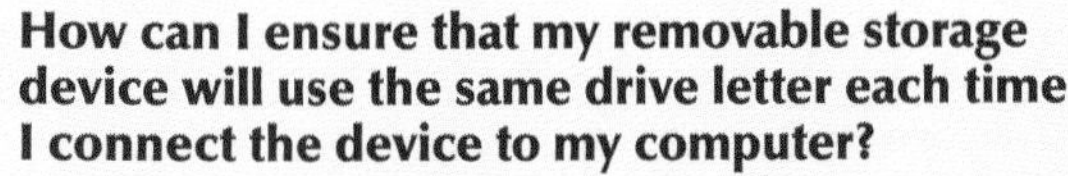

How can I ensure that my removable storage device will use the same drive letter each time I connect the device to my computer?

The Windows operating system allows you to specify a letter you want to use for a removable storage device. This ensures that the drive letter will always remain the same, no matter what other drives are installed or connected to the computer.

TAPE DRIVE

A tape drive stores and retrieves data on tape cartridges. Most people use tape drives to make backup copies of files stored on a computer.

INSTALL A TAPE DRIVE

Before installing a tape drive, turn off the computer, unplug the power cable and remove the cover from the computer case. Then ground yourself and the computer case. For information about grounding, see page 6.

1

Using a slotted screwdriver, remove the drive bay cover from the drive bay on the front of the computer. Then slide the tape drive into the drive bay.

2

Connect a cable from the power supply to the tape drive.

3

Using a ribbon cable, connect the tape drive to the computer.

4

Using small screws, secure the tape drive in the drive bay. Then replace the cover on the computer case.

INSTALL AN EXTERNAL TAPE DRIVE

Position the external tape drive on your desk. Then connect the drive to a parallel, SCSI or USB port at the back of your computer. You can then plug the power cable from the drive into an electrical outlet on the wall.

SET UP

Jumpers

Inexpensive tape drives use a floppy drive ribbon cable to connect to a computer, but many tape drives use a Small Computer System Interface (SCSI) ribbon cable. If there are devices already attached to the SCSI ribbon cable, you may need to adjust the jumpers on the tape drive. Consult the drive's documentation for information about adjusting the jumpers.

Installation Software

All tape drives include installation software you can use to install the necessary driver and set up the tape drive to work with your computer. You may also be able to use the installation software to optimize the performance of the drive.

TAPE CARTRIDGES

Inside a tape cartridge is a thin strip of plastic tape with a magnetic surface, similar to the tape found in audiotapes and videotapes. When you insert a tape cartridge into a tape drive, the tape moves across read/write heads in the tape drive. The read/write heads read and record data on the tape.

CHOOSE A TAPE DRIVE

Tape Drive Type

There are several types of tape drives available. Each type of tape drive uses its own type of tape cartridge. Some types of tape cartridges are capable of storing a great deal more data than other types. You should choose a drive that can store the entire contents of your hard drive on a single tape cartridge.

TAPE DRIVE TYPE	TAPE CARTRIDGE CAPACITY
• Quarter-Inch Cartridge (QIC)	• up to 10 GB
• Travan	• up to 14 GB
• Digital Audio Tape (DAT)	• up to 24 GB
• 8 millimeter (mm)	• up to 40 GB
• Linear Tape-Open (LTO)	• up to 100 GB

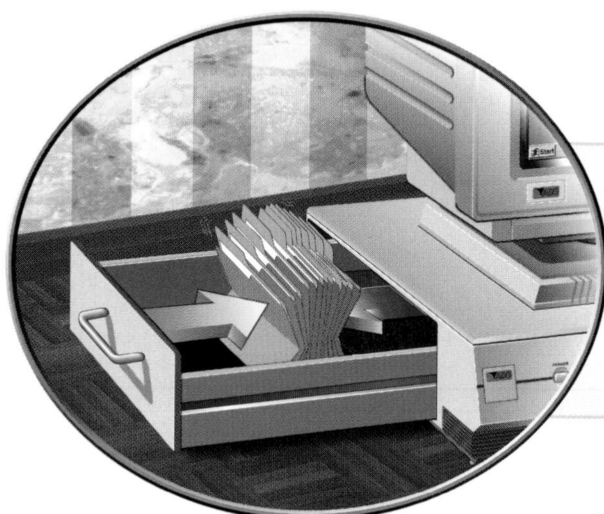

Compression

Some tape drives can compress, or squeeze together, data so a tape cartridge can store more data. Depending on the type of data you are storing, compression can almost double the amount of data the tape cartridge can hold.

Backup Software

Most tape drives come with backup software that usually has limited features. You can purchase additional backup software that allows you to perform more advanced tasks, such as scheduling your backups.

TEST AND TROUBLESHOOT

Should I test my tape drive and cartridges?

You should regularly restore data from tape cartridges to ensure that the tape drive is operating correctly and the tape cartridges are not damaged. Without regular testing, you could be performing backups on damaged cartridges without knowing there is a problem.

Why am I having problems restoring data from a tape cartridge?

The current backup software and the backup software used to store the data may be incompatible. To restore the data, you should use the same backup software that was used to back up the data originally.

How often should I clean my tape drive?

A tape drive may stop working if it is not cleaned regularly. Most tape drives need to be cleaned after a specific number of hours of use. Check the manufacturer's instructions for details on when to clean your tape drive.

You can use a cleaning cartridge to clean your tape drive. A cleaning cartridge is similar in size and shape to a tape cartridge.

CD-ROM OR DVD-ROM DRIVE

A CD-ROM drive is a device that reads information stored on CDs and CD-ROM discs. A DVD-ROM drive is a device that reads information stored on DVD-ROM discs.

INSTALL A CD-ROM OR DVD-ROM DRIVE

Before installing a CD-ROM or DVD-ROM drive, turn off the computer, unplug the power cable and remove the cover from the computer case. Then ground yourself and the computer case. For information about grounding, see page 6.

1

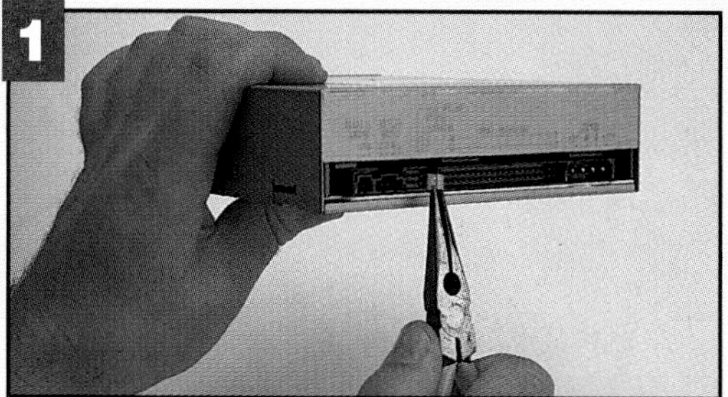

If necessary, adjust the jumpers on the back of the CD-ROM or DVD-ROM drive.

2

Using a slotted screwdriver, remove the drive bay cover from the drive bay on the front of the computer. Then slide the drive into the drive bay.

3

Connect a cable from the power supply to the CD-ROM or DVD-ROM drive.

4

Using a ribbon cable, connect the drive to the computer.

5

If necessary, connect the audio cable to the drive. Then connect the audio cable to the sound card. This allows your computer's speakers to play sound from CDs or DVD-ROM discs.

6

Using small screws, secure the drive in the drive bay. Then replace the cover on the computer case.

SET UP

Adjust Jumpers

If you use an Enhanced Integrated Drive Electronics (EIDE) ribbon cable to connect the drive and another device to the computer, you may have to change the jumpers on the devices. One device must be set as the master, while the other is set as the slave.

You may also need to adjust the jumpers on the drive if you are using a Small Computer System Interface (SCSI) ribbon cable to connect multiple devices. Each device must be assigned a unique number from zero to seven. Consult the drive's documentation for information about adjusting the jumpers.

Change Settings

Your computer may automatically detect and set up a CD-ROM or DVD-ROM drive you install. If your computer does not set up the drive, you may need to change the computer's settings. For information about computer settings, see page 146.

SPEED

The speed of a CD-ROM or DVD-ROM drive is indicated by a number followed by an X and determines how fast a disc spins. The faster a disc spins, the faster information transfers from the disc to the computer, which results in better performance. Most new CD-ROM drives have a speed of at least 32X. Most new DVD-ROM drives have a speed of at least 8X.

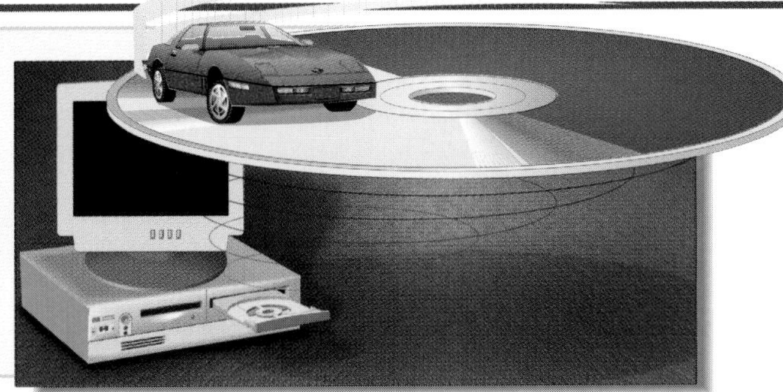

DRIVE TYPES

CD-ROM Drive

A CD-ROM drive only reads information stored on music CDs and CD-ROM discs. You cannot use a CD-ROM drive to store information on a disc.

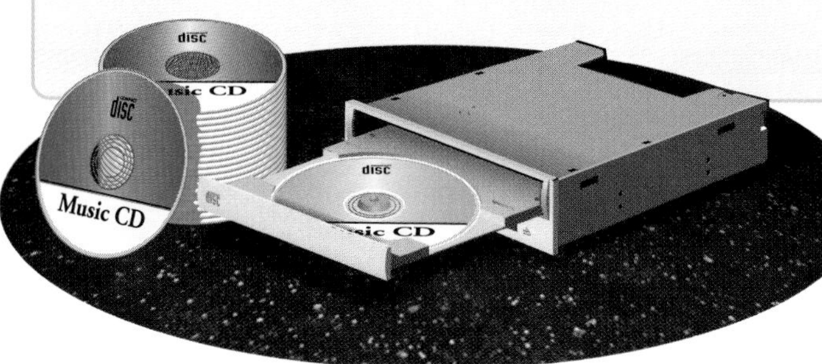

CD-Recordable Drive

A CD-Recordable (CD-R) drive allows you to store your own information on a disc. This type of drive is useful for backing up a hard drive or distributing information. A CD-Recordable drive can record information on each disc only once. A CD-Recordable disc can store up to 650 MB of data.

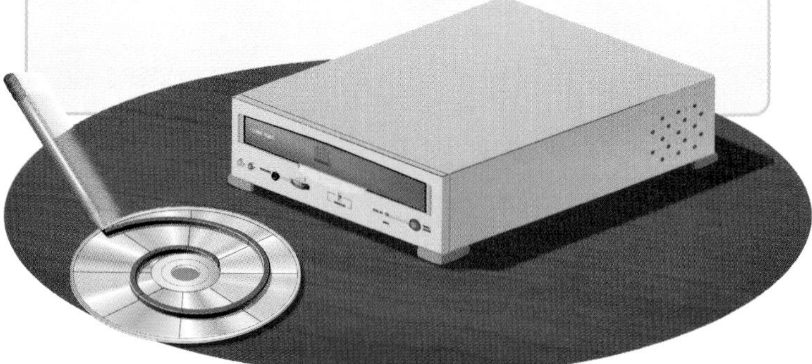

CD-Rewritable Drive

A CD-ReWritable (CD-RW) drive is similar to a CD-Recordable drive, but allows you to change the data you record on a disc many times. A CD-Rewritable disc stores the same amount of data as a CD-Recordable disc.

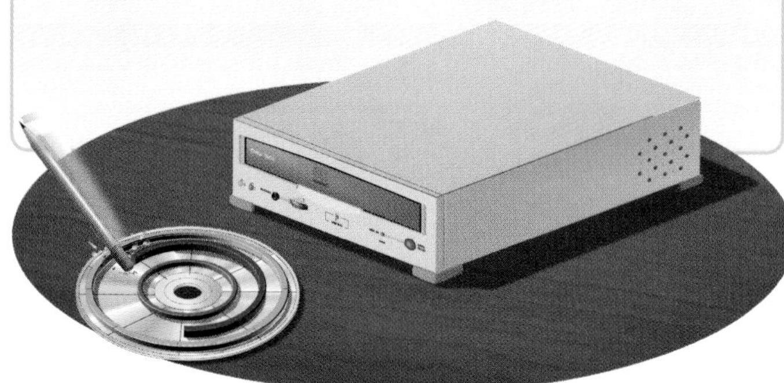

DVD-ROM Drive

A DVD-ROM drive can read CD-ROM discs, music CDs and DVD-ROM discs. A DVD-ROM disc can store up to 4.7 GB of information, including programs and multimedia.

TROUBLESHOOT AND MAINTAIN

Why can't my CD-ROM or DVD-ROM drive access information on a disc?

If your CD-ROM or DVD-ROM drive cannot access information on a disc, the disc may not be compatible with the drive. Some discs, such as discs created using a CD-Recordable or CD-Rewritable drive, are not compatible with all CD-ROM or DVD-ROM drives.

My CD-ROM or DVD-ROM drive sounds like it is constantly running. Is something wrong?

If your CD-ROM or DVD-ROM drive sounds like it is constantly running, the disc in the drive may be scratched and the drive may not be able to access the information on the disc. To prevent scratches, you should handle only the outer edge of your discs.

How do I clean my CD-ROM or DVD-ROM drive?

Over time, dust and dirt can accumulate inside a CD-ROM or DVD-ROM drive. This may prevent the drive from reading information on a disc. You should use a cleaning kit to clean the inside of your drive on a regular basis. CD-ROM and DVD-ROM drive cleaning kits are available at most computer stores.

Microsoft Internet Explorer
File Edit View Favorites Tools Help
Back Search Favorites History
Address
Go Links
Internet
PHONES
WRITING
DISC IN
OPEN CLOSE

CHAPTER 6

UPGRADE A COMPUTER

Would you like to learn how to increase your computer's capabilities? This chapter explains how to upgrade your computer's BIOS, operating system, software and more.

UPGRADE A COMPUTER

After deciding to upgrade, you should consider the various ways to upgrade your computer.

You can upgrade a computer by adding a new component or replacing a current component with one that offers more features.

DETERMINE IF YOU NEED TO UPGRADE

Consider Current Needs

You should consider how you currently use the computer and then determine if the computer could better meet your needs. For example, if you mainly use your computer to access information on the Internet, you may want to upgrade the modem to a faster one or upgrade to a high-speed Internet connection. This will allow you to transfer information to your computer faster.

Consider Future Needs

You should consider how you want to use the computer in the future. You may want to upgrade a computer that is not capable of adequately meeting your future needs. For example, if you intend to use a computer to play games, you may want to upgrade to a fast CD-ROM drive or install a high-quality sound card.

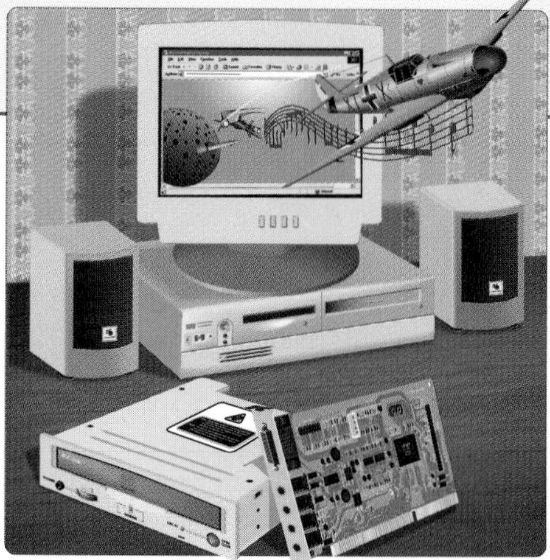

WAYS TO UPGRADE

Increase Capabilities

You can upgrade a computer by increasing the computer's capabilities, such as enhancing multimedia capabilities or increasing storage. This lets you use the computer to perform new tasks. For example, adding a TV tuner card to a computer lets you use the computer to watch television programs.

Improve Efficiency

You can improve the efficiency of a computer by upgrading a component to a faster model. Modems, CPUs and CD-ROM drives are examples of components you can replace with faster models to upgrade a computer. Adding more memory to a computer is also an effective way to improve the computer's efficiency.

Replace Failing Components

Many people upgrade their computers by replacing a failing component. For example, when a hard drive fails, you may want to consider upgrading to a hard drive with more storage capacity.

You may have no choice but to upgrade a failing component if the original model is no longer available. For example, hard drives with capacities of less than 5 GB are no longer manufactured.

Resource settings allow the devices installed on a computer to communicate with the computer.

Each device has its own unique resource settings. You can check the documentation included with a device to determine which resource settings it can use.

ADJUST RESOURCE SETTINGS

Jumpers and DIP Switches

If a device uses jumpers, you can adjust the resource settings by placing a small plastic plug over pins on the device. Other devices may require you to adjust the resource settings using a series of small switches, called DIP switches.

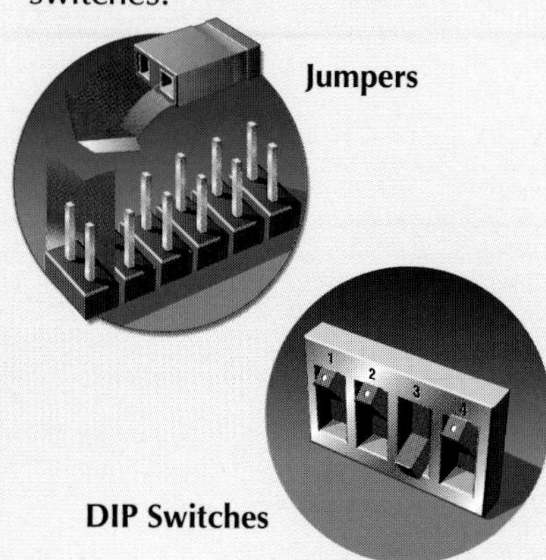

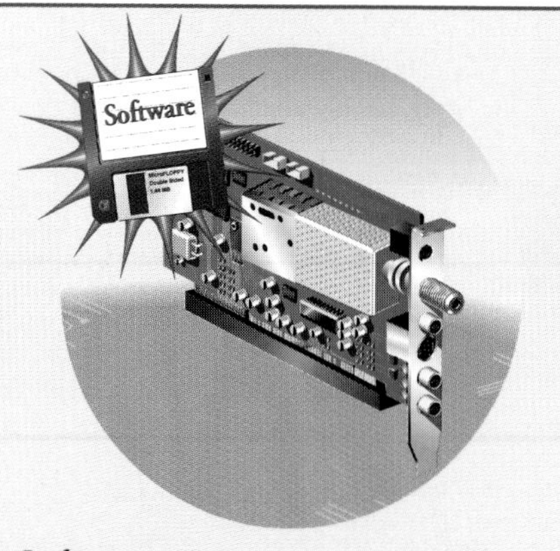

Software

Many devices come with software you can use to adjust the resource settings for the device. The software saves the resource settings on a memory chip located on the device. The memory chip can store the resource settings even when the computer is turned off.

Plug and Play

Most new computers use Plug and Play technology. When you install a Plug and Play device, the computer will detect the device and automatically adjust the resource settings for the device.

COMMON RESOURCE SETTINGS

IRQ

An Interrupt Request (IRQ) tells the computer that a device needs attention.

Common IRQ Settings	
3	Serial port 2
4	Serial port 1
5	Sound card
7	Parallel port

DMA Channel

A Direct Memory Access (DMA) channel allows a device to communicate directly with the computer's memory to speed up the processing of information.

Common DMA Channel Settings	
1	Sound card
3	Parallel port or voice modem
5	Sound card or SCSI card
6	Sound card or network interface card

I/O Address

An Input/Output (I/O) address specifies which area of memory a device uses to communicate with the computer.

Common I/O Address Settings	
220	Sound card
300	Network interface card
370	Parallel port
3F0	Serial port 1

Memory Address

A memory address indicates which area of memory a device uses to perform functions.

Common Memory Address Settings	
C0000	Video card
C8000	Hard drive
D0000	Network interface card
F0000	BIOS

You can use the Basic Input/Output System (BIOS) to change your computer's settings.

BIOS

The BIOS is a chip on your system board that allows you to access and change your computer's settings. When you install a new device on your computer, the BIOS will usually change your computer's settings so the computer can work with the new device. If the BIOS does not automatically change your computer's settings, you can use the BIOS setup program to change the computer's settings yourself.

CMOS

Your computer's settings are stored in another chip on the system board, called the Complementary Metal Oxide Semiconductor (CMOS) chip. Any changes you make to your computer's settings using the BIOS setup program are saved in the CMOS. A small battery allows the CMOS to store your computer's settings even when the computer is turned off.

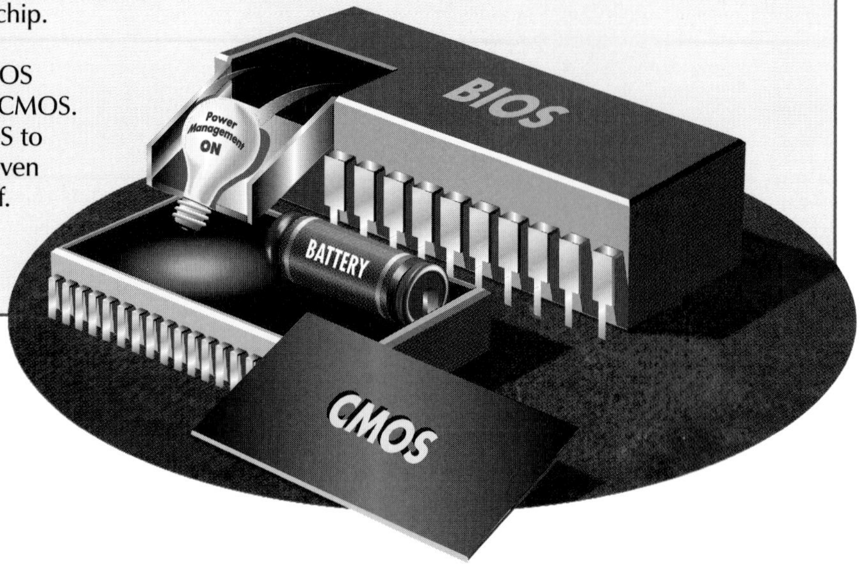

BIOS SETUP PROGRAM

Documentation

The BIOS setup program is different for many computers. You should always consult the documentation that came with your computer or system board before accessing or changing any settings in the BIOS.

Access

Most computers let you access the BIOS setup program by pressing a specific key as the computer starts. Some computers also let you use configuration software to access the BIOS setup program after the computer has started.

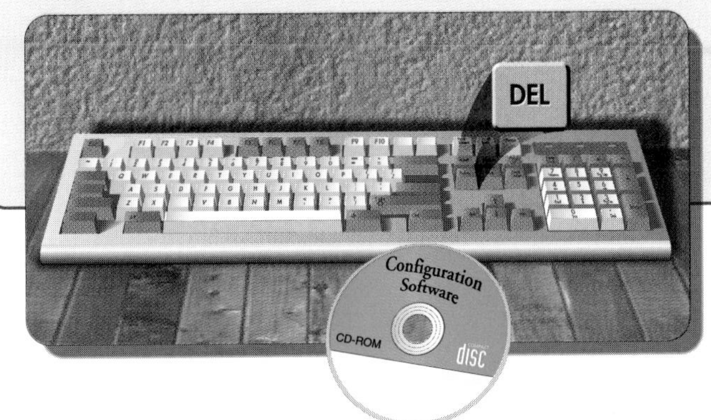

Interface

Most BIOS setup programs have a text-based interface, which allows you to select and change computer settings from a menu using the keys on your keyboard. Some BIOS setup programs have a Graphical User Interface (GUI, pronounced "gooey"), which allows you to use a pointing device to select pictures to change your computer's settings.

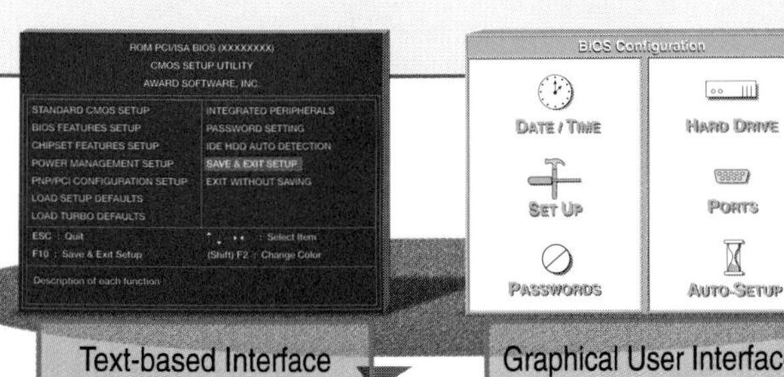

Customization

Computer manufacturers often customize the BIOS setup program to improve the performance of their products. For example, a computer that includes a non-standard feature, such as a FireWire port, will have support for the feature built into the BIOS.

COMMON COMPUTER SETTINGS

Boot Sequence

The boot sequence contains information about the order that your computer checks storage devices for an operating system when you turn on the computer. Most computers begin with the floppy drive and then check the hard drive. You can change the boot sequence to change the order that your computer checks storage devices.

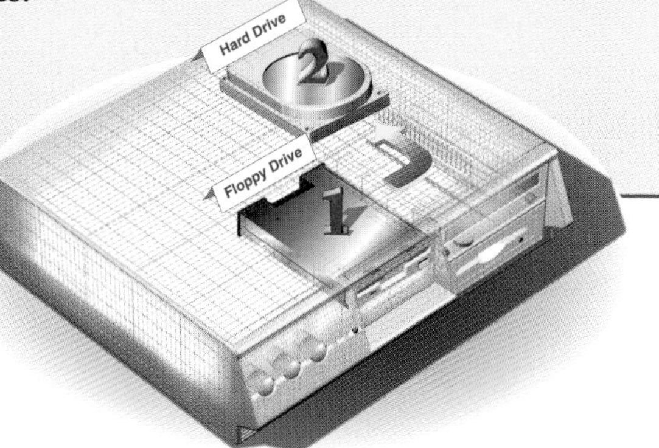

Connector

You can adjust the settings for connectors, such as USB or parallel ports, on your computer. You can also enable or disable connectors on your computer.

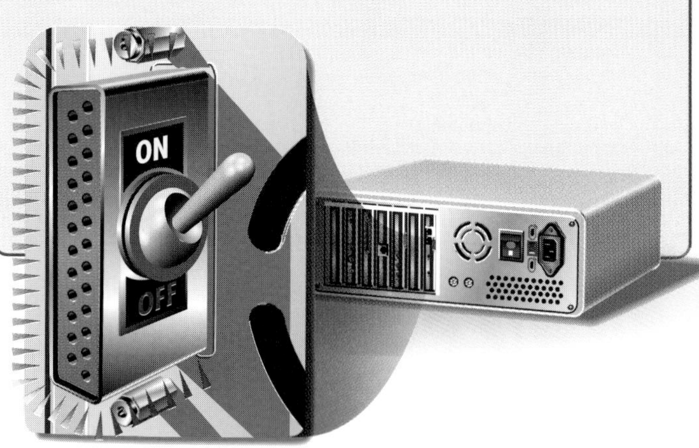

Hard Drive

You can specify the settings for your hard drive, including the number of cylinders, heads and sectors the hard drive uses. A hard drive's settings are usually printed on the drive or in the documentation included with the drive.

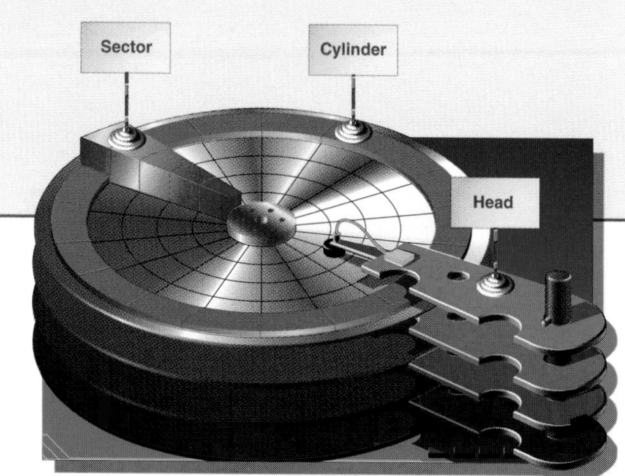

Memory Speed

The memory in most computers can operate at different speeds. Many BIOS setup programs allow you to adjust the speed of the memory.

Power Management

You can change the power management settings on your computer. Power management allows you to conserve energy by controlling how the computer uses power after a period of inactivity. For example, you can have your computer enter a low power, or standby, mode after ten minutes of inactivity.

Storage Device

You can adjust the settings for the storage devices, such as a floppy or CD-ROM drive, installed on your computer. For example, you can specify the storage capacity of a floppy drive installed on your computer.

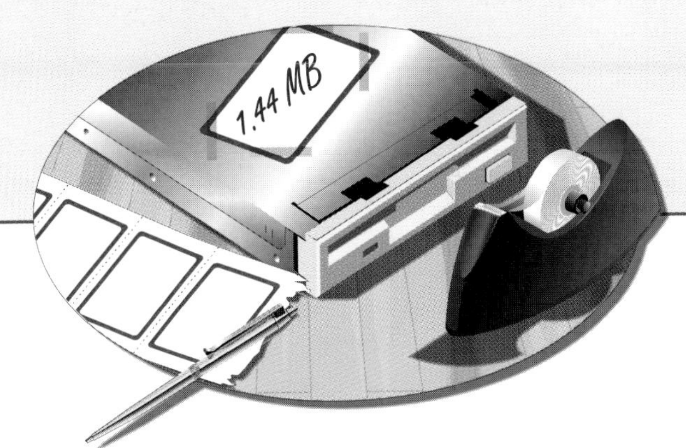

Password

You can assign a password to prevent people from accessing the BIOS setup program and changing your computer's settings. Many BIOS setup programs also allow you to assign a password to prevent other people from using your computer.

Default

Most BIOS setup programs allow you to restore the computer's default settings. This enables you to reverse any incorrect settings that have adversely affected your computer.

UPGRADE THE BIOS

You can upgrade the BIOS in your computer by reprogramming the BIOS with a newer version. You should only upgrade the BIOS if you want to be able to use a device that is not currently supported by the BIOS or correct an error.

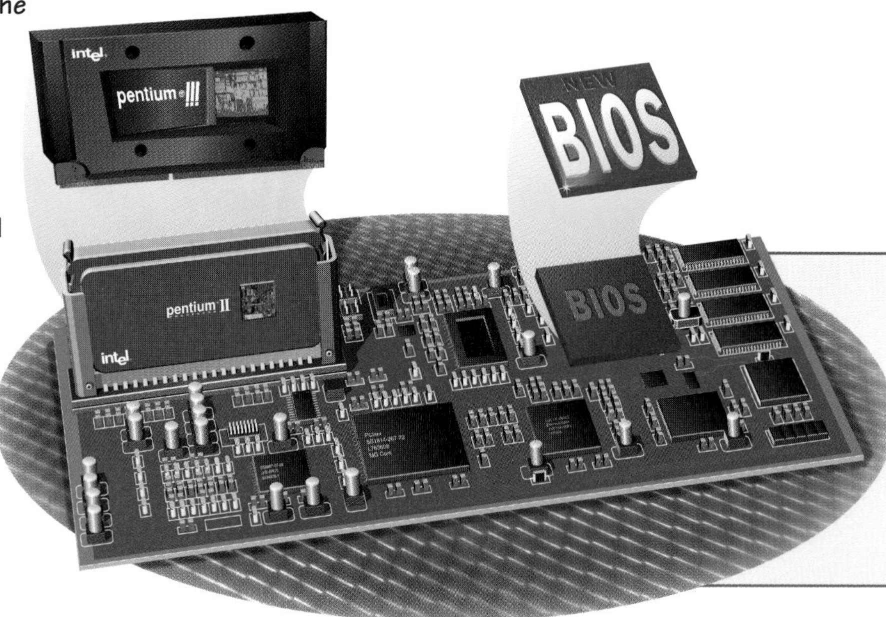

For example, the BIOS may be upgraded to allow a system board to use a new CPU that was not available when the system board was first created.

UPGRADE

Create a Startup Disk

The process of upgrading the BIOS usually involves creating a floppy disk that can be used to start the computer and automatically reprogram the BIOS. BIOS upgrades contain very detailed instructions on how to create the startup disk and how to reprogram the BIOS. These instructions should be followed very carefully.

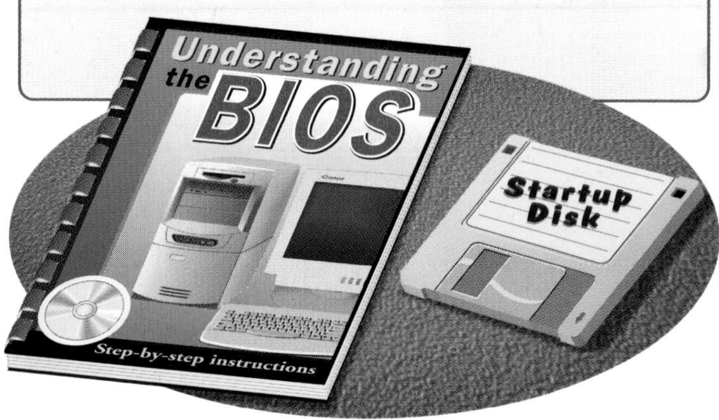

Caution

Even if two computers are similar, you should never reprogram a BIOS with an upgrade intended for another computer, as this could render your computer unusable. It is also important to ensure that power to the computer is not interrupted while you are upgrading the BIOS. This could destroy the BIOS.

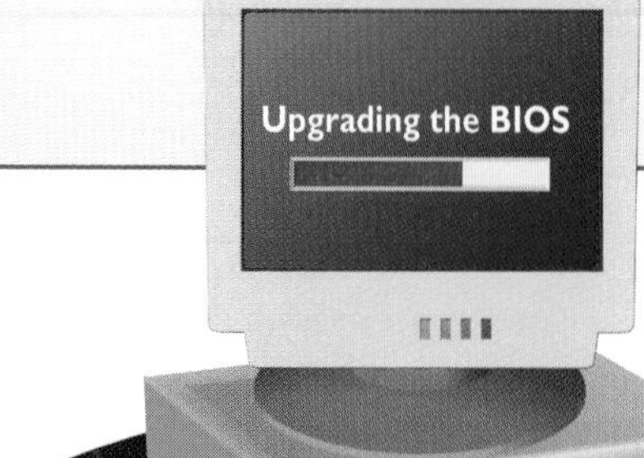

CHOOSE A BIOS UPGRADE

Where to Find BIOS Upgrades

System board manufacturers often customize the BIOS to improve the performance of their products, so the manufacturer of your system board is the best source for a BIOS upgrade. If you are unable to contact the manufacturer of your system board, the BIOS manufacturer may be able to assist you.

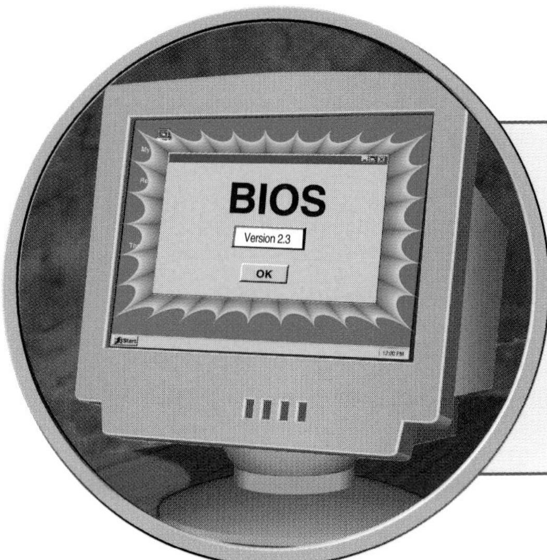

Version Number

Each BIOS has a version number, which is typically displayed as the computer is starting. You can check with the system board manufacturer to see if the version number of the BIOS in your computer is the latest one. The latest version of the BIOS includes all changes made in previous versions, so you only need to install the latest version.

Bug Fixes

Many BIOS upgrades are created to correct problems with older BIOS versions, such as an incompatibility with a specific type and brand of memory. BIOS upgrades are typically available with a list of any bug fixes that have been made since the previous version of the BIOS upgrade. Checking the list of bug fixes can help you decide whether upgrading the BIOS will fix the problem you are experiencing.

UPGRADE AN OPERATING SYSTEM

An operating system determines the hardware and software you can install on your computer. You can upgrade your operating system so you can use hardware or software that your current operating system does not support.

OPERATING SYSTEM FUNCTIONS

Control Hardware

An operating system controls the different parts of a computer system and enables all the parts to work together smoothly and efficiently.

Run Application Software

An operating system runs application software, such as Microsoft Word and Lotus 1-2-3.

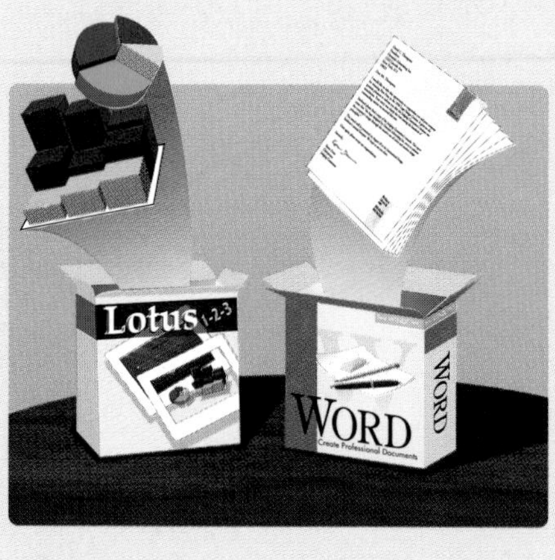

Manage Information

An operating system provides ways to manage and organize information stored on a computer. You can use an operating system to sort, copy, move, delete and view files.

UPGRADE CONSIDERATIONS

Ease of Use

Before upgrading, you should try using a computer running the operating system you want to upgrade to. This allows you to make sure the operating system is easy to use.

Minimum Requirements

You must ensure that your computer meets the minimum requirements the operating system needs to work properly. For example, most operating systems require a computer to have a certain amount of memory and hard drive space.

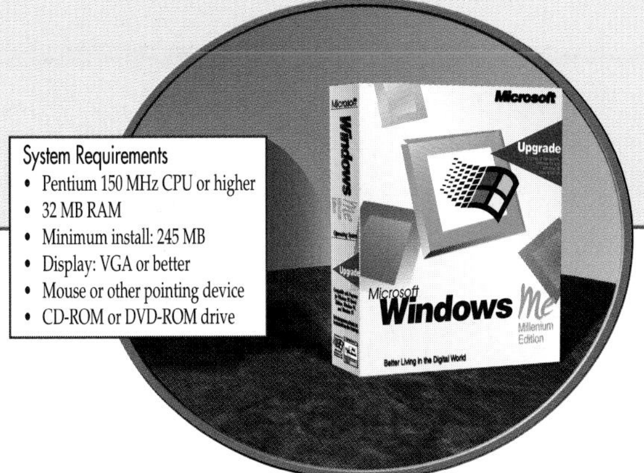

System Requirements
• Pentium 150 MHz CPU or higher
• 32 MB RAM
• Minimum install: 245 MB
• Display: VGA or better
• Mouse or other pointing device
• CD-ROM or DVD-ROM drive
Microsoft
Upgrade
Microsoft Windows Me
Millenium Edition

TROUBLESHOOT AN UPGRADE

Hardware Compatibility

If a hardware device no longer works after you upgrade your operating system, you may need to update the device's driver or change the settings for the operating system. You can contact the manufacturer of the device for an updated driver or consult the operating system documentation for information about how to change the settings. You may also need to change your computer's settings. For information about computer settings, see page 146.

Software Compatibility

If your application software is not working properly, the application may be incompatible with the new operating system. You may need to upgrade the software to work with the new operating system.

UPGRADE SOFTWARE

Upgrading software can improve the way you accomplish specific tasks on your computer. There are several issues you should consider before upgrading software.

You can buy software at computer stores. There are also thousands of programs available on the Internet.

TYPES OF UPGRADES

New Version

All software has a version number. When a manufacturer adds new features to existing software, the upgraded software is given a higher number than the previous version. This helps people identify the most up-to-date software. For example, Internet Explorer 5.5 is a more recent version of the Web browser than Internet Explorer 5.0

Patch

Manufacturers create minor software upgrades, called patches, to make corrections or improvements to software. A patch is also often referred to as a service pack. You can often find a patch on the software manufacturer's Web site. You can also contact the manufacturer to obtain a patch on a floppy disk or CD-ROM disc.

UPGRADE CONSIDERATIONS

New Capabilities

Most software is upgraded at least once every year or two to add new capabilities or improved features to the software. In some cases, the new capabilities increase the complexity of the software and can cause the software to operate slower than the previous version. You should upgrade software only when you need new capabilities.

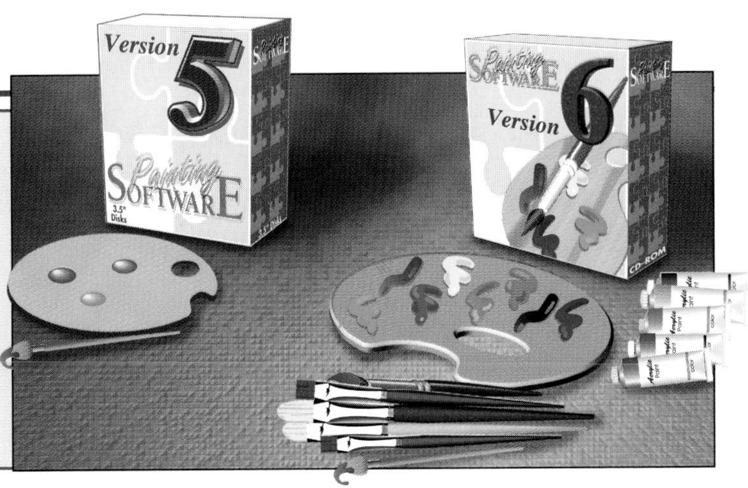

Cost

Software upgrades vary in price, but are usually less expensive than hardware upgrades. Upgrading software can be an effective way to increase the capabilities and performance of your computer without spending a lot of money. For example, instead of purchasing a new modem, you can download a faster Web browser from the World Wide Web for free.

Compatibility

If you decide to upgrade your software, make sure you choose software that is compatible with your operating system. You should also check the minimum requirements for the software upgrade. A new software version often requires more memory and hard drive space than a previous version.

Calendar
May 2001
1 2 3 4 5 6
7 8 9 10 11 12 13
14 15 16 17 18 19 20
21 22 23 24 25 26 27
28 29 30 31
TRAVAN
zip
Compressed
Air
1/4"

CHAPTER 7

REPAIR A COMPUTER

Are you interested in learning how to troubleshoot hardware and software problems, when to consult a repair service and more? Read this chapter for information.

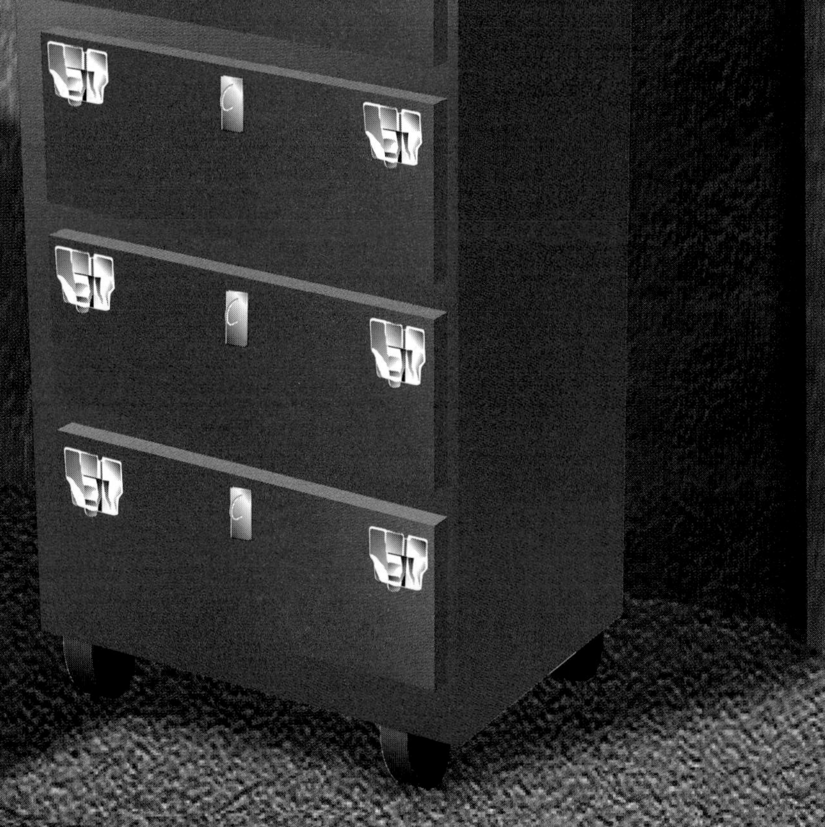

There are several common causes of hardware failure. Being aware of the causes of hardware failure can help you avoid problems.

Loose Connection

A loose connection between a computer and a component can give the appearance of a hardware failure. You should always make sure components are securely connected to the computer.

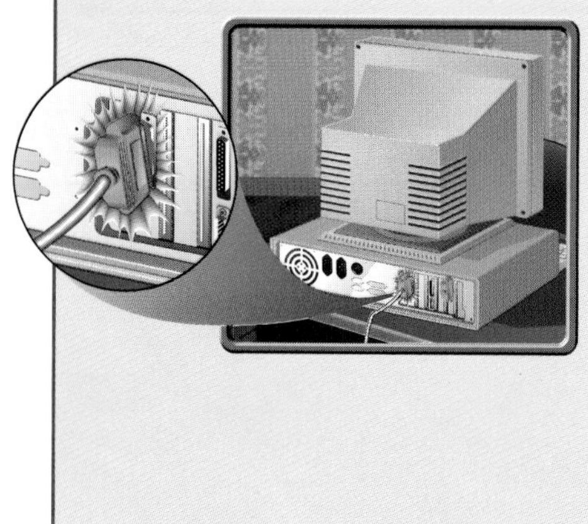

Power Fluctuations

One of the most common causes of hardware failure is repeated exposure to power fluctuations, such as spikes, surges and blackouts. You can connect a computer to an Uninterruptible Power Supply (UPS) to protect the computer from power fluctuations. For information on uninterruptible power supplies, see page 102.

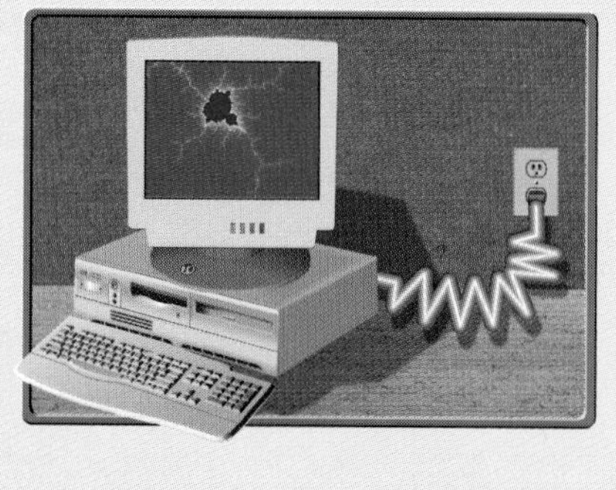

Dust and Dirt

Dust and dirt inside a computer are a common cause of hardware failure. Dust and dirt can cause increased temperatures and short-circuiting inside a computer. You should clean a computer on a regular basis to keep hardware in good working order. For information on cleaning a computer, see page 20.

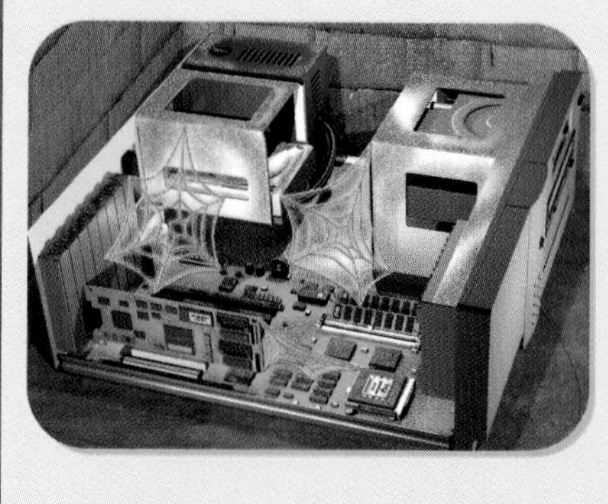

Defective Media

Defective storage media, such as a floppy disk or tape cartridge, can give the appearance of a failed storage device. You should try using a different floppy disk or tape cartridge to determine whether the media or the device is at fault.

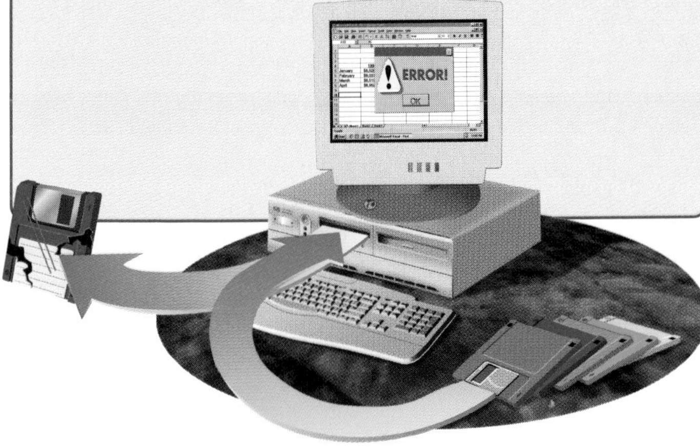

Defective Component

Defects can cause a component to fail when it is first installed in a computer or after only a short period of use. Although the quality and reliability of new components have increased in recent years, up to 10 percent of new components may be defective when they are purchased.

Component Age

Many components simply fail after they have been used for several years. Components, such as hard drives, floppy drives and fans, which contain moving parts eventually wear out. If properly maintained, most computer components can last 5 years or more.

Heat

All computer components generate heat as they operate. If the temperature in a computer gets too high, hardware failures can occur. To prevent overheating, you should always ensure that a computer has adequate ventilation and that the fan opening at the back of the computer is not blocked.

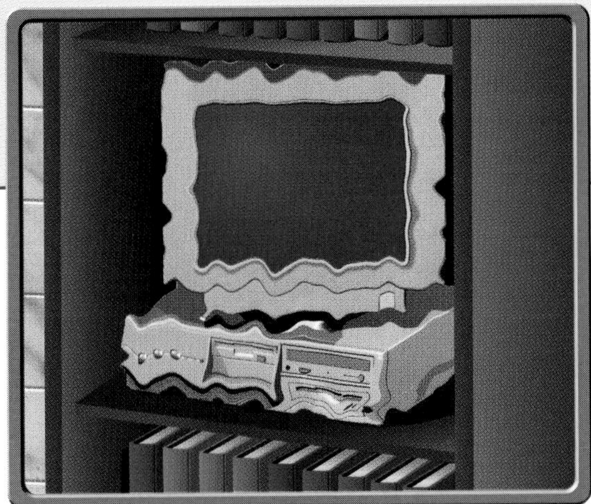

TROUBLESHOOT A HARDWARE PROBLEM

Troubleshooting can help you find the cause of a hardware problem and may help you fix the problem.

When troubleshooting a hardware problem, you should focus on one component at a time, beginning with the component you think is causing the problem.

Check the Manual

The first step in troubleshooting a hardware problem is to check the documentation for the computer or device for troubleshooting information. Manuals usually provide detailed information about the most common problems.

Check Connections

A loose connection is a common cause of hardware problems. Make sure the component is securely connected to the computer.

Check the Driver

Most computer components require software, called a driver, to operate. You should ensure you are using the correct and most up-to-date driver for the component you think is causing the problem.

Test Multiple Possibilities

Testing multiple possibilities can help you find the cause of a problem. For example, if a floppy drive cannot access data on a floppy disk, the problem may be caused by the drive or the disk. To find the cause, try using another disk. If the floppy drive cannot access data on the second disk, the drive is likely the cause of the problem.

Try Another Component

You can try using another component to troubleshoot a problem. For example, if you think the video card is malfunctioning, try replacing it with a video card you know works properly. If the problem stops, the original video card is likely the cause of the problem.

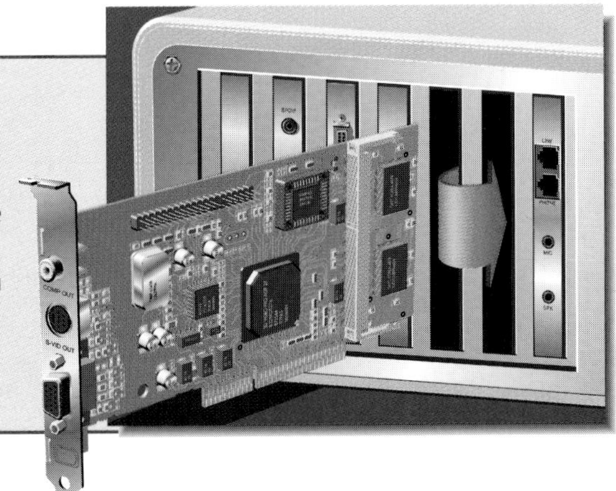

Move and Remove Components

Moving and removing components can help you troubleshoot a problem. For example, if you suspect an expansion card is causing a problem, first try moving the card to another expansion slot. If the problem stops, it may be due to the original expansion slot. If the problem persists, you can remove the expansion card and restart the computer to see if the problem still exists. If the problem stops, it is likely due to the expansion card.

TROUBLESHOOT A SOFTWARE PROBLEM

When troubleshooting a software problem, you should start with the program you most recently installed on the computer. A corrupt program may begin causing problems, such as program crashes, error messages and system lockups, shortly after the program is installed.

To avoid accidentally corrupting or deleting files your programs need to operate, you should always exit all open programs and properly shut down the operating system before turning off a computer.

Check for Viruses

Software problems may be caused by a computer virus. You can use an anti-virus program to check the computer for viruses. Most anti-virus programs also include a virus removal feature you can use if you find a virus. For information about viruses and anti-virus programs, see page 22.

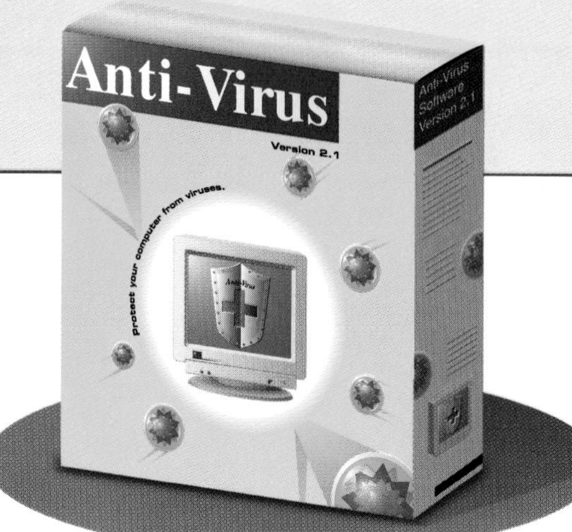

Check for Updates

Software manufacturers often create minor software updates, called patches or service packs, to fix known bugs and problems with the software. You can check the software manufacturer's Web site to see if a patch or service pack exists that fixes your problem.

Re-Install Software

If a problem occurs only when you use a specific program, you may be able to correct the problem by re-installing the software. Re-installing software replaces the program files on the computer with a new copy. If the cause of a problem is deleted or corrupted program files, re-installing the software may correct the problem.

Uninstall Software

If you suspect the problems you are experiencing are caused by a particular program, you can remove the program to see if the problems stop. Most programs come with a utility that lets you uninstall the program. Some operating systems, such as Windows Me and Windows 2000, also include an uninstall utility you can use to help remove a program.

Re-Install Operating System

If you are experiencing problems with many of the programs installed on a computer, the operating system may be the cause of the problems. An operating system can become corrupted when system files are accidentally deleted or damaged. Re-installing the operating system may resolve the problems.

DIAGNOSTIC PROGRAMS

A diagnostic program may help you locate and repair computer problems.

All personal computers have a basic, built-in diagnostic program called the Power-On Self Test (POST). For information about the POST, see page 166.

Where to Find Diagnostic Programs

Most operating systems, such as Windows Me and Windows 2000, include some diagnostic programs. You can also buy many commercial diagnostic programs on the Internet or at computer stores. Popular commercial diagnostic programs include McAfee's First Aid and Symantec's Norton Utilities.

Troubleshoot Using Diagnostic Programs

You can set up most diagnostic programs to run diagnostic tests repeatedly and report any errors that are detected. This is useful if you are trying to troubleshoot a problem that occurs from time to time and you need to run the diagnostic program for an extended period, such as overnight.

TYPES OF DIAGNOSTIC PROGRAMS

Hard Drive

A hard drive diagnostic program can help you locate and repair errors on a hard drive. Most hard drive diagnostic programs can also help improve the performance of a hard drive.

Memory

A memory diagnostic program allows you to check for errors in a computer's memory. Memory diagnostic programs are also useful for displaying the amount of memory in a computer and the amount of memory required by individual programs.

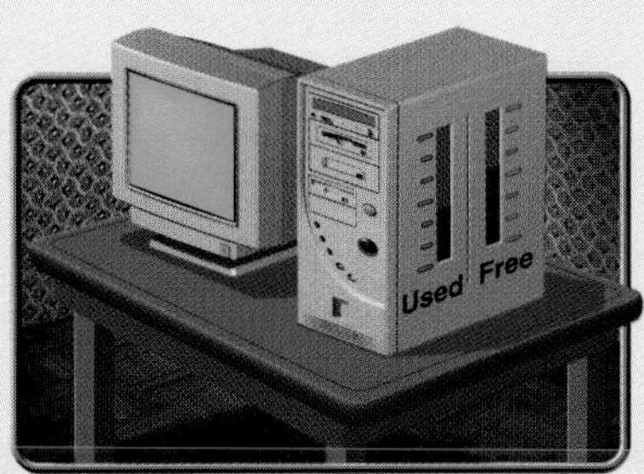

Software

Software can cause many computer problems. A software diagnostic program inspects all the software installed on a computer to ensure the software is operating correctly.

Hardware

Many computer components and devices, such as SCSI cards, network interface cards and removable storage devices, come with their own specialized diagnostic programs. These diagnostic programs allow you to test the hardware for errors.

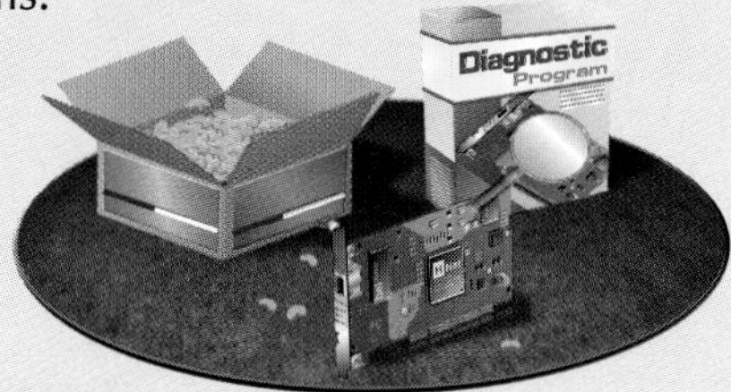

Operating System

Some operating systems have diagnostic programs that constantly monitor, diagnose and repair problems detected in the operating system.

Each time you turn on your computer, the computer performs a series of tests, called the Power-On Self Test (POST). The POST determines whether the main components in the computer, such as the system board and hard drive, are functioning properly. If a component is malfunctioning, the computer generates an error code.

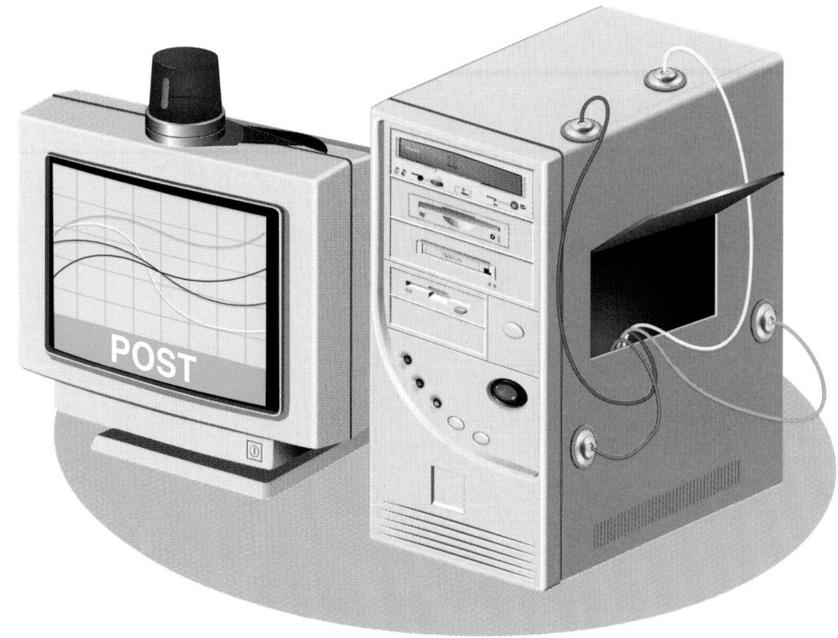

Error Codes

If the computer detects an error during the POST and the video card and monitor are working properly, the computer will display an error code on the screen.

The error codes your computer displays depend on the type of system board in the computer. For example, some computers display only an error number, while other computers may display an error number and a short message explaining the error. You should always consult the documentation that came with your computer or system board to determine the exact cause of an error and how to repair the error.

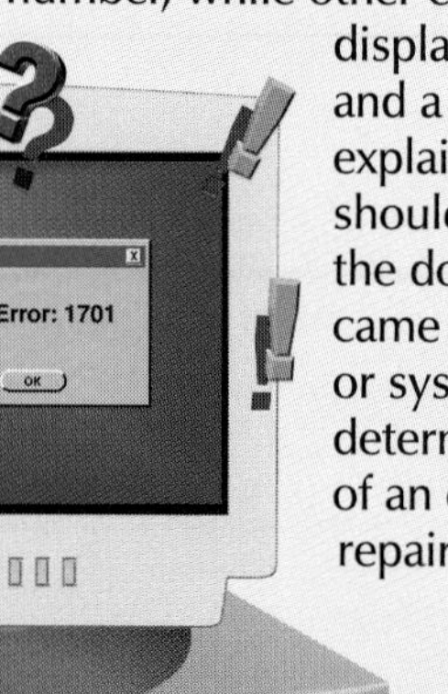

Here are some examples of common error codes.

Error Number	Problem
101 - 199	System board error
201 - 299	RAM error
301 - 399	Keyboard error
601 - 699	Floppy drive error
901 - 999	Printer port error
1101 - 1199	Serial port error
1701 - 1799	Hard drive error

Beep Error Codes

If the computer finds an error during the POST and the video card is not working properly, the computer will generate a beep error code. Beep error codes usually mean that the computer will not be able to start until the error is fixed.

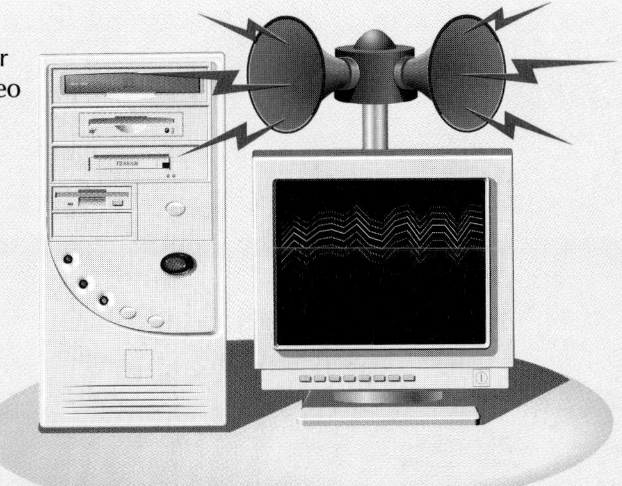

The beep error codes your computer generates depend on the type of system board in the computer. For example, some computers may generate a series of short and long beeps, while other computers generate only short beeps. You should always consult the documentation that came with your computer or system board to determine what a beep error code means before attempting to repair the error.

All computers normally generate a single beep when they start up. If a computer beeps once and continues to start up, there is no error.

Here are some examples of common beep error codes.

No. of Beeps	Problem
1	Memory error
2	Memory error
3	Memory error
4	System timer error
5	CPU error
6	Keyboard controller error
7	CPU error
8	Video card error
9	BIOS error
10	CMOS error
11	Cache memory error

A repair service is useful if you are unable to fix a computer problem yourself. There are several factors to consider before choosing a repair service.

DETERMINE IF YOU NEED A REPAIR SERVICE

Identify the Problem

When a computer problem occurs, you should troubleshoot the problem yourself. This can help you determine whether the problem is caused by a hardware failure and decide if you need a repair service. For example, if an error message appears when a floppy drive tries to access data on a floppy disk, the problem may be a failing drive or simply a damaged disk.

Consider Replacing the Component

Always consider the cost of repairing a component. Many components, such as floppy drives, are so inexpensive that repairing the component may cost more than replacing it. You might also consider upgrading a failing component. For example, buying a new, fast CD-ROM drive may cost less than repairing a slow drive.

If you choose to replace or upgrade a component, you may want to do the work yourself and avoid using a repair service.

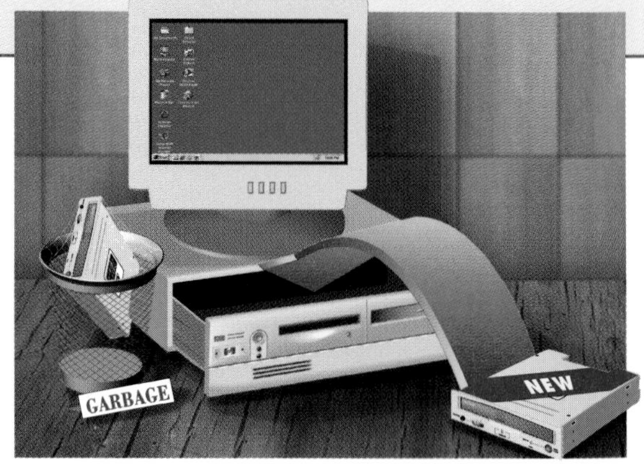

WHEN TO USE A REPAIR SERVICE

Electrical Problems

If your computer has severe electrical problems, you should take the computer to a repair service. If you attempt to repair electrical problems in your computer, you may damage the computer or suffer personal injury.

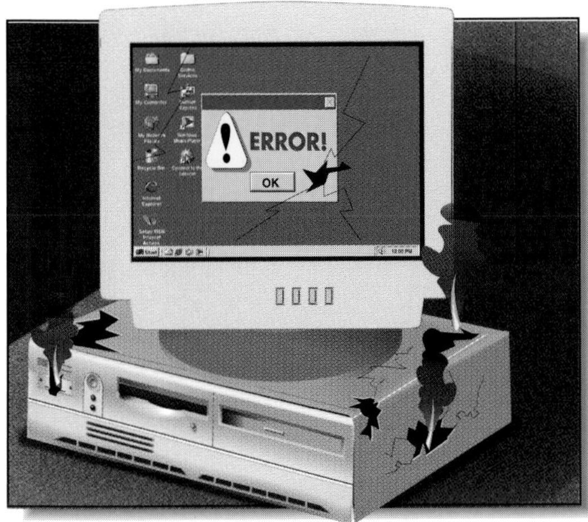

Complicated Problems

Some problems are the result of several hardware failures occurring at the same time. A problem with multiple causes can be very difficult to troubleshoot and repair. If you are unable to troubleshoot a problem yourself, you may want to use a repair service.

BEFORE GOING TO A REPAIR SERVICE

Once you decide you need a repair service, you should record information about the problem you are experiencing, such as when the problem first happened, how often the problem occurs and what steps the repair service can take to reproduce the problem. It is also helpful to provide a repair service with information about the components and programs installed on the computer. Providing the repair service with as much information as possible can help the repair service fix the problem quickly and efficiently.

CHOOSE A REPAIR SERVICE

Recommendations

You should choose a repair service that has been recommended by someone you trust. Some repair services will give you a list of customers you can contact to verify the quality of the work.

Estimates

You should use a repair service that will provide a written estimate before the work is performed. After you agree to a price, ask the repair service to contact you if the repair will cost more than the original estimate.

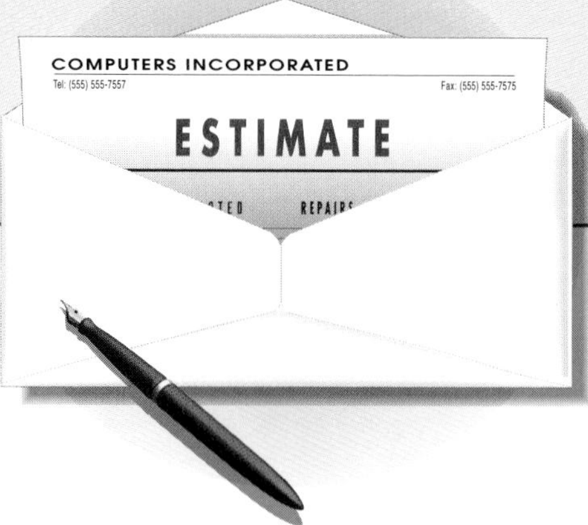

Warranty

Many repair services offer warranties, which guarantee their work for a period of time. You should look for at least a 90-day warranty, but a longer warranty is preferable.

Speed

You should use a repair service that works quickly, since you will be without the use of your computer while it is being fixed. Try to find out how long it will take a repair service to fix your computer.

TYPES OF REPAIR SERVICE

Manufacturer

If you have a problem with a component that is under warranty, you may be able to return the component to the manufacturer for replacement or repair. You may have to pay the shipping costs, which can be expensive.

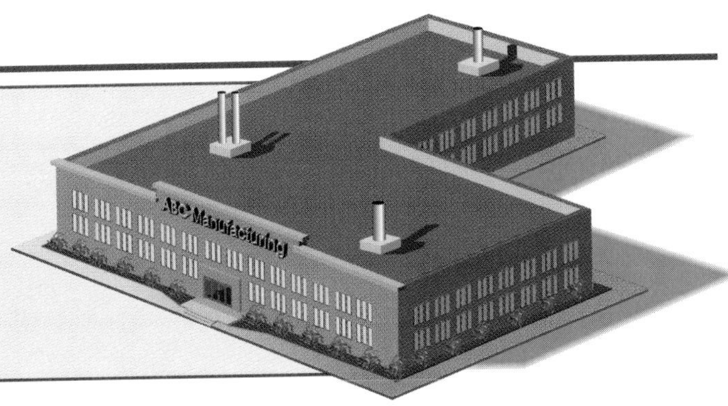

Computer Store

Most computer stores have a service department that repairs computers. Prices and quality of work vary greatly between stores. If you purchased your computer from a computer store, you can inquire at that store if they will repair the computer at a reduced cost.

Dedicated Service Company

Dedicated service companies specialize in repairing computers. Although many dedicated service companies repair computers only for businesses, some will also repair computers for individuals. Dedicated service companies usually charge more than other types of repair services, but they tend to offer better service.

AFTER A REPAIR

After a computer returns from a repair service, you should test and burn in the computer or repaired device to ensure the problem has been fixed. To burn in a computer or device, run the computer or device for an extended period of time.

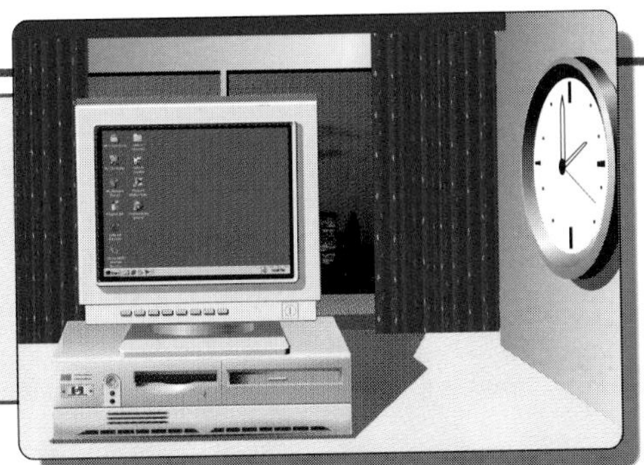

If you have a problem with a computer or component that is covered by a manufacturer's warranty, the manufacturer may repair or replace the product.

When purchasing a new computer, you may be able to purchase an extended warranty. An extended warranty sometimes covers the loan of a computer and guaranteed repair times.

Non-Warranty Problems

You should always troubleshoot a problem yourself to ensure the problem is caused by a product covered by the warranty. If you request warranty service for a problem caused by a product not covered by the warranty, you may have to pay for the time a technician spends investigating the problem.

Telephone Technical Support

Most manufacturers offer telephone technical support free of charge for products covered by a warranty. Telephone support is often the first level of technical support available to you when a hardware problem occurs.

Although the technical support is free, you may be on hold a long time. If the call is long-distance and not toll-free, it can be quite expensive.

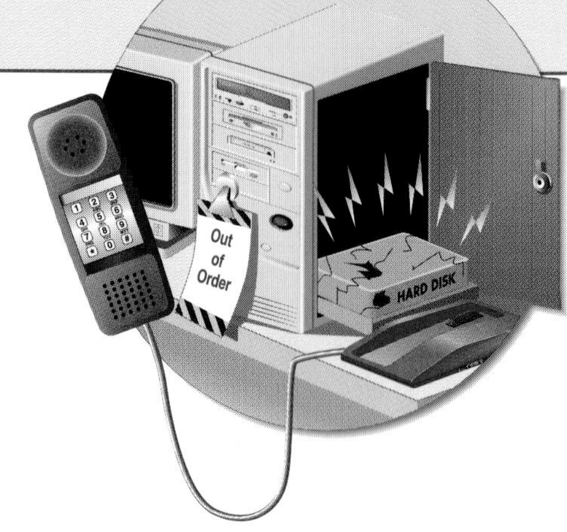

TYPES OF WARRANTY SERVICE

The warranty determines the type of warranty service you are eligible for, but a telephone technical support representative may determine the type of warranty service you receive.

On-Site Service

With on-site service, a technician comes to your home to repair or replace a product. On-site service is usually available when you buy a complete computer system. On-site technicians often carry spare parts and can usually fix problems promptly.

Ship-In Service

With ship-in service, you must send a computer or component to the manufacturer to be repaired or replaced. Many manufacturers require that you get an authorization number from a technical support representative before returning a product, and that you ship the product in the original packaging. You may also have to pay the shipping costs, which can be expensive.

Carry-In Service

Carry-in service means that you must take a computer or component to the manufacturer or the store where you purchased it to be repaired or replaced. You will usually have to leave the product for a number of days before it is repaired.

Computer Blowou
Sale 25% OFF
On all in stock software
Sale 10% OFF
On all in printers
Sale 10% OFF
On all in stock monitors
Sale 10% OFF
On all in stock computers
Monitor
Monitor
Monitor
PRINTER
Includes NetBEUI Protocol
Internet Explorer

CHAPTER 8

PURCHASE A NEW COMPUTER

Are you wondering what factors you should consider before purchasing a new computer? This chapter compares brand-name and clone computers, outlines specifications and standards and shows you how to build your own computer.

BRAND-NAME AND CLONE COMPUTERS

When purchasing a new computer, you must decide whether a brand-name or clone computer will best suit your needs.

Brand-Name

A brand-name computer is a computer made by a large computer manufacturer, such as IBM, Dell or Compaq. Brand-name computers contain only components made or approved by the manufacturer. Most computers that are sold are brand-name computers.

Clone

A clone computer was originally a computer that was not manufactured by IBM but was compatible with the first IBM personal computer. The term clone computer now refers to any computer that is not made by a large computer manufacturer.

Clone computers are becoming more popular because they can contain a variety of components from different manufacturers. This allows you to specify exactly which components you want a computer to contain.

CHOOSE A COMPUTER

Compatibility

You can upgrade a clone computer more easily than a brand-name computer because a clone computer can support a wider range of components from a variety of different manufacturers. The components in a brand-name computer are often specially designed and expensive to replace, which makes upgrading a brand-name computer more difficult.

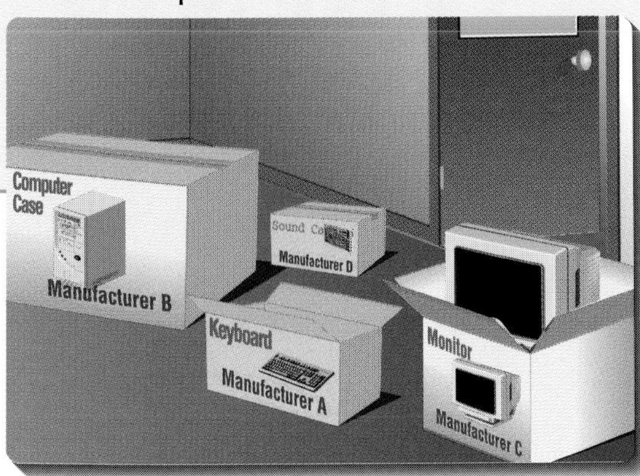

Reliability

Brand-name computers tend to be more reliable than clone computers because the large brand-name computer manufacturers have very rigorous quality control.

Cost

Brand-name computers are usually more expensive than clone computers. Although clone computers are less expensive, they are not necessarily of lower quality.

After-Sale Service

Brand-name computers usually come with better after-sale service than clone computers. Brand-name computer manufacturers usually offer an extended warranty, technical support and software support for programs packaged with the computer. This kind of after-sale service is often not available for clone computers.

Where you should buy a computer depends on your budget, whether you want a brand-name or clone computer and the type of after-sale service you require.

You should buy a computer from a business with a good reputation that has been in operation for a number of years.

Manufacturers

Many manufacturers sell computers directly to the public over the telephone or on the Internet. Buying directly from a manufacturer is usually less expensive than buying from a store. You can have the manufacturer build the computer to your specifications, but you are limited to only the components the manufacturer offers. Most manufacturers offer telephone and online technical support services, as well as repair services.

Computer Chain Stores

You can find computer chain stores in most major cities. These stores offer a wide selection of brand-name products from popular manufacturers. Chain stores tend to be more expensive than other types of stores, but usually offer good after-sale service, including introductory training classes, technical support and repair services.

Independent Computer Stores

Most independent computer stores sell less expensive clone computers and usually do not offer a wide selection of brand-name products. Independent computer stores can be an excellent source of affordable computers, but may not provide adequate after-sale service.

Department Stores

Office supply, electronic and warehouse-type department stores often have a section that sells computers. Most department stores offer brand-name computers at reduced prices, but usually do not have knowledgeable staff to answer your questions or give advice. Some department stores may provide technical support and on-site repair services.

Online and Mail-Order Companies

Most online and mail-order companies offer computers at discounted prices. Some online and mail-order companies sell only brand-name computers, while others also offer less expensive clones. Many online and mail-order companies offer telephone and online technical support services, but you may have to deal directly with the manufacturer for repairs.

You can find advertisements for reputable online and mail-order companies in most major computer publications.

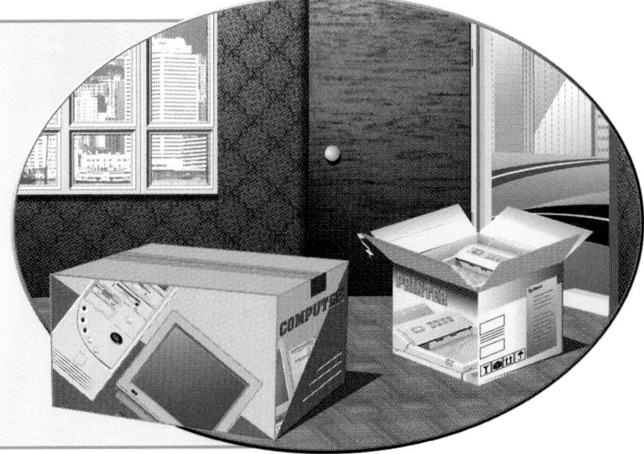

The options and features you should choose when buying a computer depend on how you plan to use the computer. There are three main uses of computers—basic, office and home.

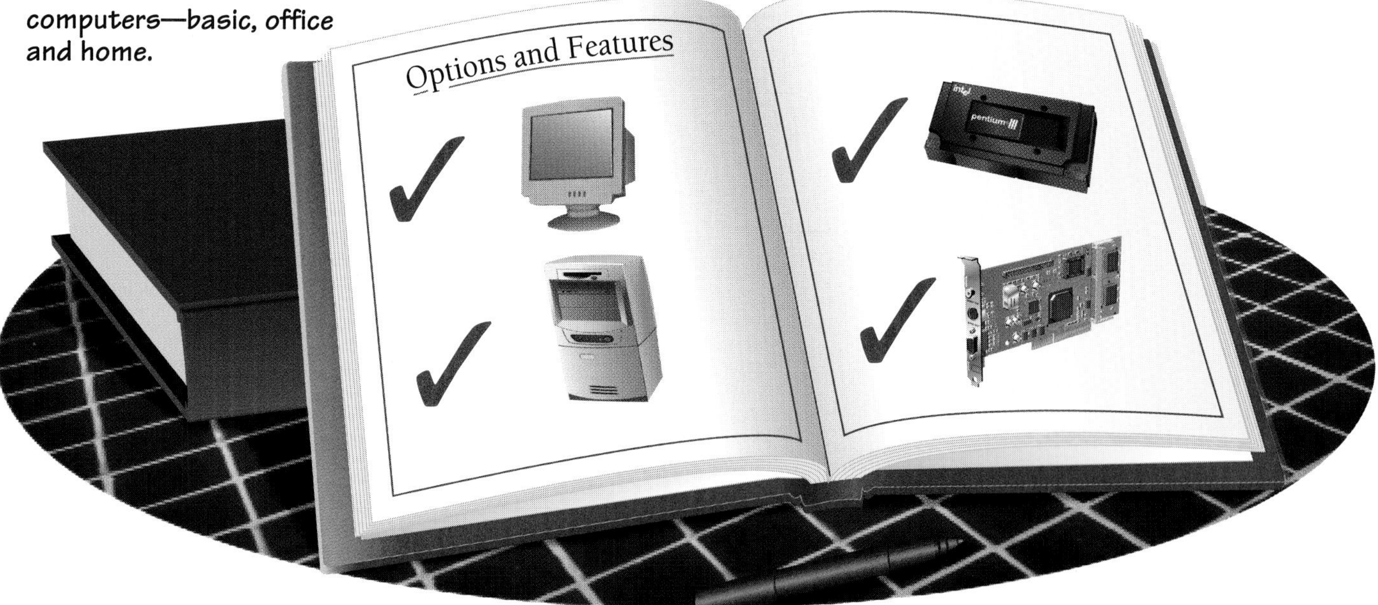

BASIC USE

An entry-level, or basic, computer is usually suitable for people new to computing. If you need a computer to perform simple tasks such as exchanging e-mail and browsing the World Wide Web, consider buying a computer with at least the specifications listed here.

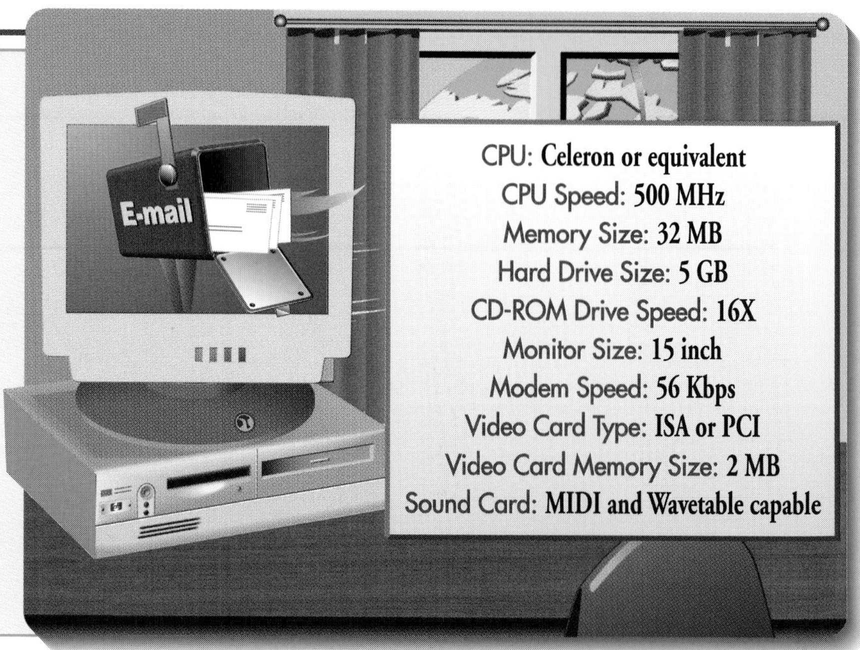

E-mail
CPU: Celeron or equivalent
CPU Speed: 500 MHz
Memory Size: 32 MB
Hard Drive Size: 5 GB
CD-ROM Drive Speed: 16X
Monitor Size: 15 inch
Modem Speed: 56 Kbps
Video Card Type: ISA or PCI
Video Card Memory Size: 2 MB
Sound Card: MIDI and Wavetable capable

OFFICE USE

Many office computers do not need to be very powerful, since they are used mostly for word processing and spreadsheet applications. If you need a computer to perform general office tasks, consider buying a computer with at least the specifications listed here.

HOME USE

Most home computers need to be powerful because they are often used for playing games and running multimedia applications. When buying a computer for home use, consider buying a computer with at least the specifications listed here.

CPU: Pentium III or equivalent
CPU Speed: 800 MHz
Memory Size: 64 MB
Hard Drive Size: 10 GB
DVD-ROM Drive Speed: 12X
Monitor Size: 15 inch
Modem Speed: 56 Kbps
Video Card Type: PCI or AGP
Video Card Memory Size: 16 MB
Sound Card: MIDI and Wavetable capable

PERSONAL COMPUTER STANDARDS

There are several standards that specify the components manufacturers should include in personal computers. You should purchase a computer that meets or exceeds the minimum requirements specified by the current standard.

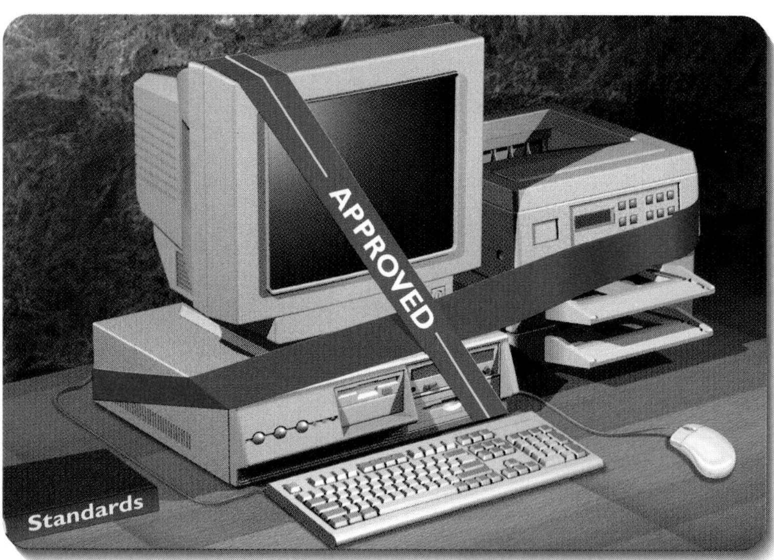

New standards are established regularly to reflect the latest developments in the computer industry. The PC 2001 standard is the most recent computer standard from Microsoft and Intel. For more information about the PC 2001 standard, visit the Web site at www.pcdesguide.org/pc2001/default.htm.

Compatibility

Personal Computer (PC) standards allow hardware and software created by different manufacturers to work together. By following a PC standard, a software manufacturer can be confident that its applications will operate properly on a computer that meets the same PC standard.

Development

PC standards help define short-term trends in the computer industry, which allows manufacturers to plan the development of new products more effectively. For example, many hardware manufacturers are developing USB-compatible devices, such as removable storage devices, to take advantage of the USB ports that are now built into new computers.

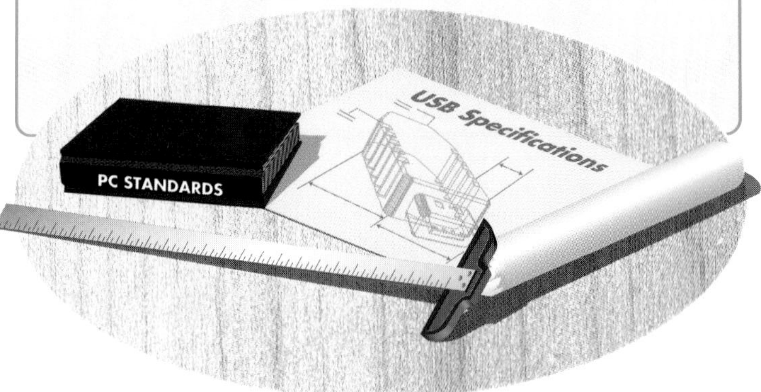

PC 2001 STANDARD

CPU Speed

Desktop computers must have a minimum CPU speed of 667 MHz. Portable computers must have a minimum CPU speed of 400 MHz.

Cache

Computers must have a minimum cache size of 128 KB.

Memory

Computers must have at least 64 MB of RAM.

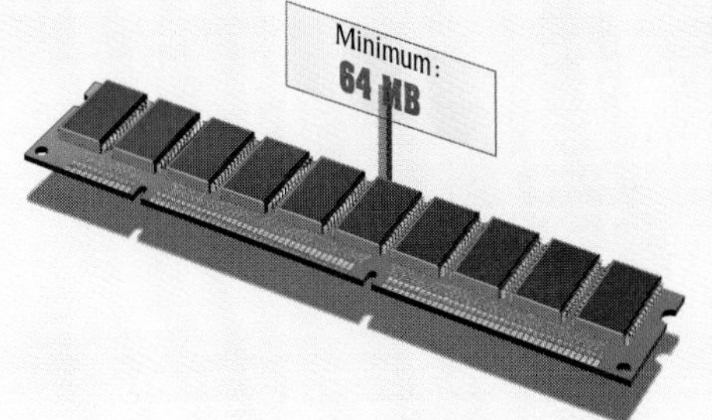

Power Management

Computers must support advanced power management features.

USB

Desktop and portable computers must have a USB bus. Desktop computers must have least 2 USB ports, while portable computers must have at least 1 USB port.

Graphics Support

Desktop computers must be able to support a minimum video resolution of 1024 x 768 and must include video playback capabilities.

Storage Devices

Desktop and portable computers must include a hard drive. Desktop computers must also include a CD-ROM or DVD-ROM drive.

A portable computer is a small, lightweight computer you can easily transport. A battery or electrical outlet supplies the power for a portable computer.

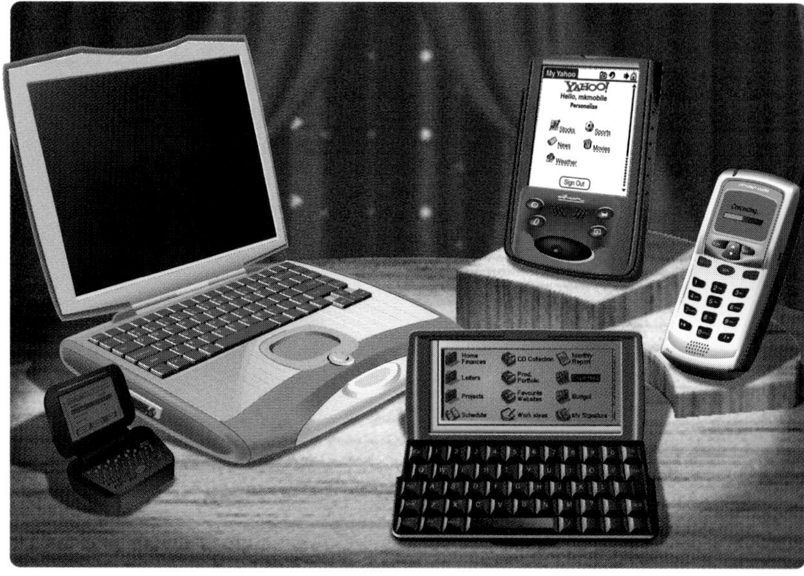

Because portable computers are much smaller than desktop computers, they require special consideration when being upgraded or repaired.

TYPES OF PORTABLE COMPUTERS

Notebook

A notebook computer, also called a laptop computer, is the most popular type of portable computer. You can buy a notebook computer with the same capabilities as a desktop computer, although notebook computers are more expensive.

A notebook computer has a built-in keyboard, pointing device and screen, eliminating the need for cables to connect these devices to the notebook.

Docking Station

You can use a docking station to connect many additional devices to a notebook at once. A docking station can also provide additional features to a notebook computer, such as networking capabilities and a full-size monitor and keyboard.

Handheld

A handheld computer is a portable computer that is small enough to carry in your hand.

Handheld computers are capable of storing thousands of addresses, appointments and memos. You can use a handheld computer to exchange electronic mail, send and receive faxes and browse the World Wide Web. Some handheld computers also come with word processing and spreadsheet applications.

You can connect a handheld computer to a desktop computer to exchange data between the two computers.

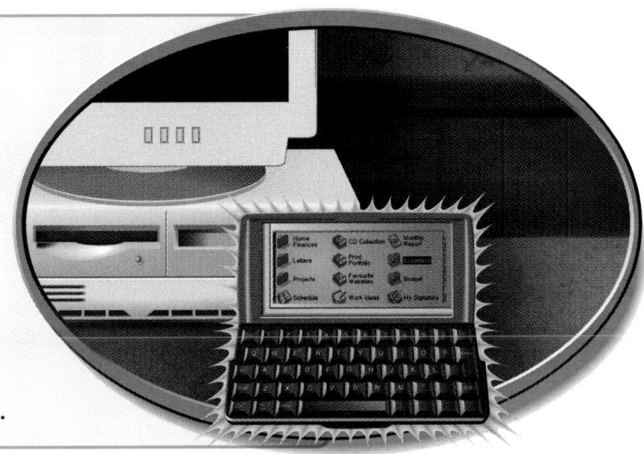

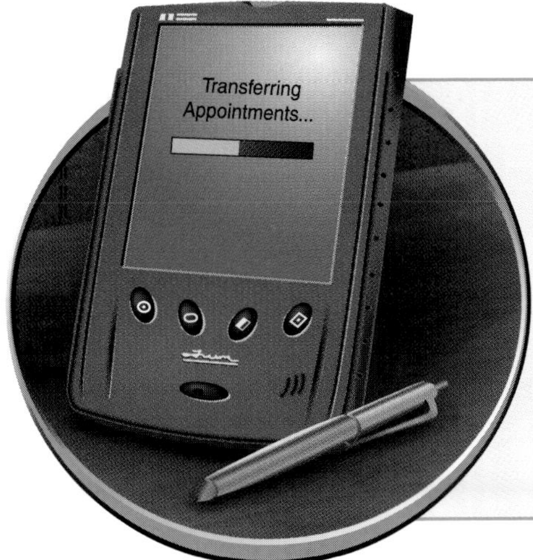

PDA

A Personal Digital Assistant (PDA) is a small handheld computer that is often used as an electronic organizer. You can connect a PDA to a desktop computer to exchange data between the two computers.

PDAs have many of the same features as handheld computers, but they do not have a built-in keyboard. You use a stylus, or electronic pen, to input data into a PDA.

Other Handheld Computers

Some mobile phones and pagers now offer computing capabilities. For example, these devices may offer scheduling software and allow you to access the Internet and exchange electronic mail.

SET UP AND TROUBLESHOOT

Set Up a Portable Computer

Most notebook computers use the same setup procedures as desktop computers. For example, before you can use a notebook computer, you must install an operating system. You may also need to adjust the computer's settings.

Handheld computers and PDAs usually have an operating system already installed. Most also have a fixed set of features that do not require you to change any settings.

Troubleshoot

If you are having problems with a notebook computer, you can use the same diagnostic programs you would use on a desktop computer. A diagnostic program may be able to help you locate and repair problems when a notebook computer malfunctions. Handheld computers and PDAs often have built-in diagnostic programs. For information about diagnostic programs, see page 164.

If you are having problems with the software you are using on a notebook computer, you can use the same software troubleshooting methods you would use on a desktop computer. For information about troubleshooting software problems, see page 162.

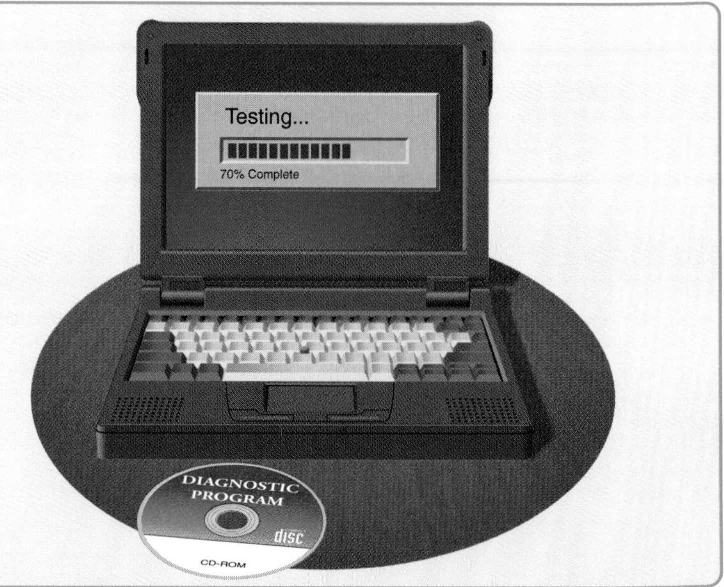

UPGRADE AND REPAIR

Upgrade

Portable computers have limited upgrade options. Most notebook computers can easily accommodate a larger hard drive or more memory, but it is more difficult to upgrade features such as the screen or processor.

Many components are designed for a specific type of notebook computer. When purchasing new components, make sure you get components that are compatible with your notebook.

Handheld computers and PDAs usually cannot be upgraded. In order to take advantage of newer features and capabilities, you may need to replace the handheld computer or PDA with a newer model.

Repair

A portable computer is more difficult to repair than a desktop computer. Compared to desktop computers, portable computers are more likely to have physical problems, such as broken cases and screens, that you cannot repair yourself.

Portable computers also have smaller internal components which are packed into a much smaller space. This can make it difficult to access components in a portable computer. Rather than attempting to repair a portable computer yourself, you should take it to a repair service. For information about repair services, see page 168.

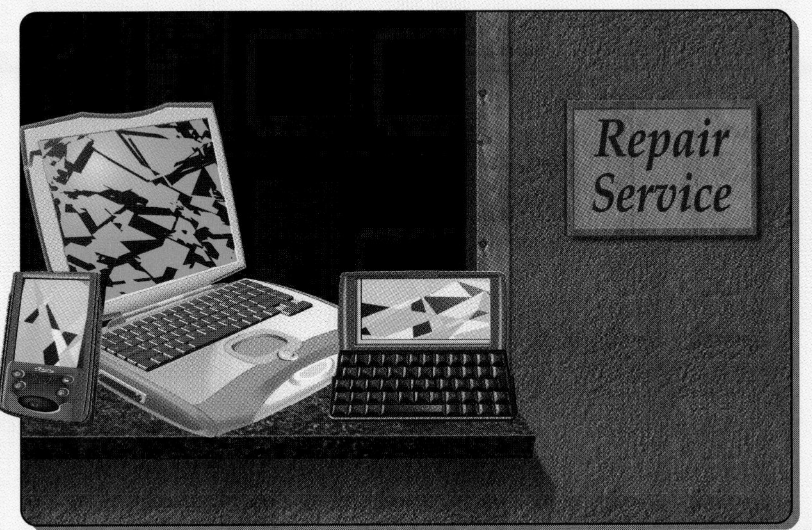

BUILD A COMPUTER

Building your own computer allows you to choose exactly which components you want to include.

Although the cost of building your own computer is only slightly less than purchasing a complete computer system, you will have a much better understanding of how a computer works when you finish.

BUILD A COMPUTER

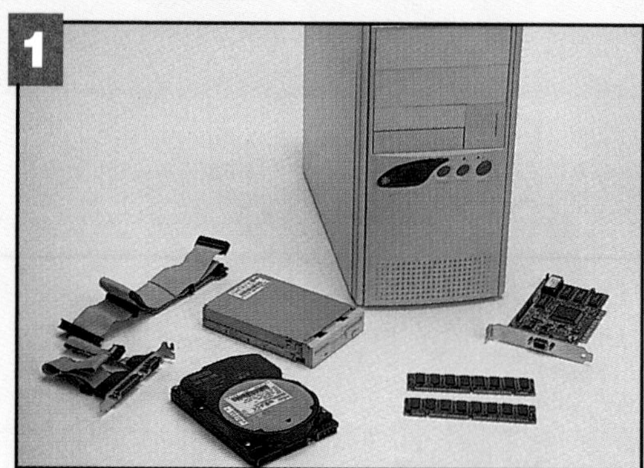

1 Determine and purchase the computer components and devices you need.

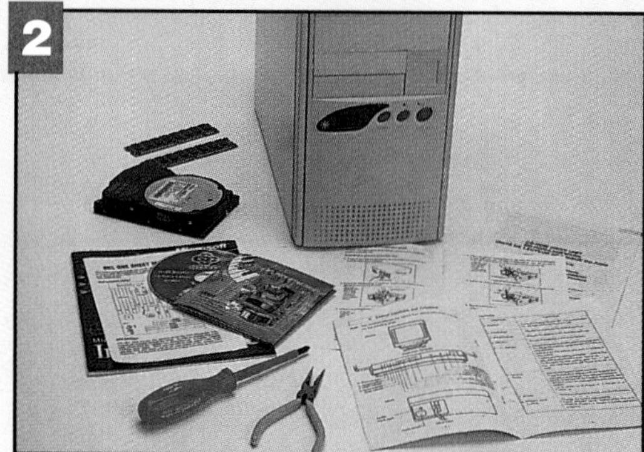

2 Gather the reference material and computer tools you need. For information about reference material, see page 14. For information about computer tools, see page 4.

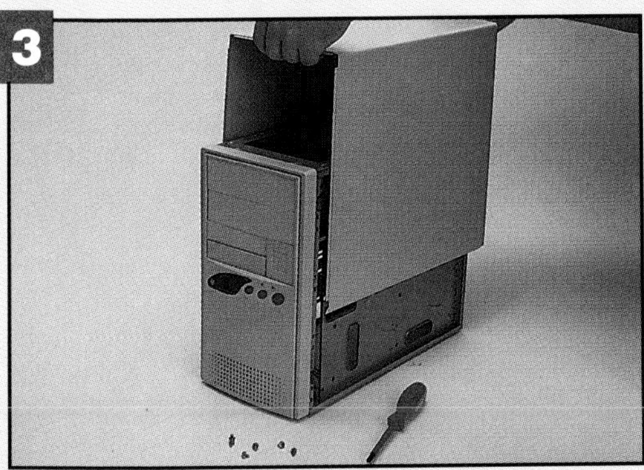

3 Remove the cover from the computer case. For information about computer cases, see page 30.

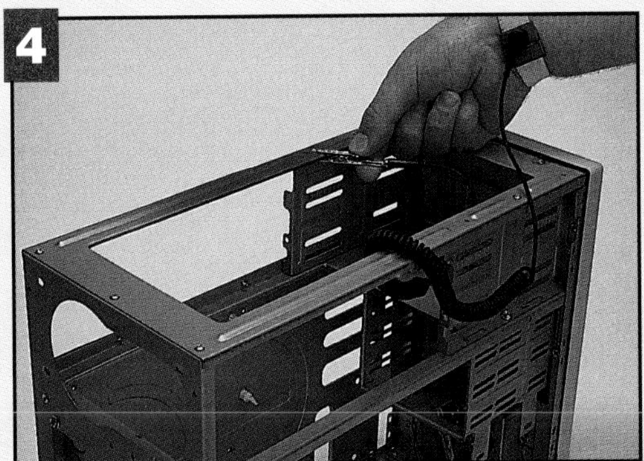

4 To prevent static electricity from damaging computer components ground yourself and the computer case. For information about grounding, see page 6.

5 Install the power supply in the computer case. For information about power supplies, see page 38.

6 Install the memory modules on the system board. For information about memory, see page 46.

7 Install the CPU on the system board. For information about CPUs, see page 42.

CONTINUED

BUILD A COMPUTER (CONTINUED)

Install the system board in the computer case. For information about system boards, see page 32.

Install the storage devices, such as a hard drive and floppy drive or CD-ROM drive, in the computer case. For information about storage devices, see page 120 to 139.

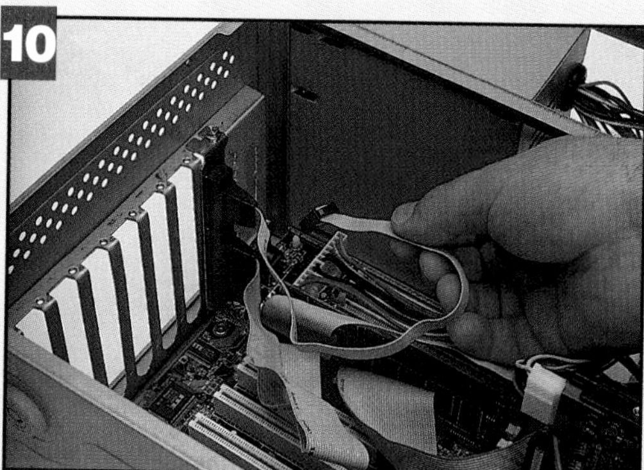

If necessary, install the internal connectors, such as a parallel or serial port, on the system board. For information about internal connectors, see page 12.

Install the video card on the system board. For information about video cards, see page 70.

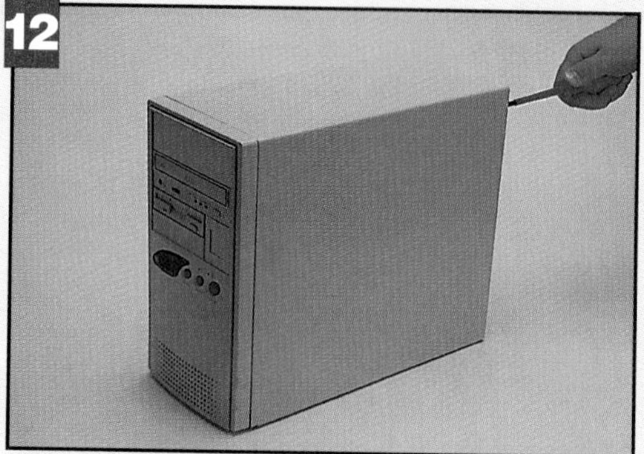

Replace the cover on the computer case.

Connect the monitor, pointing device and keyboard to the computer. For information about monitors, see page 74. For information about pointing devices, see page 60. For information about keyboards, see page 62.

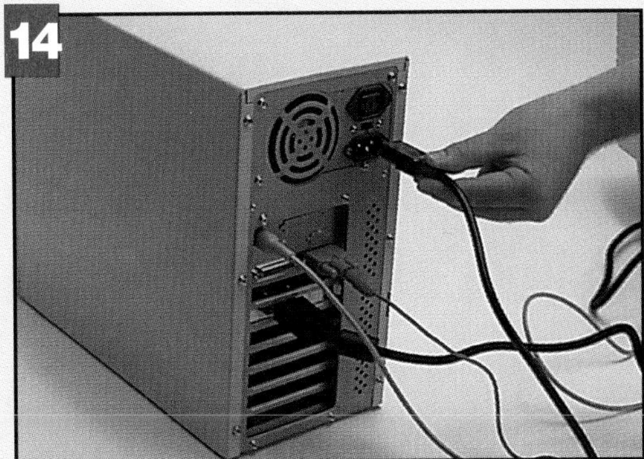

Attach the power cable to the back of the computer and then plug the power cable into an electrical outlet on the wall. Then turn on the computer.

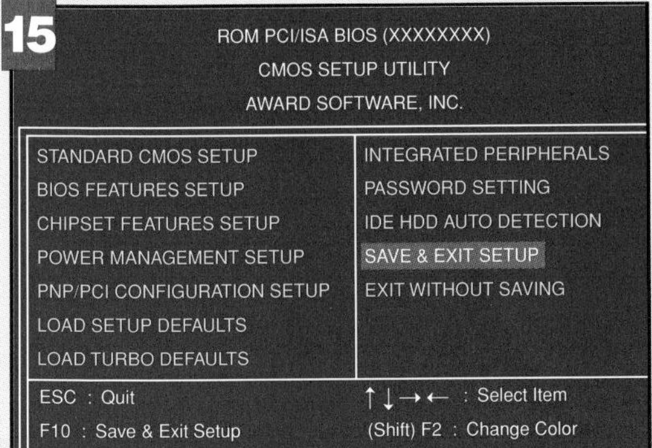

If necessary, adjust the computer's BIOS settings. For information about computer settings, see page 146.

Install the operating system. For information about operating systems, see page 152.

Install any additional external devices, such as a modem or removable storage device.

CHAPTER 9

CREATE A HOME NETWORK

Do you want to set up a home network to share information, resources and Internet connections between several computers? This chapter introduces you to network devices and protocols, as well as teaches you how to set up and test a home network.

If you have more than one computer at home, you can set up a network to share information and resources among the computers.

Set Up

You must install a Network Interface Card (NIC) in each computer you want to connect to the network. Cables are required to physically connect each computer to the network. Your network may also require a hub, which provides a central location where the cables on the network meet. If you want computers on the network to be able to connect to the Internet, one computer will need a modem or an additional network interface card to connect to the Internet.

Alternatives

There are alternatives to using network interface cards to create a network. If you are connecting two computers that use the Windows operating system, you can create a network using the Direct Cable Connection feature. This feature allows you to connect the computers using a cable that connects the computers' printer ports. While this network alternative is useful for simple file sharing, it is not appropriate for tasks such as accessing the Internet or playing multi-player games.

ADVANTAGES

Share Information and Resources

A home network enables multiple family members to share information such as schedules and resources such as storage devices. Home networks are also useful for re-using old computers and equipment. While an older computer may not have the power to play the latest games, it may still be adequate for tasks such as printer sharing.

Share an Internet Connection

If one computer on a home network has a connection to the Internet, then all computers attached to the network can share the connection to access the Internet at the same time. This is especially useful if the Internet connection is a high-speed connection, such as a cable modem or a DSL line.

Games

One of the most popular reasons for creating a home network is to take advantage of many of today's games that allow multiple players to play a game on a network.

Intelligent Devices

One of the trends of the future is the use of home networks to control intelligent devices in the home. For example, items such as lighting and security systems can be controlled using a computer. Setting up a home network will help you manage these devices.

ETHERNET NETWORK INTERFACE CARDS

You must install a Network Interface Card (NIC) in each computer you want to connect to a home network. Ethernet network interface cards are perfect for home network use.

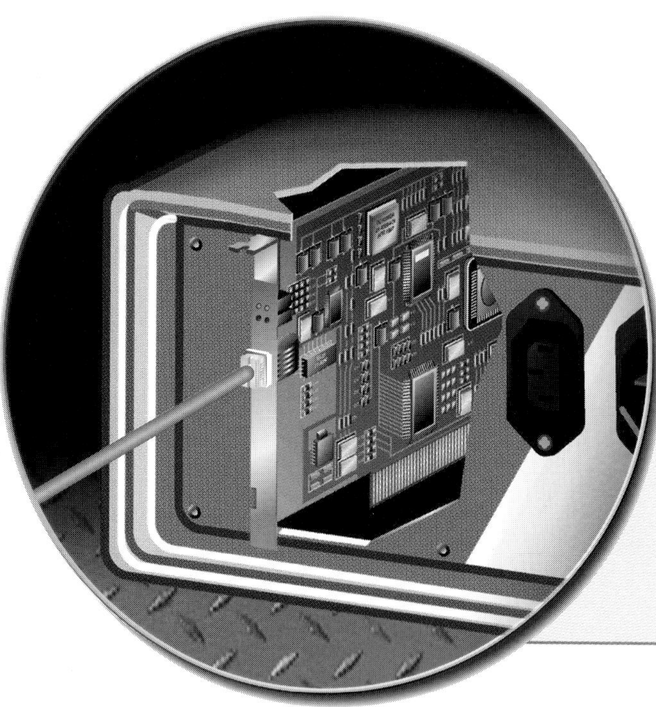

Network interface cards control the flow of information between the network and the computers. For information about installing a network interface card, see page 108.

CABLE TYPES

The network interface card you choose must be compatible with the type of cable your network will use.

Coaxial Cable

Coaxial cable is similar to television cable. Home networks connected by coaxial cable do not require any other hardware besides network interface cards, but it can be difficult to connect computers in different parts of the house.

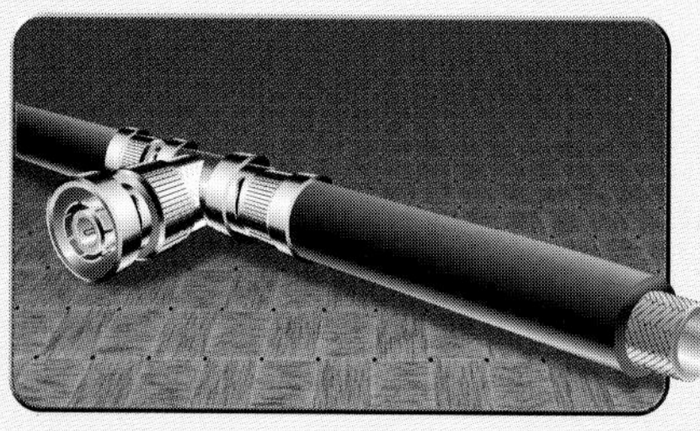

Twisted Pair Cable

Twisted pair cable is similar to telephone cable and requires the use of a network hub to connect multiple computers. Although a network created using twisted pair cable is initially more expensive, it is easier to manage and expand than a network that uses coaxial cable.

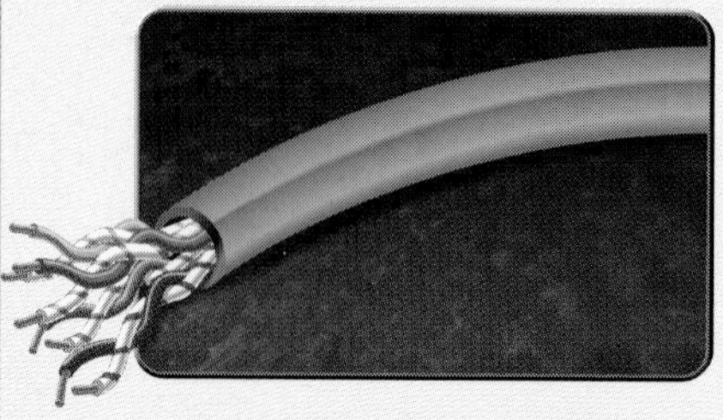

Crossover Cable

Crossover cable is a type of twisted pair cable that can connect two computers without the use of a hub. Crossover cables are available at most good electronics stores.

CHOOSE AN ETHERNET NETWORK INTERFACE CARD

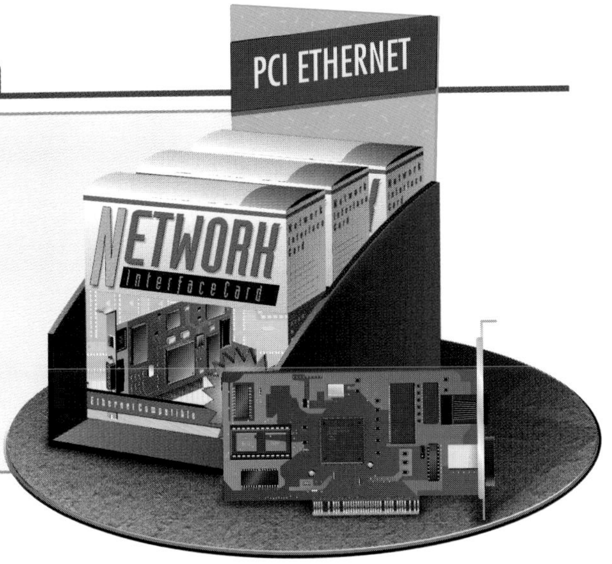

Network Interface Card Types

The type of NIC you require depends on several factors. The NIC must be compatible with the expansion slot in your computer where you will place the card. If you need the NIC to be portable, you can use a card that connects to the printer port of a computer instead of being installed in the computer. If you use a notebook computer, the computer may have a built-in network interface card or a PC Card network interface card.

Speed

Ethernet network interface cards can operate at speeds up to 1000 Mbps, but for most home networks, a speed of 10 Mbps is more than adequate. If the network will be used to frequently transfer large files and videos, you may want to consider an NIC with a speed of 100 Mbps.

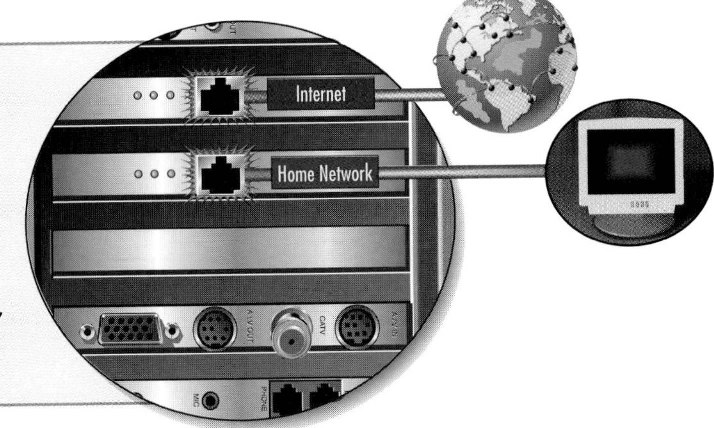

Using Multiple NICs

You may need to install more than one network interface card in a computer. For example, many high-speed Internet connections require the use of a dedicated network interface card. You also need a NIC for each network you plan to connect a computer to. When installing network interface cards, if the cards are not automatically configured, you must ensure that the resource settings for the cards do not conflict.

An Ethernet hub is a device used to connect all computers on a home network together.

A hub provides a central location where all the cables on a home network come together.

Hubs and High-Speed Connections

High-speed Internet connection devices cannot simply be connected to a hub on a home network. The devices must be connected to a computer that is connected to the hub. Some specialized high-speed devices, however, can incorporate an Ethernet hub. For information about the availability of these combined devices in your area, contact your Internet service provider, cable company or telecommunications company.

Wiring a House

In most recently built houses, it is relatively easy to run network cables through the walls to create network connections in different locations in the house. Each connection allows you to connect a computer to the hub. Connectors and cabling are available at most good electronic stores. For difficult installations, a professional cable installer should be consulted.

CHOOSE AN ETHERNET HUB

Speed

The speed of the hub determines the speed of the network interface cards that can be used on the home network. The speed of the network interface cards must not exceed the speed of the hub. For most home networks, a speed of 10 Mbps is suitable for most tasks.

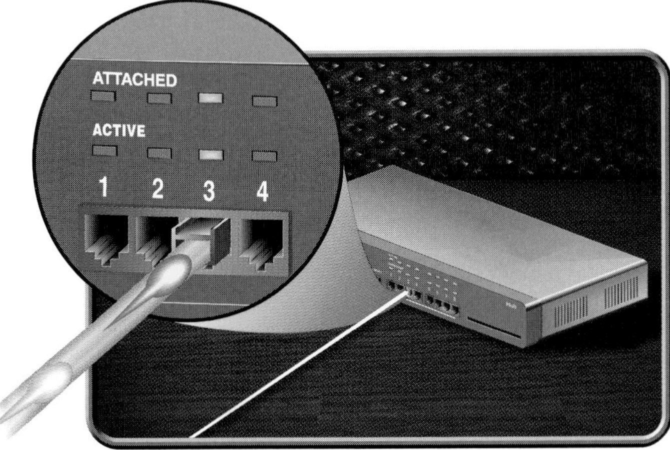

Ports

A hub contains sockets, or ports, where cables from computer devices can be plugged in. Hubs commonly have 4, 8, 16 or 24 ports. You should ensure that the number of ports on the hub meets your current and future needs.

Cable Rating

Ethernet hubs used in the home use twisted pair cable and RJ-45 connectors to attach to the network interface card and hub. Twisted pair cable is rated for different speeds. Category 5 (CAT5) rated cable is capable of transmitting information at speeds of 100 Mbps. You should use cables and connectors that are rated CAT5 to ensure that your network will be easy to upgrade in the future.

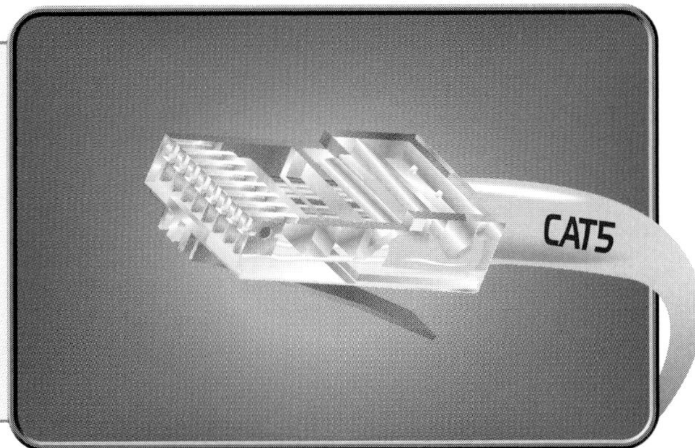

NETWORK PROTOCOLS

Once the computers and hub on a home network are connected, you need to install protocols to allow the devices on the network to exchange information. Most operating systems include the protocols you need to install.

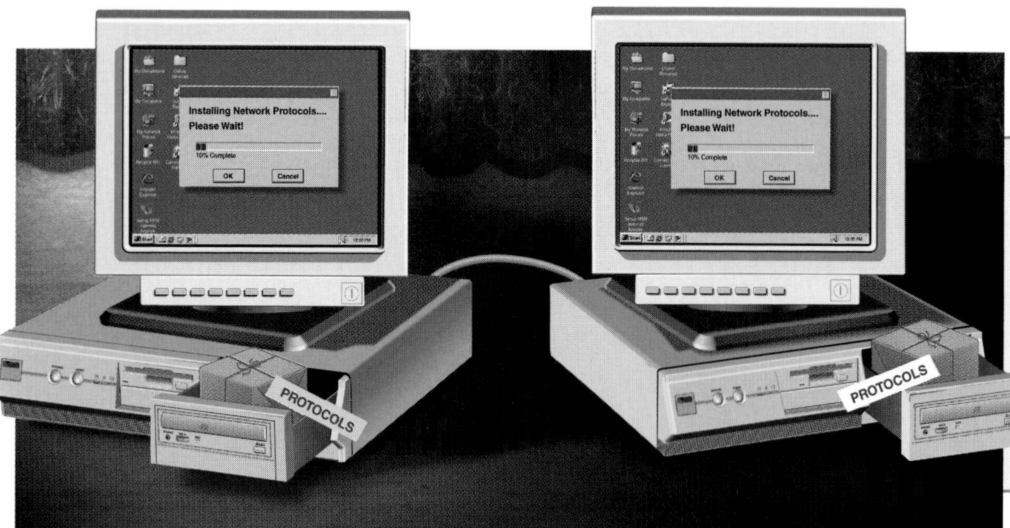

A protocol is a set of rules that determines how devices on a network communicate. Devices require specific protocols to communicate with each other. Your network may require several types of protocols to support all the devices.

TYPES OF PROTOCOLS

TCP/IP

Transmission Control Protocol/Internet Protocol (TCP/IP) is the suite of protocols that allows computers and devices to connect to the Internet. Even networks and devices that are not connected to the Internet now use TCP/IP as a standard. You should install TCP/IP so your home network will be compatible with future devices.

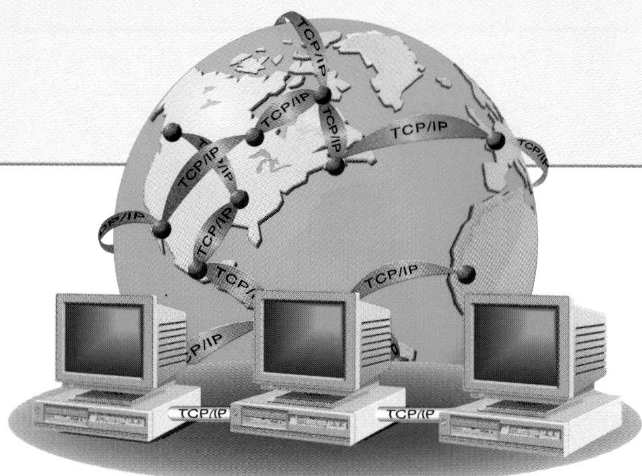

NetBEUI

NetBIOS Extended User Interface (NetBEUI), a protocol originally developed by IBM, allows computers on a Windows network to communicate. One of the benefits of using the NetBEUI protocol is that it requires very little configuration. You may only need to assign a computer and workgroup name to each computer on the network.

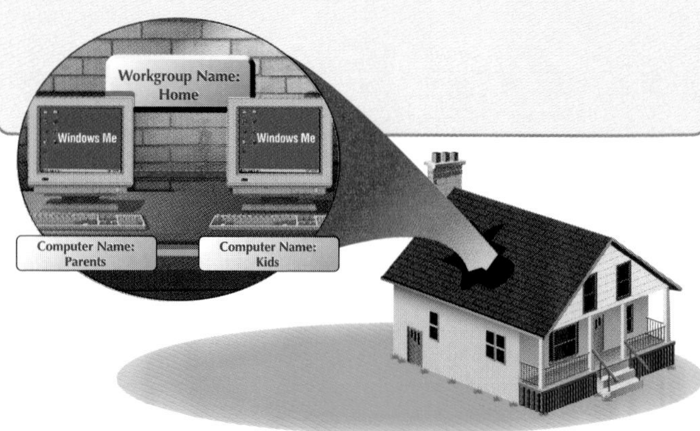

CONFIGURE TCP/IP PROTOCOLS

IP Number

On a home network that uses TCP/IP protocols, you must assign an IP number to each computer to identify the computer on the network. The first three parts of the IP number should be the same for each computer on the home network. The last part of the number should be unique for each computer. For example, the first computer on the network could have the IP number 192.168.52.1. The second computer would have the IP number 192.168.52.2.

Subnet Mask

You also need to assign a subnet mask for your home network. The subnet mask for most home networks should be set to 255.255.255.0. If your network will be connected to the Internet, your Internet Service Provider (ISP) may provide a subnet mask for your network.

Domain Name Server and Gateway

If your home network will be connected to the Internet, you may need to specify the IP number of the Domain Name Server (DNS) and gateway of your Internet service provider. Your ISP can give you the IP numbers you require.

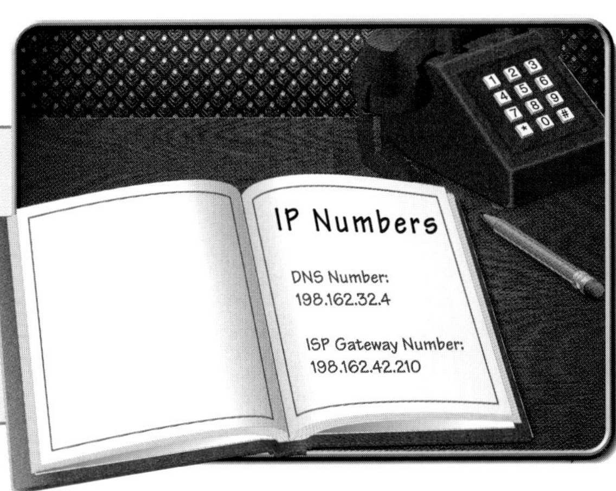

Once the entire network is installed and configured, the network should be thoroughly tested to ensure that all the devices are functioning and information is transferring properly.

Cable Tester

Faulty cables are one of the most common physical errors on a network. A cable tester is a device that allows you to verify the cable used to connect a computer to another computer or device is not broken. Each time you press the button on the cable tester, the tester verifies whether a pin on one end of a cable connects to the correct pin on the other end of the cable. This chart indicates which pins should correspond to each other for straight and crossover cables.

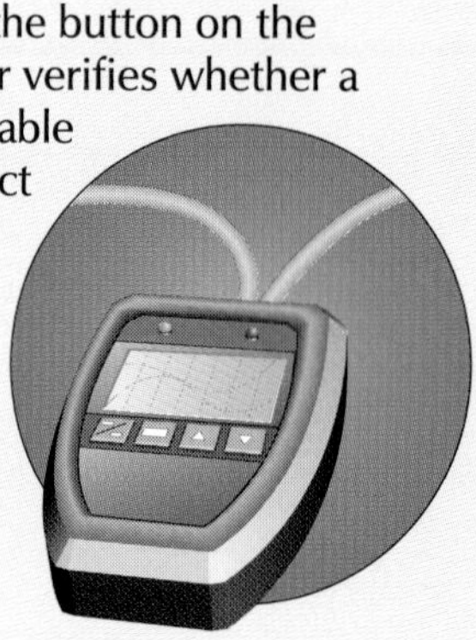

Pin Number	Straight Cable		Crossover Cable	
1	1	White/Orange	3	White/Green
2	2	Orange	6	Green
3	3	White/Green	1	White/Orange
4	4	Blue	4	Blue
5	5	White/Blue	5	White/Blue
6	6	Green	2	Orange
7	7	White/Brown	7	White/Brown
8	8	Brown	8	Brown

PING

The PING utility is an invaluable tool for establishing whether a connection between two computers or devices is functioning. PING sends information to a computer or device on a network and then reports how long it takes to receive a reply from the destination computer or device.

PING is available on computers using the TCP/IP protocol suite. To use PING, type **ping** followed by the IP number of the computer you want to contact in an MS-DOS prompt screen. If a message appears stating that the request timed out, the connection is not working.

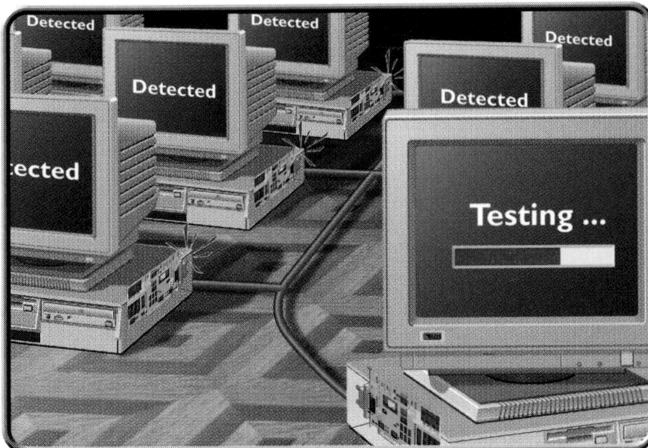

Broadcast

Many network interface cards come equipped with testing software. The software allows you to broadcast information that can be detected by similar network interface cards on the network. Broadcasts are a good way to test connections on a network.

Sniffer

If the physical connections on a network appear to be intact, you can use a sniffer program, also referred to as a protocol analyzer, to examine the information traveling along the network. A sniffer program is installed on a computer on the network and can monitor information about protocols and data on the network.

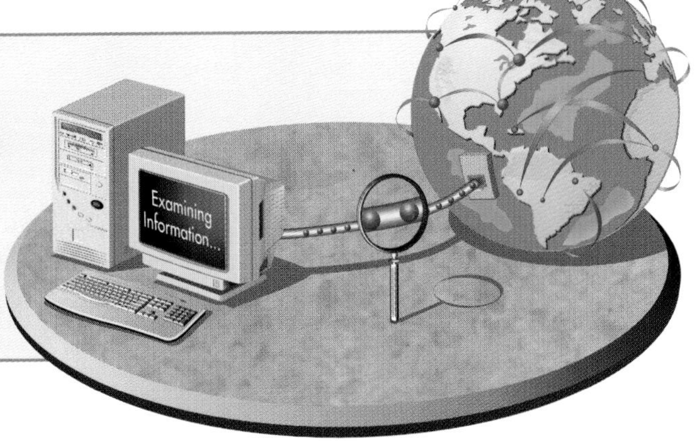

CONNECT A NETWORK TO THE INTERNET

You can set up one computer on your home network to share its connection to the Internet with other computers on the network. There is a wide variety of software available to simplify connecting a home network to the Internet.

INTERNET CONNECTION SHARING

Windows

The Internet Connection Sharing, or ICS, feature is included with Windows 98 Second Edition, Windows 2000 and Windows Me. ICS allows users of a Microsoft network to access the Internet using a single Internet connection.

UNIX

A single UNIX computer can easily be configured to connect a network to the Internet without any additional hardware or software. Many versions of UNIX, such as Red Hat Linux, are now available to the home user free of charge or at a low cost.

Third-Party Applications

You can use a program such as Qbik's WinGate or Sygate Home Network to connect a home network to the Internet if your operating system does not have built-in Internet connection sharing capabilities.

INTERNET CONNECTION SHARING CONSIDERATIONS

Share a Modem

Internet connection sharing allows any computer connected to a network to share a single modem that is connected to the Internet. This allows any computer on the network to access the Internet without having to have its own connection to the Internet and modem.

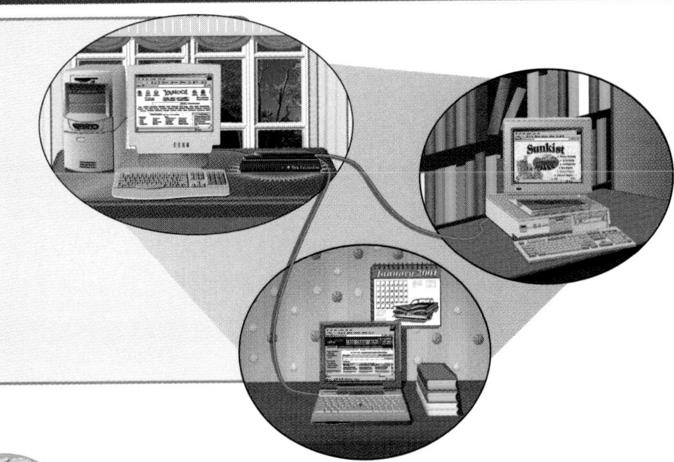

Share a High-Speed Connection

You can also share a high-speed connection, such as cable, DSL or ISDN, to access the Internet. In many cases, high-speed connections require a network interface card to connect to the high-speed device or modem. The computer with the Internet connection may require two network interface cards—one for the home network and another for the Internet connection.

ISP Account

An Internet Service Provider (ISP) is a company that provides connections to the Internet for a fee. You need only one ISP account to connect your network to the Internet. If people on the network wish to have their own e-mail accounts, each person will have to set up an e-mail address with the ISP.

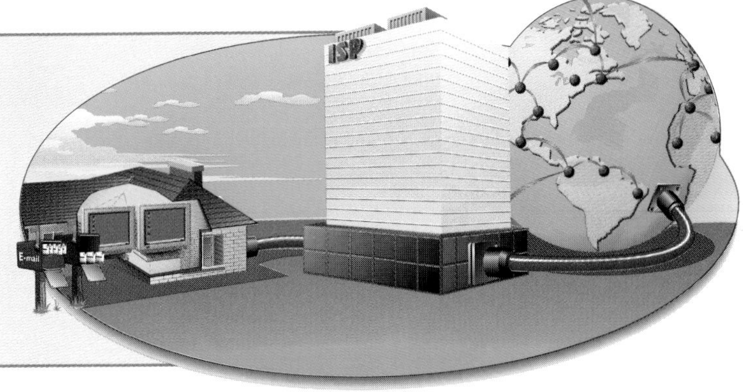

SET UP

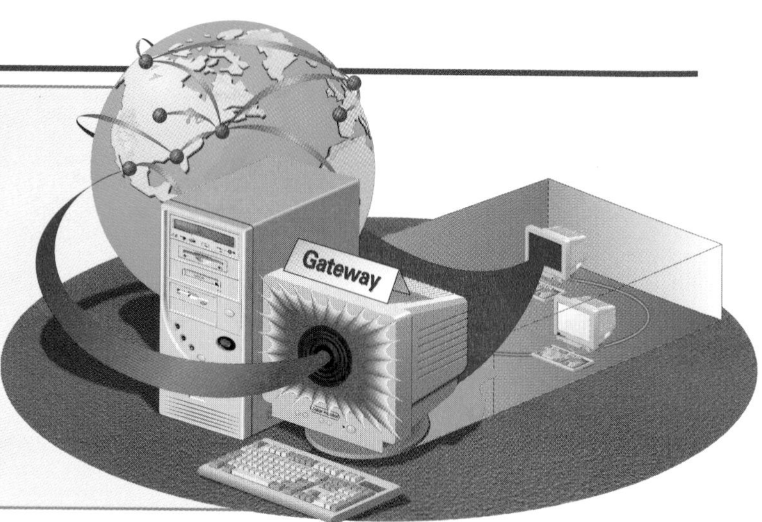

Gateway

The Internet connection sharing program is installed on the computer with the connection to the Internet, which is called the gateway computer. The gateway computer must be turned on and connected to the Internet whenever another computer on the network wants to access the Internet. Most gateway computers can be configured to connect to the Internet automatically when another computer tries to access the Internet and disconnect when there is no activity.

Client

Client software should be installed on any computer you want to use to access the gateway computer and connect to the Internet. The client software is used to configure the computer's TCP/IP settings and communicate with the gateway computer.

IP Numbers

Each computer that accesses the Internet requires its own unique IP number. The Internet connection sharing program typically sets up the IP numbers for each computer on the home network.

Multiple Platforms

Once a gateway computer has been set up to access the Internet, other computers using different operating systems can use the gateway to access the Internet. Computers running the Macintosh, DOS, UNIX and Windows operating systems can all share the Internet connection.

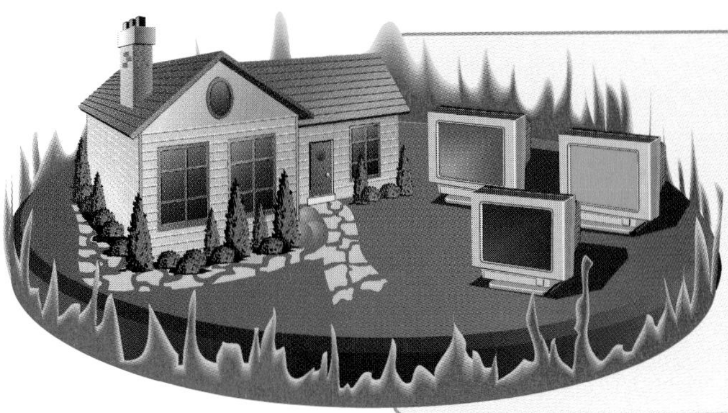

Firewalls

Many home networks that are connected to the Internet can be vulnerable to unauthorized access from other people connected to the Internet. To prevent unauthorized access to the home network, special software called a firewall can be installed. Many Internet connection sharing programs include some firewall features. You may also want to install separate firewall software on the gateway computer.

Filters

Using a single Internet connection for all the computers on a home network allows you to restrict access to specific areas of the Internet. Some Internet connection sharing programs allow you to define which Web sites users on the home network can access. This is useful if children are accessing the Internet using the home network and you wish to restrict access to inappropriate Web sites.

SET UP A HOME NETWORK

Setting up a home network is a lot less complicated than most people think.

When setting up a home network, it is a good idea to first set up all the computers and devices that will be used in one area with a good source of lighting. This will make it easier to configure and test the network prior to moving the network computers and devices to their permanent locations.

SET UP A HOME NETWORK

1 

Install the network interface cards in each computer to be connected to the network. For information about network interface cards, see page 108.

2 

Connect the network cables to the network interface card in each computer. For information about network cables, see page 196.

3 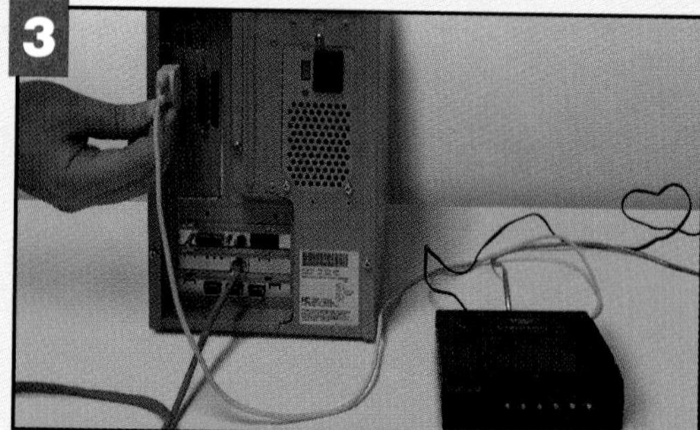

Connect any external modems or high-speed devices to the computers.

4 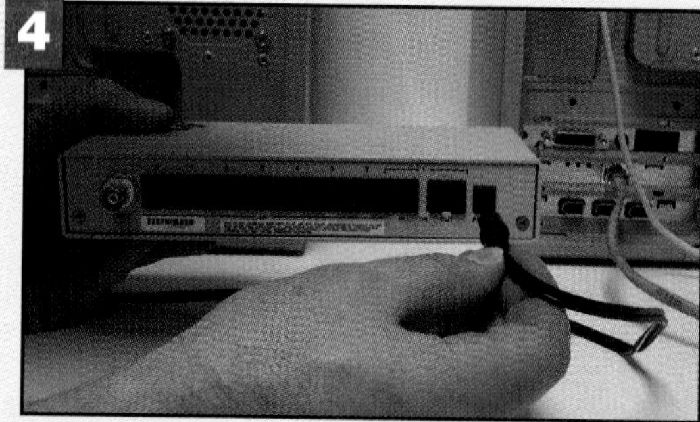

Set up the Ethernet hub for the network. For information about Ethernet hubs, see page 198.

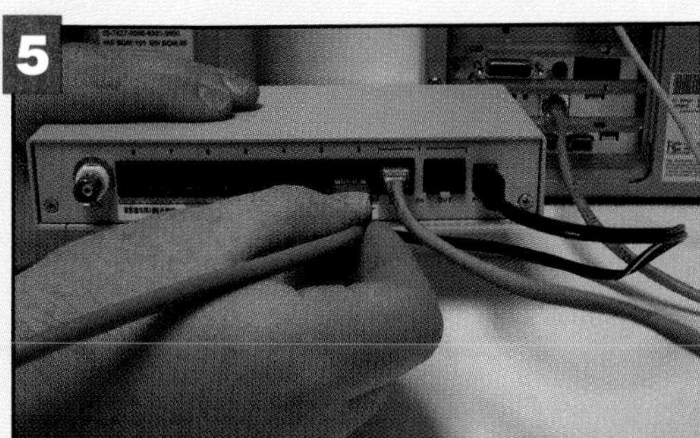

Connect the network cable from each computer or device to the Ethernet hub.

Turn on the Ethernet hub and verify that it is functioning.

Turn on each computer or device connected to the hub.

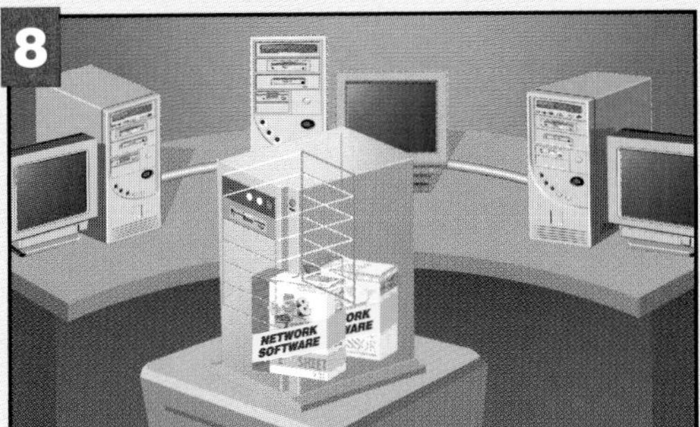

Install and configure any necessary network software on the computers, such as Internet connection sharing software.

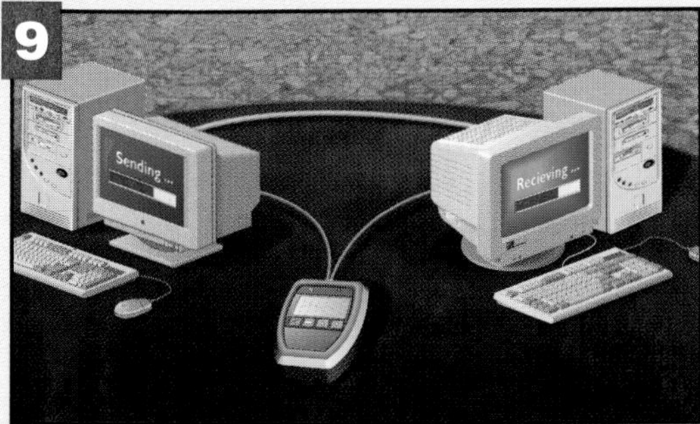

Test the network connections. For information about testing network connections, see page 202.

Once the network is working properly, move the computers and devices to their permanent locations in the home. Then reconnect all cables, if necessary and retest the connections.

S T U V W X Y Z
A B C
Manufacturers' Contact Information
JVC Digital Storage Systems
Key Tronic
Kingston Technology
Labtec
Lexmark
LG Electronics
Logitech
MAG InnoVision
Matrox Graphics
Maxtor
McAfee.com
214
Micron Technology
Microsoft
Mitsumi Electronics
NEC Technologies
Nikon
Ontrack Data International
Palm
Panasonic
Philips Electronics
PowerQuest
SOYO Computer
Symantec
Tecmar Technology
Toshiba
Tripp Lite Power Protection

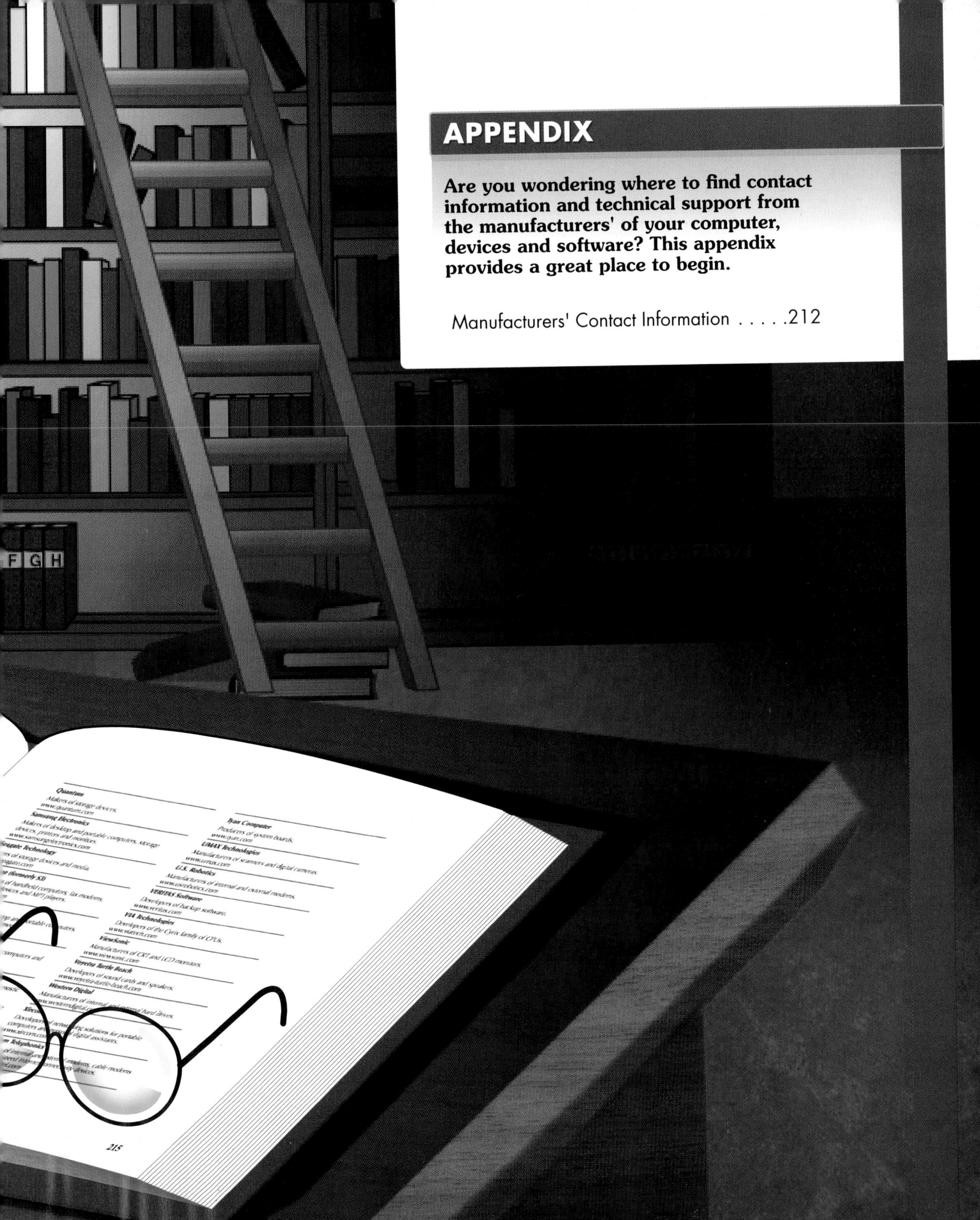

APPENDIX

Are you wondering where to find contact information and technical support from the manufacturers' of your computer, devices and software? This appendix provides a great place to begin.

MANUFACTURERS' CONTACT INFORMATION

Most manufacturers of computers and computer devices have Web sites that provide information about their products. You can visit a manufacturer's Web site to obtain information and technical support.

3Com

Providers of home networking devices and DSL modems.
www.3com.com

3dfx Interactive

Makers of the Voodoo family of 3D graphics cards.
www.3dfx.com

3Dlabs

Leading suppliers of graphics accelerator hardware and software.
www.3dlabs.com

ABIT Computer

Producers of jumperless system boards.
www.abit-usa.com

Acer

Manufacturers of desktop and portable computers.
www.acer.com

Adaptec

Makers of network storage devices.
www.adaptec.com

Agfa

Manufacturers of digital equipment, such as scanners and digital cameras.
www.agfa.com

Amazon.com

Online retailer offering handheld computers and computer software.
www.amazon.com

AMD (Advanced Micro Devices)

Developers of the Athlon family of CPUs.
www.amd.com

America Online

The world's largest Internet service provider.
www.aol.com

American Megatrends

Producers of AMIBIOS and system boards.
www.ami.com

American Power Conversion

Providers of uninterruptible power supply (UPS) systems.
www.apcc.com

Apple Computer

Developers of Macintosh computers and accessories and QuickTime multimedia software.
www.apple.com

AST Computers

Manufacturers of desktop and portable computers.
www.ast.com

ASUSTek Computer

Producers of system boards and portable computers.
www.asus.com

ATI Technologies

Suppliers of 3D graphics and multimedia technology.
www.atitech.com

Belden

Manufacturers of computer cable and cord products.
www.belden.com

Black Box Network Services

Providers of network services.
www.blackbox.com

Canon

Manufacturers of printers, scanners and digital cameras.
www.canon.com

CDW (Computer Discount Warehouse)

Online and mail-order retailers of computer products.
www.cdw.com

Compaq

Manufacturers of desktop and portable computers.
www.compaq.com

CompUSA

Online and mail-order retailer of computer products.
www.compusa.com

CompuServe

Internet service provider with worldwide presence.
www.compuserve.com

Corel

Developers of CorelDRAW and WordPerfect software and Corel LINUX operating system.
www.corel.com

Creative Labs

Manufacturers of the SoundBlaster family of sound cards, as well as CD-ROM and DVD-ROM drives, MP3 players and video cards.
www.creative.com

CTX International

Makers of CRT and LCD monitors.
www.ctxintl.com

Dell Computer

Manufacturers of desktop and portable computers.
www.dell.com

DTK Computer

Producers of desktop computers, system boards and monitors.
www.dtkcomputer.com

Duracell

Manufacturers of high-performance batteries.
www.duracell.com

EarthWeb

Providers of online services to businesses as well as comprehensive reference libraries.
www.earthweb.com

Eastman Kodak

Developers and manufacturers of digital cameras and photo CDs.
www.kodak.com

Epson

Makers of printers and digital cameras.
www.epson.com

Exabyte

Makers of backup devices and media.
www.exabyte.com

Gateway

Manufacturers and retailers of desktop and portable computers.
www.gateway.com

Gigabyte Technology

Producers of system boards.
www.giga-byte.com

Hewlett-Packard

Makers of printers, scanners, desktop and portable computers and storage devices.
www.hp.com

Hitachi

Makers of handheld and portable computers and storage devices.
www.hitachi.com

IBM

Manufacturers of desktop and portable computers, printers, monitors and software.
www.ibm.com

Imation Enterprises

Makers of storage devices.
www.imation.com

Intel

Developers of the Pentium and Celeron family of CPUs as well as system boards.
www.intel.com

Iomega

Makers of Zip and Jaz removable storage devices and media.
www.iomega.com

JVC Digital Storage Systems

Makers of CD-R and CD-RW drives.
www.jvc.net/ds2

Key Tronic

Manufacturers of keyboards and mice.
www.keytronic.com

Kingston Technology

Manufacturers of memory products.
www.kingston.com

Labtec

Manufacturers of speakers, headphones and microphones.
www.labtec.com

Lexmark

Manufacturers and developers of ink-jet, laser and dot-matrix printers.
www.lexmark.com

LG Electronics

Makers of monitors and storage devices.
www.lgeus.com

Logitech

Manufacturers of mice, keyboards, joysticks and speakers.
www.logitech.com

MAG InnoVision

Manufacturers of CRT and LCD monitors.
www.maginnovision.com

Matrox Graphics

Manufacturers of video cards.
www.matrox.com/mga

Maxtor

Manufacturers of internal and external hard drives.
www.maxtor.com

McAfee.com

Developers of VirusScan anti-virus scanner and First Aid diagnostic software.
www.mcafee.com

Micron Technology

Designers and manufacturers of memory products.
www.micron.com

Microsoft

Developers of the Windows family of operating systems, as well as application software and input devices.
www.microsoft.com

Mitsumi Electronics

Makers of storage and input devices.
www.mitsumi.com

NEC Technologies

Makers of CRT and LCD monitors, printers, scanners and storage devices.
www.nectech.com

Nikon

Manufacturers of digital cameras.
www.nikon.com

Ontrack Data International

Developers of backup and diagnostic software.
www.ontrack.com

Palm

Manufacturers and developers of Palm handheld computers and the Palm OS.
www.palm.com

Panasonic

Makers of CRT and LCD monitors, portable computers, scanners, printers and storage devices.
www.panasonic.com

Philips Electronics

Manufacturers of speakers, sound cards, monitors and storage devices.
www.philips.com

PowerQuest

Developers of backup and hard drive management software.
www.powerquest.com

Quantum

Makers of storage devices.
www.quantum.com

Samsung Electronics

Makers of desktop and portable computers, storage devices, printers and monitors.
www.samsungelectronics.com

Seagate Technology

Makers of storage devices and media.
www.seagate.com

SONICblue (formerly S3)

Manufacturers of handheld computers, fax modems, home network devices and MP3 players.
www.sonicblue.com

Sony Electronics

Makers of monitors, desktop and portable computers, storage devices and storage media.
www.sony.com

SOYO Computer

Producers of system boards, portable computers and personal digital assistants.
www.soyo.com

Symantec

Developers of the Norton family of anti-virus, diagnostic and network protection software.
www.symantec.com

Tecmar Technology

Manufacturers of tape drives and cartridges.
www.tecmar.com

Toshiba

Makers of desktop and portable computers, digital cameras and storage devices.
www.toshiba.com

Tripp Lite Power Protection

Providers of uninterruptible power supply (UPS) systems.
www.tripplite.com

Tyan Computer

Producers of system boards.
www.tyan.com

UMAX Technologies

Manufacturers of scanners and digital cameras.
www.umax.com

U.S. Robotics

Manufacturers of internal and external modems.
www.usrobotics.com

VERITAS Software

Developers of backup software.
www.veritas.com

VIA Technologies

Developers of the Cyrix family of CPUs.
www.viatech.com

ViewSonic

Manufacturers of CRT and LCD monitors.
www.viewsonic.com

Voyetra Turtle Beach

Developers of sound cards and speakers.
www.voyetra-turtle-beach.com

Western Digital

Manufacturers of internal and external hard drives.
www.westerndigital.com

Xircom

Developers of networking solutions for portable computers and personal digital assistants.
www.xircom.com

Zoom Telephonics

Makers of internal and external modems, cable modems and high-speed Internet connectivity devices.
www.zoomtel.com

INDEX

F

G

H

I

J

K

L

M

N

O

P

Q

R

S

T

U

V

W

Z

ORDER FORM

Hungry Minds™

TRADE & INDIVIDUAL ORDERS
Phone: **(800) 762-2974**
or **(317) 572-3993**
(8 a.m.–6 p.m., CST, weekdays)
FAX : **(800) 550-2747**
or **(317) 572-4002**

EDUCATIONAL ORDERS & DISCOUNTS
Phone: **(800) 434-2086**
(8:30 a.m.–5:00 p.m., CST, weekdays)
FAX : **(317) 572-4005**

CORPORATE ORDERS FOR 3-D VISUAL™ SERIES
Phone: **(800) 469-6616**
(8 a.m.–5 p.m., EST, weekdays)
FAX : **(905) 890-9434**

Qty	ISBN	Title	Price	Total

Shipping & Handling Charges

	Description	First book	Each add'l. book	Total
Domestic	Normal	$4.50	$1.50	$
	Two Day Air	$8.50	$2.50	$
	Overnight	$18.00	$3.00	$
International	Surface	$8.00	$8.00	$
	Airmail	$16.00	$16.00	$
	DHL Air	$17.00	$17.00	$

Subtotal ______________

CA residents add applicable sales tax ______________

IN, MA and MD residents add 5% sales tax ______________

IL residents add 6.25% sales tax ______________

RI residents add 7% sales tax ______________

TX residents add 8.25% sales tax ______________

Shipping ______________

Total ______________

Ship to:

Name ______________________________

Address ______________________________

Company ______________________________

City/State/Zip ______________________________

Daytime Phone ______________________________

Payment: ☐ Check to Hungry Minds (US Funds Only)
☐ Visa ☐ Mastercard ☐ American Express

Card # ______________ Exp. ________ Signature ______________________

maranGraphics®